REVISION WORKBOOK

Company Law

CONSULTANT EDITOR: LORD TEMPLEMAN
EDITOR: JACQUELINE WILKINSON
BA, PhD, Solicitor

OLD BAILEY PRESS

OLD BAILEY PRESS
200 Greyhound Road, London W14 9RY

1st edition 1997

© Old Bailey Press Ltd 1997

Previous editions published under The HLT Group Ltd.

ISBN 1 85836 231 8

British Library Cataloguing-in-Publication.

A CIP Catalogue record for this book is available from the British Library.

Printed and bound in Great Britain.

Contents

Acknowledgement

Some questions used are taken or adapted from past University of London LLB (External) Degree examination papers and our thanks are extended to the University of London for their kind permission to use and publish the questions.

Caveat

The answers given are not approved or sanctioned by the University of London and are entirely our responsibility.

They are not intended as 'Model Answers', but rather as Suggested Solutions.

The answers have two fundamental purposes, namely:

a) To provide a detailed example of a suggested solution to an examination question, and

b) To assist students with their research into the subject and to further their understanding and appreciation of the subject of Laws.

Introduction

This Revision WorkBook has been designed specifically for those studying company law to undergraduate level. Its coverage is not confined to any one syllabus, but embraces all the major company law topics to be found in university examinations.

Each chapter contains a brief introduction explaining the scope and overall content of the topic covered in that chapter. There follows, in each case, a list of key points which will assist the student in studying and memorising essential material with which the student should be familiar in order to fully understand the topic. Recent cases and statutes are noted as necessary. However, on the assumption that the student will already possess a textbook/casebook and, for the sake of simplicity, case law has been kept to the bare minimum.

Additionally in each chapter there is a question analysis which looks at past examination questions on similar topics in company papers. The purpose of such a question analysis is to give an appreciation of the potential range of questions possible, and some idea of variations in wording, different formats in questions and alternative modes of combining different issues in one question.

Each chapter will end with at least one, and usually several, typical examination questions, together with skeleton solutions and suggested solutions. Wherever possible, the questions are drawn from University of London external company law papers 1990–96. However it is inevitable that, in compiling a list of questions by topic order rather than chronologically, not only do the same questions crop up over and over again in different guises, but there are gaps where questions have never been set at all.

Undoubtedly, the main feature of this Revision WorkBook is the inclusion of as many past examination questions as possible. While the use of past questions as a revision aid is certainly not new, it is hoped that the combination of actual past questions from the University of London LLB external course and specially written questions, where there are gaps in examination coverage, will be of assistance to students in achieving a thorough and systematic revision of the subject.

Careful use of the Revision WorkBook should enhance the student's understanding of company law and, hopefully, enable him to deal with as wide a range of subject matter as anyone might find in a company law examination, while at the same time allowing him to practise examination techniques while working through the book.

In this revised edition the final chapter contains the complete June 1996 University of London LLB (External) Company Law question paper, followed by suggested solutions to each question. Thus the student will have the opportunity to review a recent examination paper in its entirety, and can, if desired, use this chapter as a mock examination – referring to the suggested solutions only after first having attempted the questions.

Abbreviations

Throughout this Company Law Revision WorkBook the abbreviations CA and IA are used for Companies Act and Insolvency Act respectively. If examination candidates choose to use similar abbreviations when answering examination questions, the full name of the relevant Act should always be given alongside the abbreviated form where it first appears, as in the suggested solutions in this book.

How to Study Company Law

Company law is a subject which is heavily regulated by statute – companies do not exist at common law. Students coming fresh to the subject may therefore get the impression that a knowledge of the statutes is the most important asset for a company lawyer. This is not entirely true. Although the statutes form the basis of the subject, there is also a vast amount of case law, some of which interprets the statutes, while other parts lay down principles which are not to be found in the statutes at all. The subject is one which may also overlap with other areas of law, in particular equity and trusts and contract. There are also occasional criminal liabilities, but it is safe to say that most undergraduate company law courses place relatively little emphasis on these (with the possible exception of insider trading).

Another problem is that the amount of statutory regulation and case law has grown substantially in the past decade, and continues to grow. Because of this it is important for students to look for underlying principles in the subject. If these are grasped, it may well be possible to work out a sensible answer to a problem question even when much of the detailed law has been forgotten. Thus, it is important to know that company law normally operates on a principle of majority rule, that directors are in a fiduciary position in the company, and that the ultimate control rests in the general meeting.

Another important theme running through company law is that of maintaining a balance between the interests of shareholders, creditors and directors. Many apparently complex problems can be reduced to examples of this conflict.

In examinations essay questions tend to fall into two types. One type asks for an account of a particular area of the law. In attempting these questions it is important to identify carefully which area is being asked about and to stick to the point – company law topics are often interwoven, and it is easy to be lured into irrelevancy. It is also necessary to know the material thoroughly. These questions should be avoided by students who are relying on grasp of principle rather than detailed knowledge. The second type of essay question asks about issues of policy, often couched in terms which suggest that the law in a particular area is defective. Obviously, some knowledge of the law is required to answer these questions, but they are also suitable for those with a good grasp of principle.

Problem questions frequently cover a number of different areas. For this reason it is important to look closely at them and to ensure that all the areas are covered. In particular, remember to look at the situation from the point of view of all the parties. Remember that the remedies available to the company are not necessarily the same as those available to the shareholders, and that the directors are separate from the company. Some problems may ask about actions which appear to prejudice the creditors, even though the creditors are not mentioned in the problem: remember to consider their remedies as well.

Revision and Examination Technique

(A)   REVISION TECHNIQUE

Planning a revision timetable

In planning your revision timetable make sure you do not finish the syllabus too early. You should avoid leaving revision so late that you have to 'cram' – but constant revision of the same topic leads to stagnation.

Plan ahead, however, and try to make your plans increasingly detailed as you approach the examination date.

Allocate enough time for each topic to be studied. But note that it is better to devise a realistic timetable, to which you have a reasonable chance of keeping, rather than a wildly optimistic schedule which you will probably abandon at the first opportunity!

The syllabus and its topics

One of your first tasks when you began your course was to ensure that you thoroughly understood your **syllabus**. Check now to see if you can write down the **topics** it comprises from memory. You will see that the chapters of this WorkBook are each devoted to a syllabus topic. This will help you decide which are the key chapters relative to your revision programme. Though you should allow some time for glancing through the other chapters.

The topic and its key points

Again working from memory, analyse what you consider to be the key points of any topic that you have selected for particular revision. Seeing what you can recall, unaided, will help you to understand and firmly memorise the concepts involved.

Using the WorkBook

Relevant questions are provided for each topic in this book. Naturally, as typical examples of examination questions, they do not normally relate to one topic only. But the questions in each chapter *will* relate to the subject matter of the chapter to a degree. You can choose your method of consulting the questions and solutions, but here are some suggestions (strategies 1–3). Each of them pre-supposes that you have read through the author's notes on key points and question analysis, and any other preliminary matter, at the beginning of the chapter. Once again, you now need to practise working from *memory*, for that is the challenge you are preparing yourself for. As a rule of procedure constantly test yourself once revision starts, both orally and in writing.

Strategy 1

Strategy 1 is planned for the purpose of *quick revision*. First read your chosen question carefully and then jot down in abbreviated notes what you consider to be the main points at issue. Similarly, note the cases and statutes that occur to you as being relevant for citation purposes. Allow yourself sufficient time to cover what you feel to be relevant. Then study the author's *skeleton solution* and skim-read the *suggested solution* to see how they compare with your notes. When comparing consider carefully what the author has included (and concluded) and see whether that agrees with what you have written. Consider the points of variation also. Have you recognised the key issues? How relevant have you been? It is possible, of course, that you have referred to a recent case that *is* relevant, but which had not been reported when the WorkBook was prepared.

Strategy 2

Strategy 2 requires a nucleus of *three hours* in which to practise writing a set of examination answers in a limited time-span.

Select a number of questions (as many as are normally set in your subject in the examination you are studying for), each from a different chapter in the WorkBook, without consulting the solutions. Find a place to write where you will not be disturbed and try to arrange not to be interrupted for three hours. Write your solutions in the time allowed, noting any time needed to make up if you *are* interrupted.

After a rest, compare your answers with the *suggested solutions* in the WorkBook. There will be considerable variation in style, of course, but the bare facts should not be too dissimilar. Evaluate your answer critically. Be 'searching', but develop a positive approach to deciding how you would tackle each question on another occasion.

Strategy 3

You are unlikely to be able to do more than one three hour examination, but occasionally set yourself a single question. Vary the 'time allowed' by imagining it to be one of the questions that you must answer in three hours and allow yourself a limited preparation and writing time. Try one question that you feel to be difficult and an easier question on another occasion, for example.

Misuse of suggested solutions

Don't try to learn by rote. In particular, don't try to reproduce the *suggested solutions* by heart. Learn to express the basic concepts in your own words.

Keeping up-to-date

Keep up-to-date. While examiners do not require familiarity with changes in the law during the three months prior to the examination, it obviously creates a good impression if you can show you are acquainted with any recent changes. Make a habit of looking through one of the leading journals – *Modern Law Review, Law Quarterly Review*, the *Company Lawyer* or the *New Law Journal*, for example – and cumulative indices to law reports, such as the *All England Law Reports* or *Weekly Law Reports*, or indeed the daily law reports in *The Times*. The *Law Society's Gazette* and the *Legal Executive Journal* are helpful sources, plus any specialist journal(s) for the subject you are studying.

(B)   EXAMINATION SKILLS

Examiners are human too!

The process of answering an examination question involves a *communication* between you and the person who set it. If you were speaking face to face with the person, you would choose your verbal points and arguments carefully in your reply. When writing, it is all too easy to forget *the human being who is awaiting the reply* and simply write out what one knows in the area of the subject! Bear in mind it is a person whose question you are responding to, throughout your essay. This will help you to avoid being irrelevant or long-winded.

The essay question

Candidates are sometimes tempted to choose to answer essay questions because they 'seem' easier. But the examiner is looking for thoughtful work and will not give good marks for superficial answers.

The essay-type of question may be either purely factual, in asking you to *explain the meaning* of a certain doctrine or principle, or it may ask you to *discuss* a certain proposition, usually derived from a quotation. In either case, the approach to the answer is the same. A clear programme must be devised to give the examiner the meaning or significance of the doctrine, principle or proposition and its origin in common law, equity or statute, and cases which illustrate its application to the branch of law concerned.

The problem question

The problem-type question requires a different approach. You may well be asked to advise a client or merely discuss the problems raised in the question. In either case, the most important factor is to take great care in reading the question. By its nature, the question will be longer than the essay-type question and you will have a number of facts to digest. Time spent in analysing the question may well save time later, when you are endeavouring to impress on the examiner the considerable extent of your basic legal knowledge. The quantity of knowledge is itself a trap and you must always keep within the boundaries of the question in hand. It is very tempting to show the examiner the extent of your knowledge of your subject, but if this is outside the question, it is time lost and no marks earned. It it inevitable that some areas which you have studied and revised will not be the subject of questions, but under no circumstances attempt to adapt a question to a stronger area of knowledge at the expense of relevance.

When you are satisfied that you have grasped the full significance of the problem-type question, set out the fundamental principles involved.

You will then go on to identify the fundamental problem, or problems posed by the question. This should be followed by a consideration of the law which is relevant to the problem. The source of the law, together with the cases which will be of assistance in solving the problem, must then be considered in detail.

Very good problem questions are quite likely to have alternative answers, and in advising A you should be aware that alternative arguments may be available. Each stage of your answer, in this case, will be based on the argument or arguments considered in the previous stage, forming a conditional sequence.

If, however, you only identify one fundamental problem, do not waste time worrying that you cannot think of an alternative – there may very well be only that one answer.

The examiner will then wish to see how you use your legal knowledge to formulate a case and how you apply that formula to the problem which is the subject of the question. It is this positive approach which can make answering a problem question a high mark earner for the student who has fully understood the question and clearly argued his case on the established law.

Examination checklist

1   Read the instructions at the head of the examination carefully. While last-minute changes are unlikely – such as the introduction of a *compulsory question* or *an increase in the number of questions asked* – it has been known to happen.

2 Read the questions carefully. Analyse problem questions – work out what the examiner wants.

3 Plan your answer *before* you start to write. You can divide your time as follows:

   (a) working out the question (5 per cent of time)

   (b) working out how to answer the question (5 to 10 per cent of time)

   (c) writing your answer

   Do not overlook (a) and (b)

4 Check that you understand the rubric *before* you start to write. Do not 'discuss', for example, if you are specifically asked to 'compare and contrast'.

5 Answer the correct number of questions. If you fail to answer one out of four questions set you lose 25 per cent of your marks!

Style and structure

Try to be clear and concise. Basically this amounts to using paragraphs to denote the sections of your essay, and writing simple, straightforward sentences as much as possible. The sentence you have just read has 22 words – when a sentence reaches 50 words it becomes difficult for a reader to follow.

Do not be inhibited by the word 'structure' (traditionally defined as giving an essay a beginning, a middle and an end). A good structure will be the natural consequence of setting out your arguments and the supporting evidence in a logical order. Set the scene briefly in your opening paragraph. Provide a clear conclusion in your final paragraph.

Table of Cases

Table of Statutes

1 Corporate Personality

1.1 Introduction

Corporate personality may be defined as the doctrine that a company is for legal purposes an independent person having an existence separate from that of the human beings who own, manage and serve it. For the most part the doctrine is well settled, though there are still some difficulties is working out certain of the implications of the doctrine. These difficulties are considered in the key points section (1.2) below.

1.2 Key points

a) *Concept of incorporation*

A company is formed by the process of 'incorporation'. This is an administrative procedure, and its correct completion is both necessary and sufficient for the company to exist as an independent legal entity.

b) *Legal capacity and personality*

Once a company is duly incorporated it has both legal personality and legal capacity.

Legal personality means that the company exists as a legal person. It is distinct from its shareholders, directors and employees. As a separate person it has its own interests, which must be considered separately from those of the humans involved with it.

Legal capacity means that the company can own property and can make contracts in its own name and on its own behalf. In practice this will be done through the agency of human beings, but it is essential to understand that as a matter of law these acts will be the acts of the company.

c) *Groups of companies*

Particular difficulties arise where there are groups of companies. A company may own some or all of the shares in another company. Where one company has a majority of the shares in another company the first is said to control the second and the two companies form a group. In practice groups of many companies are found.

In principle each company in the group remains a separate legal entity, with its own property and its own rights and liabilities. This principle is sometimes used as a way of minimising or avoiding liabilities, and this may lead to an argument that some or all of the companies in a group should be regarded as a single entity. This is considered further under 'the veil of incorporation' below.

1

d) *The veil of incorporation*

When a company has been formed it is said to be protected by the 'veil of incorporation'. This means that it is not open to outsiders to argue that the company is really the same person as those controlling it (*Salomon* v *Salomon* [1897] AC 22). The *Salomon* principle was recently re-emphasised in *Polly Peck International plc (In Administration)* [1996] 2 All ER 433.

The corollary to this fundamental principle is that a company's directors and shareholders may contract with it (*Lee* v *Lee's Air Farming Ltd* [1961] AC 12), do not generally incur liability for its debts or defaults, and are not entitled to its property (*Macaura* v *Northern Assurance Co* [1925] AC 619). There are exceptions to this principle:

i) Agency

A company may be found to be acting as the agent of its principal shareholders and/or directors, although there is no general presumption that this is so; for an explanation of the principles see *Smith, Stone & Knight* v *Birmingham Corporation* [1939] 4 All ER 116.

ii) Trust

Where shares in a company are held on trust, the court may occasionally be prepared to look at the terms on which they are held (*Abbey Malvern Wells Ltd* v *MLGP* [1951] Ch 728), but it seems that this exception will apply only rarely.

iii) Statute

Some statutory provisions, eg Insolvency Act 1986, ss212–215 and Companies Act 1985, ss24, 349(4) and 117(8), impose personal liability on directors or members in certain circumstances.

iv) Interpretation

The court may look to the 'economic reality' to assist it in interpreting statutes, contracts and other documents (*DHN Food Distributors* v *Tower Hamlets London Borough Council* [1976] 3 All ER 462, where a group was treated as a single economic unit for the purposes of a statutory compensation payment).

v) Corporate façade

This is said to be the only true case of 'piecing' or 'lifting the veil' where a company has been used as a 'mere façade' to conceal the true facts. Examples include using a company as a vehicle to: avoid a conveyance (*Jones* v *Lipman* [1962] 1 WLR 832); evade a covenant in restraint of trade (*Gilford Motor Co Ltd* v *Horne* [1933] Ch 935); avoid payment of damages (*Creasey* v *Breachwood Motors* [1992] BCC 625); and gain an advantage improperly (*Re FG Films* [1953] 1 WLR 483).

While the Court of Appeal in *Adams* v *Cape Industries plc* [1991] 1 All ER 929 refused to accept that the court can lift the veil whenever it is 'necessary to achieve justice' (per Cumming-Bruce LJ in *Re a Company* [1985] BCLC 333), it nevertheless declined to give any guidance on how the court should decide when the company has been used as a 'mere façade'. However, it seems there is nothing wrong per se in a company arranging its affairs in reliance on the *Salomon* principle so as to minimise or avoid its liabilities.

1.3 Recent cases

Mephistopholes Debt Collection Services (A Firm) v *Lotay* (1994) The Times 17 May – only a company enjoys separate legal personality.

Polly Peck International plc (In Administration) [1996] 2 All ER 433 – *Salomon* principle upheld.

Re H (Restraint Order: Realisable Property) [1996] 2 All ER 391 – the Court of Appeal regarded property of certain companies as that of shareholders where there was evidence that the company structure had been used to avoid excise duty.

Seaboard Offshore Ltd v *Secretary of State for Transport* [1994] 2 All ER 99 – a company was not vicariously liable for the acts of all its employees.

1.4 Analysis of questions

The topic of corporate personality has appeared regularly on the London paper and is popular everywhere.

1.5 Questions

QUESTION ONE

No, limited in certain aspects

'B C Hunt has written of "that brilliant intellectual achievement of the Roman lawyers, the juristic person, a subject of rights and liabilities as a natural person". Although so anticipated, to some extent, the achievement is no less remarkable in English law where a corporate legal entity has been evolved which has shown itself to be fully adequate to meet the vastly greater and more complex needs of modern times and, so far, capable of adaptation and development to maintain its usefulness.' *?*

Discuss with reference to the development of the corporate entity doctrine in English company law.

University of London LLB Examination
(for External Students) Company Law June 1995 Q1

General Comment

The proposition requires an overview of the origin and rationale for the *Salomon* principle and of the circumstances in which the courts will look behind the corporate veil.

Skeleton Solution

Outline of *Salomon* principle – brief rationale for the idea – examples of lifting the veil – group activities – deliberate abuse of corporate form to avoid obligations or restrictions – judicial analysis of facts on agency or instrument basis – statutory incursions into the principle – abuse of controlling positions within closely held companies.

Suggested Solution

The development of the concept of corporate legal entity owes much to *Salomon* v *Salomon* (1897), where the House of Lords established the principle that incorporation creates a legal entity completely separate and distinct from its members. There is no agency or fiduciary relationship created between company and member, and the fact of incorporation, without more, does not make the members liable for company debts beyond the limit of their share

3

more, does not make the members liable for company debts beyond the limit of their share liability. This, and the development of limitation of liability by share or guarantee, has created a highly flexible method of conducting business of almost unlimited scope and scale. The system offers considerable protection to creditor, member, employee and director, while maintaining a form that is subject to the control of the law to a remarkable degree. The true worth of the system can be seen in cases where there is attempted abuse of limited liability or company law, or where injustice would follow too strict an application of the principle. The courts are quite willing to lift the 'veil of incorporation' in appropriate cases and certain situations illustrate this well:

a) *Corporate groups and dominance by holding companies*

The leading case is *Smith, Stone & Knight* v *Birmingham Corporation* (1939), where the court reviewed the question of a holding company's entitlement to disturbance compensation for property occupied in the name of, and for the purposes of, a subsidiary. The judgments suggest tests to ascertain the reality of who traded there: was it a truly independent subsidiary or a mere corporate shadow of the holding company? The court looked behind the veil and saw clearly that the subsidiary had little existence beyond paper and that the holding company should succeed in getting compensation. A similar result was seen in *DHN Food Distributors* v *Tower Hamlets London Borough Council* (1976). Significant factors in such a consideration are the incidence of day-to-day control and management or lack of it. The financial substructure of the subsidiary was looked at in *Re FG Films* (1953) and *Littlewoods Mail Order Stores Ltd* v *Inland Revenue Commissioners* (1969). If, however, a holding company transfers property legally to its subsidiary to gain a perceived business advantage, it cannot expect the courts to lift the veil for the purpose of regaining an immunity for unlimited tortious liability which it lost in transferring the property: *William Cory & Sons Ltd* v *Dorman Long & Co Ltd* (1936).

b) *Abuse of corporate form to evade obligations or restrictions*

In *Re Bugle Press Ltd* (1961), the court lifted the veil to disclose a company acquired and used for the sole purpose of taking advantage of statutory rights available to takeover bidders. The company was used by holders of 90 per cent of the shares in the target company who could not, without this device, bring themselves within s428 Companies Act (CA) 1985 as an 'offeror'. The court refused to sanction such tactics. A fairly common abuse is the transfer of property into or out of companies to prevent creditors, trustees in bankruptcy or other claimants succeeding to it or acquiring it. In this situation the court will look at the reality of the transaction, and disregard abuse and sham as in *Jones* v *Lipman* (1962), (attempt to avoid specific performance of house transfer). In *Wallersteiner* v *Moir (No 1)* (1974), a most serious abuse of the corporate form required the court to pierce the veil.

c) *Judicial analysis of facts on agency or instrument basis*

Despite the pronouncements to the contrary in *Salomon*, the courts will, where appropriate, give serious consideration to whether a company can be the agent or instrument of its members. Agency arguments particularly appeal to the courts in taxation cases, as in *Apthorpe* v *Peter Schoenhofen Brewing Co Ltd* (1899) and *Firestone Tyre and Rubber Co* v *Llewellin* (1957), but arguments in the group cases seem also to rest upon agency. Nevertheless, the courts look for much more than mere shareholding to show agency, particularly between holding company and subsidiary. In *Kodak Ltd* v *Clark* (1902), a 98 per cent holding of the shares in an American subsidiary was not enough to make it an agency relationship. In *Lennard's Carrying Co Ltd* v *Asiatic Petroleum Co Ltd* (1915), the point is made that if a company is truly the creature of its controller or owner, then it will be liable for his acts or omissions in using the medium of the company to achieve his ends.

d) *Statutory intervention upon the doctrine*

Statute has created significant inroads upon the corporate entity doctrine both in the area of pending or actual insolvency as well as in cases of fraudulent, negligent or abusive control and manipulation of companies. In cases of fraudulent or wrongful trading under ss213, 214 and 216 Insolvency Act (IA) 1986 (restrictions upon use of company names), personal liability for the debts of the company can be visited upon directors and shadow directors (s214 IA 1986) and those persons along with others (s216 IA 1986). In various other breaches of company legislation, personal liability for debt or loss can be imposed upon directors and controllers but these matters are not so much a lifting of the veil but rather a statutory provision of remedies to prevent the *Salomon* principle being invoked as a defence.

e) *Abuse of controlling positions within closely held companies*

Cases such as *Scottish Co-operative Wholesale Society Ltd* v *Meyer* (1959) and *Ebrahimi* v *Westbourne Galleries Ltd* (1973) show the possibilities for the unconscionable and unfair prejudice to the legitimate expectations of members of closely-held companies by the simple expedient of controlling members conducting the affairs of the company in an abusive way. On one view, such acts are the acts of the company itself, but the corporate entity is flexible enough to allow the courts to use equitable principles to prevent abuse without destroying the essential principle of majority control. This has also led to the statutory protections provided by ss459, 460 and 461 CA 1985 and the whole development of the law on minority protection illustrates the capacity of the corporate entity doctrine to be successfully adapted to the almost limitless range of company types and sizes whilst preserving the possibility for judicial intervention against abusive control.

In summary, it is submitted that the proposition of B C Hunt is eminently supportable.

QUESTION TWO

Brandy plc is a large public company with a sound and prosperous reputation, as wine suppliers, importers and distributors. Chablis Ltd, and Muscadet Ltd are two of its wholly owned subsidiaries which specialise in the growth and manufacture of particular kinds of wines. The directors of Chablis and Muscadet have always been nominated by Brandy from its own Board of Directors and all profits made by the subsidiaries have been paid directly to the parent company. All decisions by the subsidiaries were required first to be approved by Brandy plc and any overdrafts and other liabilities – such as covenants in leases – were always guaranteed by Brandy. Brandy had also made substantial loans to its subsidiaries, which loans were secured by fixed and floating charges over all the assets of the subsidiaries.

Poor grape harvests in 1982 and 1983 placed the businesses of Chablis and Muscadet in serious jeopardy, but as their connection with Brandy (which itself was actually going through a particularly flourishing period) was well known, creditors continued to extend credit to the subsidiaries. Eventually, however, Chablis and Muscadet were wound up as insolvent, with barely sufficient assets to cover outstanding loan commitments to Brandy.

Advise the liquidator who has been urged by all the creditors, other than Brandy, to do all he can to recover their money.

University of London LLB Examination
(for External Students) Company Law June 1985 Q6

General Comment

This was a somewhat unusual problem question in that it addressed only the specific area of parent subsidiary relationships. (It should be noted that 'parent company' is now a defined term with a different meaning, and is now incorrect usage in this context. The correct term is 'holding company', as defined by Companies Act 1985, s736.) There is a good deal to write about, but candidates should be careful to confine their answers to the points which the question actually raises. The following is suggested as a good attempt at the question.

Skeleton Solution

Principle of corporate personality – subject to exceptions – holding company-subsidiary is one possible exception – factors relevant in parent-subsidiary cases – element of direction by holding company – policy issue as to piercing the veil in these cases – authorities on both sides – English law has no clear theory on the point – probably no piercing of the veil here.

Suggested Solution

In principle these companies must be treated as separate legal entities – *Salomon* v *Salomon* (1897) – but the liquidator will wish to show that this is a case where the veil of incorporation should be lifted so as to treat the companies as a single entity and treat Brandy plc as being liable for the debts of its subsidiaries. Although the *Salomon* v *Salomon* principle is well established (see most recently *Polly Peck International plc (In Administration)* (1996)) it is also settled that there are a number of exceptions, and the question is whether any of them applies here. *DHN* v *Tower Hamlets* (1976) shows that the holding company-subsidiary relationship is one which is potentially susceptible to the lifting of the veil – obviously there are cases where it would be unrealistic to accept separate legal personality for group companies (*Holdsworth* v *Caddies* (1955)). However, in *Adams* v *Cape Industries* (1991) the *DHN* case was considered by the Court of Appeal not to be a true case of 'lifting the veil' but a decision on the relevant statutory provisions, and the decision itself was doubted by the House of Lords in *Woolfson* v *Strathclyde Regional Council* (1978). The clearest exposition of the principles in this area was given by Atkinson J in *Smith, Stone & Knight* v *Birmingham Corporation* (1939), when he listed six factors which are relevant in deciding whether to lift the veil on a group of companies. However, the only one of these which is of real relevance to the present case is whether the profits of the subsidiary were made by the holding company's skill and direction (compare, for example, *Firestone Tyre and Rubber Co* v *Llewellin* (1956) and *Re FG Films* (1953).) Clearly there is in the present case some element of direction by the holding company.

The difficulty in this case may be summed up by saying that there are two mutually contradictory views of group structure: either may be adopted in any given case, and it is difficult to predict in advance what a court will do. On the side of the formalistic *Salomon* v *Salomon* (1897) analysis it may be argued that the creditors of each company in the group will not necessarily be the same, so that it would be unfair to treat all the companies together (*Charterbridge Corporation* v *Lloyds Bank* (1970)) and this may be so even in the case of a wholly owned subsidiary (*Lonrho* v *Shell* (1980)). Further, the Court of Appeal made it clear in *Adams* that a company is entitled to organise its affairs on the assumption that the court will apply the *Salomon* principle, and only if it is satisfied that there is a 'mere façade' will the veil be lifted.

The argument on the other side is that it may be equally unfair to insist too strictly on the doctrine of corporate personality. To quote Templeman LJ in *Re Southard & Co Ltd* (1979), English law allows a holding company to spawn a litter of subsidiaries and then strangle the runt, ie to let the weakest of the subsidiaries go to the wall. This may be seen as unfair to creditors of the weak subsidiary and likely to encourage holding companies to engage in unsound speculative ventures through the medium of a subsidiary. A further point made by Templeman LJ in that case is that it is often a matter of chance whether business is conducted through a branch or through a subsidiary, and it would be wrong to allow fundamental consequences to hinge on that choice. Another argument sometimes presented in this context is that groups of companies have to file group accounts and can therefore be treated as a single entity. However, it must be pointed out that these group accounts are in addition to accounts for each individual company, not in substitution for them, a fact which somewhat weakens the force of this argument.

It also appears that the court cannot, as was once thought, lift the veil merely because justice requires it. As things stand at present it must be said that the liquidator's chances of persuading the court to life the veil are not good. There are some indications of control on the part of Brandy plc, but it is not thought that these are sufficient to warrant lifting the veil of incorporation.

QUESTION THREE

Jim owned and ran a radio repair business. It was quite successful but Jim was worried about the long term prospects because of the far reaching changes being made in radio technology. Jim foresaw the eventual decline of his type of business and decided that while it was still relatively prosperous, he would transfer it to a company (especially incorporated for the purpose). Of the nominal capital of £100, ten £1 shares were issued to Jim and one to his wife. Jim was elected the sole director of the company and the company employed three mechanics. Although, the business was worth approximately £50,000, the company agreed to buy it from Jim for £80,000. In exchange for the business, the company issued a debenture for £80,000 to Jim, secured by a fixed charge on the company's fixed assets and a floating charge on all its other assets.

In January 1987, a fire in the workshop caused extensive damage to the premises (which were at all material times owned by Jim and which the company was licensed to use for the purpose of its business). The business had to cease operating for 4 weeks resulting in a loss of some £10,000, and physical damage to the premises amounted to £15,000. Jim had effected insurance against such risks, both to the premises and to the business, but when the business was sold to the company, there was no assignment of the benefit of the insurance policy to the company, nor did the company effect its own insurance against such risks. The insurance company is now refusing to pay out in respect of the loss suffered by the company from the interruption to the business.

In January 1988, the local council gave notice of its intention to exercise its compulsory purchase powers to expropriate the premises but offered compensation which took account only of the fact that Jim owned the premises and refused to consider compensation for the loss of the right to use the premises for business purposes which would result from the expropriation.

From January to April 1988, the business continued to decline and despite advice to the contrary from his accountant and workforce, Jim continued to trade through the company in the hope that it would return to solvency. In May, however, the company went into a creditor's voluntary winding up with debts exceeding assets by close to £100,000.

Discuss the following:

a) a claim by the liquidator against the insurance company in respect of the loss arising out of the interruption of the business owing to the fire.

b) a claim by the liquidator against Jim in respect of the company's debts.

c) a claim by Jim against the local council for compensation in respect of the loss of business user rights arising out of the expropriation of the premises.

University of London LLB Examination
(for External Students) Company Law June 1988 Q4

General Comment

This is a more typical problem question on corporate personality. The incorporation of an existing business which subsequently declines is similar to the facts in *Salomon* v *Salomon* (1897), and the question invites consideration of three specific areas where the doctrine of corporate personality can have important practical consequences.

Skeleton Solution

General principle of corporate personality – some exceptions. Agency possible in insurance policy, but this is contrary to authority. Claim probably fails – Insolvency Act may be available against Jim for wrongful trading: action for fraudulent trading unlikely to succeed – Jim will want veil lifted for compensation purposes – agency possible but unlikely.

Suggested Solution

It is a well established principle of company law that a company is an independent legal person, separate from its members and directors – *Salomon* v *Salomon* (1897). The usual consequence of this is that the members of a company are not liable for the debts and other obligations of a company – their liability is limited to the amount which they have agreed to pay for their shares. Conversely, the members cannot in their own name enforce any duties owed to the company.

However, this general principle is subject to exceptions, and three of those exceptions arise for consideration in the present problem. The first issue is whether the liquidator can claim against the insurance company for the loss of business arising from the fire. The difficulty is that the insurance was taken out in Jim's name rather than in that of the company. The situation is therefore similar to that in *Macaura* v *Northern Assurance Co* (1925), where the controlling shareholder was held unable to recover for a loss to the company's timber, since he lacked any insurable interest in it. Although that case may be seen as turning upon a technicality of the law of insurance, the validity of that technicality nevertheless depends upon a finding that the company is a distinct legal person from its controlling shareholder, which is an application of the doctrine of corporate personality. As *Macaura* v *Northern Assurance Co* is a decision of the House of Lords, it is submitted that the liquidator's claim against the insurance company must fail.

The second question is whether the liquidator can make Jim personally liable for any or all of the debts of the company. Again this would be a departure from the *Salomon* v *Salomon* (1897) principle, since members' liability is normally limited to the value of their shares, whilst directors as such are not generally liable at all for the company's debts. In this case, though, ss213 and 214 of the Insolvency Act 1986 are relevant. Section 213 imposes liability in the case of fraudulent trading by a company on anyone who was knowingly a party to such trading; but it seems that this section will only apply where it is possible to establish fraud in the criminal law sense, and this is always difficult. Section 214 imposes liability on a director who has engaged in wrongful trading (see *Re Produce Marketing Consortium Ltd* (1989)). This requires only that the director knew or should have known (apparently an objective test) that the company was unable to pay its debts. On the facts stated in the question there appears to be a significant risk that Jim will be held to be guilty of wrongful trading, though the likelihood of a successful action for fraudulent trading is slight.

The third question is whether Jim can claim to be identified with the company for the purpose of claiming compensation from the planning authority. It may be noted that this is one of the rare cases where the controlling shareholder will want the veil of incorporation lifted – there is no element here of protecting third parties. Probably Jim's strongest argument is that the company occupied the premises as agent for him, an approach which succeeded in *Smith, Stone & Knight* v *Birmingham Corporation* (1939) and in *DHN* v *Tower Hamlets* (1976). Strictly speaking this is not a case of lifting the veil, since it recognises the existence of two independent parties (how else could there be an agency relationship?) but the overall result will be what Jim wants. It is difficult to predict what view the court would take, but it is submitted that it would be unduly generous to allow the claim for compensation.

QUESTION FOUR

Health Industries plc is a large well-established drug company which is the head of a large group of companies including Property Limited, a wholly-owned subsidiary which owns all the premises used by Health Industries in its business, and Testing Limited, another wholly owned subsidiary which was set up specifically to carry out commercially risky ventures in the search for profitable new drugs. The Board of Directors of Health Industries consists of seven members, but the managing director, Larry Lincoln, is the dominant force. The board generally agrees with his proposals and he has become clearly associated in the mind of the public with Health Industries plc.

Last year the local authority governing the area where Health Industries carries on part of its business expropriated certain land under its statutory powers as part of a slum clearance programme. This included land owned by Property Limited. The compensation offered under the scheme established by the expropriating statute provided for compensation to be paid to 'the owner of the expropriated land according to the open market value of the land plus the assessed damages for any loss of profits suffered by the owner'. The compensation offered by the local authority to Property Limited has ignored the loss, amounting the £150,000, suffered by Health Industries plc in having to relocate its operations elsewhere.

More recently, Testing Limited undertook experiments to try to develop a drug to cure certain types of cancer. In a high profile advertising campaign, Larry Lincoln made a personal appeal on behalf of Testing Limited for volunteers for this experiment. The advertising campaign ran for several days on television and in national newspapers, and 100 volunteers were selected. The experiment went disastrously wrong; several volunteers died, others were permanently maimed. The experiment was not properly researched and there is clear evidence of negligence. Testing Limited has assets of £2,000 to £3,000 and now faces claims of several millions. Test cases have been brought against both Testing Limited and Health Industries plc.

Advise Health Industries plc.

University of London LLB Examination
(for External Students) Company Law June 1992 Q7

General Comment

This question is about separate corporate legal personality and its exceptions and ramifications. Any serious student of company law must have considered the topic, and ought not to have had difficulty in obtaining at least a fairly good mark.

Skeleton Solution

Separate personality of a company – exceptions – illustrative cases.

Suggested Solution

An incorporated company is in law an entirely distinct and separate legal person from its members. In *Salomon* v *Salomon* (1897) Mr Salomon, who had previously carried on a boot and shoe business as an individual, caused a company to be incorporated and became the holder of almost all of its shares. He then sold and transferred his business to the company and took a secured debenture on its assets for the unpaid balance of the purchase price. When the company became insolvent, the House of Lords held that Mr Salomon, as a secured creditor, had a prior claim to the assets to the claims of the company's unsecured creditors; as distinct legal persons Mr Salomon and the company could trade with each other notwithstanding Mr Salomon's control of the company.

Lee v *Lee's Air Farming Ltd* (1961), or analogous cases, could also be cited and discussed with advantage.

The *Salomon* principle will equally well apply to Health Industries plc and its two wholly owned subsidiaries; each company is a distinct legal person.

Nevertheless, there are circumstances in which the courts will not apply the doctrine of corporate personality distinct from that of membership. An illustrative case is *Gilford Motor Co Ltd* v *Horne* (1933) where the court refused to allow an individual who was bound by a valid restrictive covenant to evade performance by forming a company, with himself as its only substantial shareholder, which would proceed to break the covenant. How wide are the circumstances, apart from fraud, in which the courts will disapply the *Salomon* principle is unclear.

As regards the expropriation of land owned by Property Ltd, it is clear that Property Ltd, which is not a trader, has not lost any profits thereby. But if Health Industries plc and Property Ltd were to be regarded in this context as a single entity, a loss of profit would be incurred. There are two contrasting cases on this point and in the context of similar facts to these of our problem. In *DHN* v *Tower Hamlets* (1976) the Court of Appeal allowed the holding company to claim compensation for disturbance to the business which it carried out on land compulsorily to be acquired from its wholly owned subsidiary. But in *Woolfson* v *Strathclyde Regional Council* (1978) the court declined to allow a claim where the circumstances were in many respects similar save that there the company which ran the business did not control the owners of the land. *Woolfson*'s case casts some doubt upon the *Tower Hamlets* decision; nevertheless it is submitted that, unless and until it is overruled, the *Tower Hamlets* ruling governs this part of the problem. The Court of Appeal in *Adams* v *Cape Industries plc* (1991) accepted that in cases turning on the construction of a statute, contract or other document the court may look at the economic reality and treat a group of companies as a single economic unit, treating *Tower Hamlets* as such a case. Alternatively it may be possible to show that the subsidiary was acting as the agent of the parent company, as was found to be the case in *Smith, Stone & Knight* v *Birmingham Corporation* (1939). (This, if established, would be another ground for claiming loss of profit from the land acquisition.) The relevant factors listed in *Smith*'s case cannot be easily applied to our problem, since in *Smith*'s case each company was carrying on a business and naturally the judgment was directed to that situation.

Finally, it may be mentioned that a director is not, as such, liable for torts committed by the company of which he is a director; he would be liable if he authorised the tort or personally took part in controlling it. It does not appear that Larry Lincoln has done either of these things.

2 The Memorandum of Association and Legal Capacity

2.1 Introduction

The memorandum and articles of association together are the constitution of the company, the former specifying the form and legal capacity this artificial legal person is to have, and the latter regulating its internal dealings. Both are registered at Companies House. Alterations to the memorandum, legally the most important of the two documents, must follow specified procedures depending on the clause to be altered.

For many years, the ultra vires rule (explained below), centring on the objects clause in the memorandum of association, often thwarted attempts by third parties to sue the company in contract and generated an enormous body of case law containing many fine distinctions. The rule, although it still exists, has been deprived of its teeth by the Companies Act (CA) 1989.

2.2 Key points

a) *The objects clause*

The objects clause in the memorandum is probably its most important clause. Under s5 CA 1985, it could only be altered for specified purposes and only by following the correct procedure, which includes a special resolution and a right for a dissenting minority to apply to the court for cancellation. The objects clause in the memorandum gives a company its legal powers. It states what businesses the company is formed to carry on and what powers it may exercise in the course of carrying on those businesses.

b) *Ultra vires*

The ultra vires rule states that a body must not act outside the powers (sometimes also referred to as capacity or authority) bestowed on it. Applied to companies it has meant that a company cannot carry on any business not specified in its objects clause (*Ashbury Railway Carriage and Iron Co v Riche* (1875) LR 7 HL 653), cannot exercise any power not mentioned, unless the court is prepared to imply it, nor exercise a power it possesses in pursuit of any unspecified object. Gratuitous payment by companies, such as pensions and payments to employees on the transfer of a business, have often been disallowed where there was no power to make them, on the ground that such payments could not be for the benefit of the company (see, eg, *Parke v Daily News* [1962] Ch 927). The immediate practical result was increasingly long objects clauses as companies strove to include any business they might wish to carry on, or power they might wish to exercise, together with a catch-all clause permitting the company to carry on any business which the directors thought fit (known as *Bell Houses* clause after *Bell Houses Ltd* v *City Wall Properties Ltd* [1966] 2 QB 656, the case in which it was first sanctioned).

Nevertheless, companies were still caught by the rule and, when it applied, any contract made in the course of carrying on the unauthorised business or exercising the unauthorised power was void, ie neither the company nor the other party to the transaction could enforce it.

The apparent harshness of this rule to third parties was justified by the rule that since the memorandum is a public document everyone is deemed to have knowledge of its contents (constructive notice). However, the courts recognised that the rule could be unfair, and a considerable body of case law was generated.

c) *Directors' powers*

Closely connected with the problem of ultra vires is that of directors' authority. The directors are agents of the company and clearly the company as principal cannot give directors powers which it does not itself have. Thus, directors who act ultra vires the company are clearly exceeding their powers (or authority) and are personally liable.

However, directors, like other agents, can exceed or breach their authority in other ways. They can only exercise powers delegated to them. This need not be a problem because usually all the powers of managing the company are bestowed on the directors by the articles of association. However, these powers are given to the board collectively, and a director who acts independently of the board exceeds his authority. Second, the company may have reserved certain powers to itself, or laid down a specific procedure to be followed before certain acts can be done or contracts made. If this is ignored, again the directors exceed their authority. Third, a director may not have been validly appointed.

The problem for the other party to transactions where the active directors lack express authority is whether the company is bound by the transaction. A director, like other agents, may have implied (usual) or ostensible authority, which may make the transaction enforceable against the company (see, eg, *Freeman & Lockyer* v *Buckhurst Park Properties (Mangal) Ltd* [1964] 2 QB 480). Moreover, the rule in *Royal British Bank* v *Turquand* (1856) 6 E & B 327 states that a third party is not concerned to see that internal procedures have been followed, where he is not an 'insider' and could not have known whether they had been followed or not. Thus, certain transactions were enforceable even where the directors had exceeded their authority. Nevertheless, third parties could still be caught by the complex rules and could only hope that the company would ratify the transaction or rely on their remedies against the directors personally.

A clumsy attempt was made to deal with the problem in the notorious s9(1) European Communities Act 1972. The section was fraught with interpretative difficulties (for a discussion see *International Sales & Agencies Ltd* v *Marcus* [1982] 3 All ER 551), but the section was nevertheless carried through into the 1985 legislation and became s35 CA 1985.

d) *The position of the members*

Ultra vires is an exception to the rule in *Foss* v *Harbottle* (see chapter 12: *Minorities*), thus members can sue individually to restrain an ultra vires transaction, to rescind or to sue the directors for misfeasance. An ultra vires transaction cannot be ratified.

Where directors have exceeded their authority, the company may sue them for misfeasance but, if the directors have ostensible or implied authority, the company will be bound by the transaction. The members may be able to cure a defect in a transaction which is not ultra vires by ratification or by following the necessary procedure.

e) *The Prentice Report*

The Prentice Report ('Reform of the Ultra Vires Rule', DTI, 1987) recommended that companies should have the capacity to do any act whatsoever and need no longer have an objects clause, but unfortunately this was at variance with European Community law. Many of the recommendations in the Report were carried through into new legislation in 1989, but the Government did not go so far as abolishing objects clauses, nor even the ultra vires rule.

f) *The 1989 Act and the present law*

The CA 1989 dealt with both the problems of third parties to ultra vires transactions and transactions involving lack of authority of directors. It did so by retrospectively inserting provisions into the CA 1985. The principal points to note are:

i) Section 3A says a company may state that its object is to carry on business as a 'general commercial company'. The effect is that its object is to carry on any trade or business whatsoever and to have the power to do all such things as are incidental or conducive to carrying on any trade or business. This is an attempt to make long objects clauses redundant in many cases.

ii) Under s35(1) CA 1985 (a new s35 is substituted in the Act by s108 CA 1989), the validity of any act done by a company shall not be called into question on the ground of lack of capacity by reason of anything in the company's memorandum. This effectively (if not actually) abolishes the ultra vires rule and now neither the company itself nor a third party can use ultra vires to challenge the validity of a transaction.

iii) Subsection 35(2) preserves the members' right to restrain an action which (but for s35(1)) would be a breach of the ultra vires rule, unless the action is fulfilling a pre-existing legal obligation of the company.

iv) Under subsection (3), any act of the directors (even an ultra vires one) can be ratified by special resolution but, unless a separate special resolution is passed absolving them, the directors remain personally liable.

v) The new s35A substitutes the following for the old s35 formula:

'(1) In favour of a person dealing with the company in good faith, the power of the board of directors to bind the company, or authorise others to do so, shall be deemed to be free of any limitation under the company's constitution.'

While this formula is not entirely problem-free, it includes a guide to interpretation (in subsection (2)) and should prove a better attempt to legitimate, so far as third parties are concerned, unauthorised contracts made by directors.

vi) Section 35B states that a party to a transaction is not bound to enquire whether that transaction is permitted by the company's memorandum or as to any limitation on the powers of the board to bind the company where the transaction falls within s35A. Even where s35A does not provide protection, s711A(1) effectively abolishes the doctrine of constructive notice as it relates to documents available for inspection at Companies House, but third parties must make such enquiries as ought reasonably to be made.

vii) The distinction between 'outsiders' and 'insiders' in the rule in *Turquand*'s case (as modified in *Morris* v *Kanssen* [1946] AC 459) is expressly retained. Should the other party to the transaction be a director, a 'connected person' or a company associated with a director, that party will not receive the protection of s35A and may have to account to the company or indemnify it if it sustains a loss. Nevertheless, the transaction may be ratified by special resolution (if it exceeds the company's own capacity) or ordinary resolution.

viii)Companies are now specifically empowered to make provision for employees or former employees of the company or its subsidiaries, in connection with cessation of business or the transfer of its undertaking, even though such provision may not be in the best interests of the company.

2.3 Analysis of questions

Once a fertile ground for questions, the topic has in recent years produced only two, one problem and one essay. It is thought unlikely that the essay question will be repeated in the future but there is still scope for setting problem questions along the lines of the one reproduced below. The candidate needs to demonstrate an understanding of the consequences of the ultra vires rule and abuse of directors' authority and explain how the Companies Act 1989 has affected these consequences.

2.4 Question

The objects clause of the memorandum of association of Southerly Breezes Ltd contains only the following:

i)   The objects of the company are to manufacture and sell sailing yachts.

ii) The company shall have power to do any act which is incidental or conducive to the attainment of the above objects.

The company is currently successfully engaged in its business of making and selling sailing yachts. Emily and Roland are the directors of the company but own no shares in it. In 1991 they were approached by Gina, a close friend of Roland, who was seeking a guarantee of a loan of £100,000 which she was negotiating with Spartan Bank plc. The directors said 'a friend in need is a friend indeed' and, having sent a copy of the memorandum of the company to the bank, caused the company to give a guarantee to the bank in respect of the £100,000.

In March 1993 Gina was made bankrupt and the bank commenced an action against the company on the guarantee. In May 1993 a specially convened meeting of the shareholders of the company passed the following resolutions by 51 per cent majority vote:

a)   Ratifying the directors' actions in giving the guarantee and authorising payment under it.

b)   Authorising a donation of £25,000 to the general funds of the Green Party.

Harvey, who is holder of 49 per cent of the shares, voted against the resolutions at the meeting. Advise him as to whether there are any legal grounds for getting the resolutions set aside.

University of London LLB Examination
(for External Students) Company Law June 1993 Q6

Company Law

General Comment

A question requiring the candidate to illustrate a clear understanding of ultra vires, directors' authority, and the effect on the rules of Companies Act (CA) 1989. Candidates are asked to advise a minority shareholder rather than the third party to the transactions, which is more usual.

Skeleton Solution

Objects clause – corporate gifts – capacity – express and implied powers – ultra vires – breach of authority – ss35 and 35A CA 1985 – ratification.

Suggested Solution

This question focuses on express and implied powers, the problems of a company's capacity and breach of directors' authority from a member's point of view. Both transactions are effectively gifts.

The capacity of a company to perform acts and enter into contracts is prescribed by the objects clause in its memorandum of association. An objects clause typically contains objects, which are the businesses a company is empowered to carry on and powers, which are the acts a company is permitted to do in pursuit of its objects. A company acts outside its powers (ultra vires) if it carries on any business or exercises any power not authorised by its objects clause (*Ashbury Railway Carriage and Iron Co v Riche* (1875)), or even if it exercises a power contained in its objects clause if it does so for an unauthorised object (*Introductions Ltd v National Provincial Bank* (1970)).

At common law, various consequences result from a company acting ultra vires. First, any contract made in the course of acting ultra vires is void and unenforceable by either the company or the other party (unless the latter can show he is not affected by constructive notice of the company acting ultra vires). Second, directors being agents of the company, can only exercise powers delegated to them. The company cannot, however, delegate powers it does not itself have, and thus by acting ultra vires the company, the directors exceed their own authority. As a result, they are personally liable to third parties, to the company and to members. Third, as the company does not have the powers itself, the general meeting cannot (at common law) ratify the directors' abuse of authority.

However, even where the company does have the capacity to do a particular act by virtue of its objects clause, the act may still be a breach by the directors of their authority for it may not have been done in the proper way, or it may have been done for improper purposes, for example. Agency rules apply at common law to cover this type of situation. If the director or directors who make the contract appear to the other party to have the authority to do so (ostensible authority) then the company will be bound by the contract *(Freeman & Lockyer v Buckhurst Park Properties (Mangal) Ltd* (1964)). As between the company and the directors, however, the active directors in the transaction are personally liable to the company for any loss which it may suffer, although the company may ratify an abuse of authority (if it is not also ultra vires) by ordinary resolution, binding itself under the contract.

As will be explained below, the common law consequences of both ultra vires acts and acts which exceed the directors' authority have been affected by the Companies Act (CA) 1989.

The two transactions here must be treated separately. Resolution (a) is concerned with ratification of an act already performed by the directors, and resolution (b) with an act to be performed by the company itself.

As regards the guarantee, Southerly Breezes Ltd has only one object in paragraph (i) of its objects clause. It also has one very wide power in paragraph (ii) which is unlikely to be construed as a substantive object and must therefore be an ancillary power (*Re Horsley & Weight Ltd* (1982)). Therefore, while paragraph (ii) could comprise the guaranteeing of loans, to be intra vires they should be connected with the business of manufacturing and selling sailing yachts.

Some case might be made out that the loan was in connection with the business of the company but, on the facts given, it seems most likely that it was not and the exercise of the power to guarantee the loan would therefore have been ultra vires and the guarantee void.

However, s108 CA 1989 inserted some new provisions (s35 and s35A) into the CA 1985 aimed at validating ultra vires transactions and others that exceed or breach directors' authority. Section 35(1) provides that the validity of any act done by a company shall not be called into question on the ground of lack of capacity by reason of anything in the company's memorandum. In this case this means that the company cannot use the ultra vires rule to avoid payment under the guarantee. This is relevant since, if the guarantee was validly given, it matters little as between the members and the bank whether it was retrospectively ratified.

Nevertheless, it could still be argued that the directors have exceeded their authority, not only by acting ultra vires but by using their power to give guarantees for an improper purpose. This would not be enough to invalidate the guarantee if they had ostensible authority. However, a claim that they had ostensible authority might be countered by saying that the bank had a copy of the memorandum of the company and knew the contents of its objects clause. Depending on what the loan was for, it could be argued that the bank ought to have known that the directors did not have authority to guarantee it, or at least should have been 'on enquiry'.

The CA 1989 again comes to the bank's aid because s35A CA 1985 (also inserted by s108 CA 1989) states that:

'(1) In favour of a person dealing with a company in good faith, the power of the board of directors to bind the company, or authorise others to do so, shall be deemed to be free of any limitation under the company's constitution.'

In addition, s35B states that a party to a transaction is not bound to enquire whether that transaction is permitted by the company's memorandum. Good faith is presumed and s35A(2) states that a party shall not be regarded as acting in bad faith by reason only of knowing that an act is beyond the powers of the directors under the company's constitution.

The result is that the company probably has no option but to honour the guarantee in any case, causing it a loss of £100,000. While members have their right preserved under s32 CA 1985 to obtain an injunction to restrain the commission of an ultra vires act, such as payment under the guarantee, this right is not available if the company is fulfilling a pre-existing legal obligation. If the guarantee is validated by s35(1) and s35A as appears to be the case, the company cannot challenge the payment and must suffer a loss. The question is whether that loss could or should be recovered from the directors.

The sole purpose of resolution (a) seems to be to absolve the directors from liability. While s35(3) permits the company to ratify even an ultra vires act, it must do so by passing a special resolution (although an ordinary resolution would suffice were it not ultra vires). Furthermore, such ratification does not relieve the directors of personal liability and a separate special resolution must be passed in order to do so. In this case, the meeting has merely passed an ordinary resolution. As Harvey holds 49 per cent of the shares, the necessary special resolution could not be passed without his support. Thus, the resolution is invalid and the directors remain personally liable. While the action would usually need to be brought by the company by virtue of the rule in *Foss* v *Harbottle* (1843), and the majority appear to support what the directors have done, Harvey has two points in his favour. First, the passing of a resolution by the incorrect majority is an exception to the rule (*Edwards* v *Halliwell* (1950)), and an individual member can bring an action to have the offending resolution declared invalid. Second, ultra vires is also an exception.

Turning to resolution (b), there is no express power to make this payment. When the court can imply a power to make gratuitous payments has been the subject of much judicial and academic debate. In *Hutton* v *West Cork Railway Co* (1883) Bowen LJ said that there should be 'no cakes and ale except such as are required for the benefit of the company', and political donations might in some circumstances be regarded as being generally for the company's benefit. In *Re Lee, Behrens & Co Ltd* (1932), Eve J laid down a three-stage test in order to determine the validity of corporate gifts. Besides being for the benefit of the company and bona fide they should also be reasonably incidental to the carrying on of the company's business, but in *Rolled Steel Products (Holdings) Ltd* v *British Steel Corporation* (1986) Slade J in his turn called the *Behrens* test 'misleading'. If on a true construction of the company's memorandum the act was capable of being performed as reasonably incidental to the attainment of its objects, it would not be ultra vires simply because the directors performed it for purposes other than those specified in the memorandum. Whether or not it is for the company's benefit may therefore be irrelevant.

Thus, if it is not capable of being reasonably incidental to the company's objects (and it is hard to see how it can be), the donation to the the Green Party is likely to be ultra vires. If the donation has not already been made then it may be open to Harvey to apply for an injunction against the directors to restrain payment under s35A(4) CA 1985. He may also have the resolution declared invalid, since the general meeting has no power to authorise an ultra vires payment.

If the £25,000 has already been paid, although s35(1) would seem to preclude recovery from the recipients, Harvey may seek to bring a derivative action against Emily and Roland to recover the sum. Harvey should also be advised that any derivative action may now be brought under s459 CA 1985, which enables the court to authorise any individual to bring proceedings on behalf of the company: s461(2)(c).

3 The Articles of Association

3.1 Introduction

This chapter deals with the problems arising from the provisions contained in a company's articles of association, and in particular from the concept that these articles form a contract involving the members and the company.

3.2 Key points

a) *Companies Act 1985 s14*

This section provides that the memorandum and articles of association are a contract binding as if they had been signed and sealed by every member of the company. In *Wood v Odessa Waterworks Co* (1889) 42 Ch D 636 it was held that this provision must be read as if it also deemed the company to have signed and sealed the articles. The contract is multi-partite, involving the members inter se and each member individually with the company.

The s14 contract may be enforced by any member of the company, but there is some uncertainty as to the rights which may be enforced by means of s14. One view is that s14 may only be used in connection with what are sometimes termed 'membership rights', ie those rights whose violation will affect the member in his capacity as a member. However, it is suggested that the better view is that the rights of the member include the right to have the company's affairs managed in accordance with any provisions in the articles, irrespective of theoretical debates about the nature of membership rights.

The narrower view of the s14 contract rests on the decision of Astbury J in *Hickman v Kent or Romney Marsh Sheepbreeders' Association* [1915] 1 Ch 881, whilst the broader view appears in *Salmon v Quin & Axtens* [1909] AC 442. Later cases provide support for both interpretations and, while judges generally express the narrower proposition, there is much academic support for the wider view.

Suing on the basis of 'membership rights' under the s14 contract is one way of circumventing the rule in *Foss v Harbottle* (see chapter 12: *Minorities*), and the debate therefore has more than mere academic significance. The court has generally refused to enforce 'non-membership rights' contained in the articles, however. In *Eley v Positive Government Security Life Assurance Co* (1876) 1 Ex D 88 it was held that the s14 contract could not be used to enforce the right, contained in the articles, to be the company solicitor. This refusal to allow 'outsiders' to sue on the contract extends equally to directors (see, eg, *Beattie v Beattie* [1938] P 99), but articles have been allowed to evidence the terms of an agreement between the company and its directors (*Re New British Iron Co, ex parte*

Beckwith [1898] 1 Ch 324). This problem in relation to directors has declined in importance, since virtually all directors now have service contracts. However, the articles may be held to supplement a service contract as in *Re Richmond Gate Property Co Ltd* [1965] 1 WLR 335. One should also bear in mind that removing a director from office even in accordance with the articles may be a breach of his service contract, entitling him to claim damages (*Southern Foundries Ltd* v *Shirlaw* [1940] AC 701).

Case law suggests that there are certain respects in which the s14 contract differs from an ordinary contract. Thus, it is not subject to rectification, even where it appears that the normal requirements for this remedy are fulfilled: *Scott* v *Frank Scott (London) Ltd* [1940] Ch 794. Nor can damages be awarded against the company for a breach of the contract, since this would be a misuse of the company's funds: *Houldsworth* v *City of Glasgow Bank* (1880) 5 App Cas 317.

b) *Altering the articles*

Section 9 Companies Act (CA) 1985 permits the alteration of the articles by special resolution. Difficulties sometimes arise where it is alleged that the majority has made an alteration for the purpose of treating the minority unfairly. *Allen* v *Gold Reefs of West Africa* [1900] 1 Ch 656 establishes that the power to alter the articles must be exercised bona fide in the best interests of the company.

The modern tendency is not to have in articles of association the type of provision which was subject to a challenged alteration in many of the older cases. Instead, such provisions, concerning expulsion of directors, voting rights, etc, are more usually found in directors' service contracts or shareholders' agreements. Cases of challenged alterations to articles are therefore now infrequent. Moreover, the court has generally upheld alterations where the plaintiff cannot show bad faith was involved, which has often discouraged litigants. Variation of class rights (ie membership rights attaching to a particular class of shares), involving an alteration to articles, might give scope for a legal challenge under this heading. (As to class rights, see further chapter 6: *Shares*.) Action under s459 CA 1985 (conduct unfairly prejudicial to members) would now, however, seem to be the best method of challenging most alterations.

Any provision in the articles purporting to make them unalterable is void. However, there is no objection to weighted voting rights (*Bushell* v *Faith* [1970] AC 1099). By the same token, it seems, shareholders may enter enforceable agreements as to how they will vote in the event of a resolution to alter the articles but, if the company is made a party to such a shareholders' agreement so as to fetter its statutory right to alter the articles, the agreement will be void, at least as concerns the company, according to the House of Lords' judgment in *Russell* v *Northern Bank Development Corporation Ltd* [1992] 1 WLR 588.

3.3 Analysis of questions

This topic has appeared six times since 1983, only once as an essay question (on the s14 contract). As the problems below demonstrate, the tendency has been to combine the topic with others, especially class rights and minority remedies.

3.4 Questions

QUESTION ONE

Panorama Ltd has articles of association in the form of Table A with the addition of the following provision:

> In the event of any shareholder wishing to transfer his shares, the directors shall purchase them at a fair value.

The company has issued 5,000 shares – 2,000 each to James and Jill and 1,000 to Denis. All three are directors and Denis was appointed as the company's managing director at a salary of £30,000 a year. The company has become very prosperous and a recent valuation of the company's assets suggests that the shares are worth £50 each.

Unfortunately, disagreement has arisen between James and Jill on the one hand and Denis on the other. James and Jill have threatened Denis with dismissal without compensation and have refused to consider Denis's demand that they purchase his shares for £50,000. Denis is also owed £10,000 in respect of salary arrears.

Advise Denis. Ignore any remedies Denis might have as a minority shareholder.

University of London LLB Examination
(for External Students) Company Law June 1990 Q4

General Comment

The wording of this question has a trap for the unwary – namely the last sentence, 'Ignore any remedies Denis might have as a minority shareholder.' The candidate must ensure he or she does not immediately charge down the wrong track; this is a question predominantly about articles.

Skeleton Solution

Threatened with dismissal – articles' provision: major portion of marks will be for this – salary arrears.

Suggested Solution

Denis almost certainly wishes to leave the company, but at a proper level of compensation and remuneration. James and Jill are in effect 'ganging up' on Denis and hence it would be unsatisfactory for him to remain as managing director. There are three issues: dismissal without compensation; the purchase of Denis's shares; the salary arrears.

i) *Threatened dismissal*

Without embarking on a full analysis of employment law, generally one has to have been employed for two years in order to bring proceedings for unfair dismissal. However, a managing director does not qualify as a 'company employee' for all purposes: *Re Newspaper Proprietary Syndicate Ltd* (1900). Further, most managing directors have fixed term contracts and dismissal after, say, two years of a five year contract, will entitle the dismissed managing director to the remaining three years' pay (subject to his or her mitigating the loss). If Denis has such a contract he is advised to take action against Panorama Ltd in the event he is dismissed: s303 Companies Act 1985.

Doubtless the prosperity of the company is due in no small part to Denis's efforts as managing director, and the level of compensation he is entitled to should reflect this.

ii) *Purchase of Denis's shares*

Denis is advised that he should try to sell his shares to the directors for a fair value, in accordance with the articles of association. However, James and Jill are refusing to consider his demand. A fair value would be £50, because that is what they are worth. Therefore James and Jill are ignoring the company's articles: *Re a Company* (1983); *Re London School of Electronics Ltd* (1986). The articles are part of the contract between the members of a company, and each member has the right to have the articles observed by the company and the other members. Nothing in the rule in *Foss* v *Harbottle* (1843), ie that the proper plaintiff in an action for a wrong done to a company, is the company itself, prevents Denis from suing to enforce the articles. This is because Denis would be suing in his own right to enforce a contractual obligation owed to him.

Cases in which the courts have prevented the company from ignoring its members are *Pender* v *Lushington* (1877); *Wood* v *Odessa Waterworks Co* (1889); *Salmon* v *Quin & Axtens* (1909).

Of course James and Jill may attempt to change the articles to take out this, for them, troublesome provision. They have 80 per cent of the shares between them and hence could pass a special resolution at a general meeting to change the articles, in accordance with s9 Companies Act 1985. However such alteration must be done in good faith and for the benefit of the company as a whole: *Allen* v *Gold Reefs of West Africa* (1900). This can include removing a director when the other directors agree: *Shuttleworth* v *Cox Bros & Co (Maidenhead) Ltd* (1927). However, the provision here, that of purchasing shares, is less clear; merely because one shareholder is a 'victim' is not sufficient for bad faith. In *Sidebotham* v *Kershaw, Leese & Co* (1920) a shareholder competing in business was forced by a change in the articles to transfer his shares at a fair value to the other shareholders. The meaning of 'in good faith and for the benefit of the company as a whole' was further expounded in *Greenhalgh* v *Arderne Cinemas Ltd* (1951). The proposed change must be for the benefit of a hypothetical individual member. Here, Denis would stand a fighting chance of showing bad faith on the part of the other two directors.

iii) *Denis's salary arrears*

Denis should sue the company for these – as Panorama Ltd is trading profitably he should not be unduly concerned that the company may be unable to satisfy any judgment against it. This should be fairly straightforward as there is unlikely to be a defence to this claim, and if he issued proceedings he would probably succeed on a summary judgment.

QUESTION TWO

Ox Ltd was formed in 1986 and carries on a business manufacturing nuts and bolts. The memorandum of association provides, inter alia, that the share capital of the company is divided into 50,000 £1 ordinary shares and 10,000 £1 preference shares. Further, the preference shares are there expressed to carry rights to a 16 per cent preference dividend. All the share capital has been issued.

In 1989, after lengthy negotiations, Ox Ltd purchased a factory from Pin Ltd, a company which has owned 5,000 of the ordinary shares in Ox Ltd since its formation in 1986. As part of the consideration for the purchase, it was agreed that the articles of association of Ox Ltd would be altered so as to give Pin Ltd special pre-emption rights in the event of other members of Ox Ltd wishing to sell their shares. The alteration of articles was carried out by Ox Ltd early in 1990.

The board of directors of Ox Ltd now wish to remove from the articles the rights of Pin Ltd in respect of pre-emption, although they are aware that Pin Ltd would oppose this. They also wish to reduce the preference dividend from 16 per cent to 10 per cent. They have heard that 85 per cent of the preference shareholders would be prepared to accede to this reduction since they have all become aware that the company is in financial difficulties and wish to help it. The remaining 15 per cent of the preference shareholders would be opposed to this reduction.

Advise the directors.

University of London LLB Examination
(for External Students) Company Law June 1993 Q7

General Comment

A question requiring the candidate to look very carefully at the problem. Once the 'perception threshold' of the question is broken the solution is not too difficult. A question likely to be avoided by many candidates and therefore an opportunity for the individual to distinguish him/herself. Variation of class rights is covered in chapter 6: *Shares.*

Skeleton Solution

Articles of association – restrictions on alteration – bona fide for the benefit of the company; subjective or objective test.

Ascertainment of class rights – variation of class rights – what alterations constitute a variation?

Rights of dissenting minority.

Suggested Solution

The directors of Ox Ltd ('the company') wish to alter its articles in order to achieve two things: firstly they wish to divest Pin Ltd of the pre-emption rights acquired on its sale of the factory to the company: secondly they wish to reduce the dividend attaching to the preference shares from 16 per cent to 10 per cent. We are told that both Pin Ltd and 15 per cent of the preference shareholders are unlikely to acquiesce to the alterations. There is therefore a possibility that the alterations might be challenged by either of the above groups on the basis that they constitute a variation of a class right necessitating approval by that class alone, and/or that the alterations are not in any event 'bona fide for the benefit of the company'.

Dealing firstly with the alteration removing Pin Ltd's rights of pre-emption, by virtue of s9 CA 1985 any alteration to the articles requires a special resolution. As owner of 20 per cent of the ordinary shares in Ox Ltd, Pin Ltd is prima facie unable to defeat the resolution for alteration. Pin Ltd may however contend that the pre-emption rights currently enjoyed by it are 'class rights' attached to the shares currently held and therefore that any variation will require observance of the procedure for variation laid down in the articles or, alternatively, observance of s125 CA 1985. Are the rights enjoyed by Pin Ltd class rights?

Class rights are more often easier to recognise than to define. Frequently (although not invariably) the rights are expressly defined in the articles. Farrar (*Farrar's Company Law*, 3rd ed, p222) states that 'dissimilar interests alone, not arising from legal rights under the corporate constitution, cannot generally be regarded as sufficient ground for the separation of classes'. There was until recently little authority as to what constitutes a class. A thorough review however was undertaken by Scott J in *Cumbrian Newspapers Group Ltd v Cumberland and Westmorland Herald Newspaper and Printing Co Ltd* (1986) who adopted a tri-partite classification. Of particular significance to Pin Ltd in the present case is the third category of rights upheld by Scott J in this case. These were rights which although not attached to any particular class of shares were conferred on the beneficiary qua member. In that case the rights were enjoyed on condition that the plaintiff held at least 10.67 per cent of the issued ordinary share capital of the company. Applying this to the facts of the problem it can be seen that the pre-emption rights acquired by Pin Ltd were not referable to (and were unconnected with) its pre-existing membership of the company. They are not therefore rights enjoyed qua member and for that reason neither are they class rights. This alteration at least cannot therefore be a variation of a class right. Thus the only remaining option available to Pin Ltd is to contend that the alteration is not bona fide for the benefit of the company.

The duty of shareholders to vote bona fide in the interests of the company has received a chequered treatment in the authorities over the years. The duty was firmly established by the Court of Appeal in *Allen v Gold Reefs of West Africa* (1900). The principal difficulty lies in knowing whether the test is to be applied according to the subjective view of the members or an objective view.

In *Shuttleworth v Cox Bros & Co (Maidenhead) Ltd* (1927), the Court of Appeal preferred not to interfere where there were grounds on which a reasonable shareholder would come to the same conclusion. This is at odds with the ratio of the Court of Appeal in *Greenhalgh v Arderne Cinemas Ltd* (1951) in which Lord Evershed MR adopted the test of the hypothetical shareholder, ie to ask whether what was proposed was for that person's benefit. The test proposed in *Greenhalgh* (above) is of little value where there is a conflict as in the instant case between two groups. Lord Evershed MR did however indicate that discriminatory conduct might be a ground for intervention. In the instant case it is not known exactly why Ox Ltd wishes to remove the pre-emption rights or exactly how it is intended to be beneficial to the company. Pin Ltd would therefore appear to be in a position to commence proceedings under s459 CA 1985 in order to seek redress.

The reduction of the preference dividend from 16 per cent to 10 per cent is undoubtedly a variation of the rights attaching to those shares: *House of Fraser plc v AGCE Investments Ltd* (1987); ie variation presupposes existence of the right, variation of the right, and the continued existence of the right. The resolution effecting the variation must therefore comply with any procedure laid down in the articles dealing with variation (if there is one): s125(4) CA 1985. If the articles do not provide any procedure for variation s125(2) provides a statutory procedure: this requires either a special majority of the holders of the class to consent in writing or an extraordinary resolution passed at a separate class meeting. The 15 per cent preference holders who object may apply to the court to have variation cancelled within 21 days of the consent/resolution being given/passed: s127(1) and (2). Where this mechanism is invoked the variation is of no effect unless approved by the court.

QUESTION THREE

Lorry Ltd is operating a road haulage business. It has an issued share capital of 900 £1 shares. Alan, Barry and Colin own 300 shares each. The articles of association of the company provide that, 'Alan, Barry and Colin are to be the directors of the company and each is to receive a salary of £25,000 per annum.'

The company was formed in 1987 and was immediately successful. Every year Alan, Barry and Colin have each drawn £25,000. No dividends have been paid on their shares but the huge profits of the company have been ploughed back into the business, so that now each £1 share is represented by assets worth about £1,000, and thus the total asset value of the company is about £900,000.

In 1990 Colin quarrelled with Alan and Barry over matters of business policy. After that, they made it difficult for Colin to have any real share in the management of the business because, although they still had regular weekly directors' meetings at which they were all present, Alan and Barry discussed and made all the business decisions in advance and invariably outvoted Colin at the board meetings. At first Colin complained bitterly about this, but after some months he lost all interest in the business and has not now attended a board meeting for nearly two years.

In recent months Colin has suspected that Alan and Barry have been diverting the company's haulage contracts to a newly formed company registered with the name Lorry (London) Ltd of which Alan and Barry are the sole shareholders and directors. Last week Colin confronted Alan and Barry with this and there was a violent quarrel. They have just written to him informing him that he is 'sacked as director and will receive no more salary from the company'.

Advise Colin.

University of London LLB Examination
(for External Students) Company Law June 1993 Q4

General Comment

An eye for the salient facts and an appreciation of the limits of the remedies available are required.

Skeleton Solution

The s14 contract – 'outsider rights' – contracts extrinsic but identical to the articles.

Shareholder remedies – s459 CA 1985 – s122 IA 1986 and limitations thereon – interrelation between derivative action and s459.

Suggested Solution

Colin has a plethora of remedies available to him. There are three main issues: (1) does Colin have a contractual remedy against Lorry Ltd on the basis of a contract contained in the articles?; (2) is exclusion from the board actionable qua member?; and (3) can Colin pursue any remedy against Alan and Barry on behalf of Lorry Ltd?

1)   Section 14 CA 1985 gives contractual effect to the memorandum and articles between the members inter se, and between the members and the company. The effect is that every member has a contractual right to enforce observance of the articles: *Wood* v *Odessa Waterworks Co* (1889). There are however important restrictions on the type of right which may be enforced. Most significantly the rights enforceable are only those which affect the member in his capacity as member: *Eley* v *Positive Government Security Life Assurance Co* (1876). In the instant case the relevant article provides that Colin is to be director. The

right is therefore not conferred qua shareholder and prima facie Colin has no action on the basis of the contract contained in the articles.

There are however two further possibilities. The first is that Colin may be able to bring an action qua member to have the articles enforced (the fact that this will result in his being reinstated as a director being incidental to the action). There is no direct authority in Colin's favour in point although the House of Lords in *Quin & Axtens* v *Salmon* (1909) upheld the plaintiff's injunction qua member although it affected him principally qua director. The second possibility is that the court would be prepared to imply a contract extrinsic but identical to the articles, alterable unilaterally by the company: *Re New British Iron Co, ex parte Beckwith* (1898). On this basis Colin would at least be able to recover any arrears of salary.

2) As a shareholder Colin has potentially at his disposal two important remedies. He may petition the court for a just and equitable winding up of Lorry Ltd pursuant to s122(1)(g) IA 1986. Alternatively he may bring proceedings under s459 CA 1985 for unfairly prejudicial conduct. Frequently the same set of facts will give rise to the availability of either remedy. Exclusion from participation in management was recognised as a ground for just and equitable winding up (at least in relation to quasi-partnership companies) by the House of Lords in *Ebrahimi* v *Westbourne Galleries Ltd* (1973). As a condition precedent to granting relief the court will require to be satisfied as to the existence of one or more of the following criteria: (a) the company should have been formed on the basis of a personal relationship involving mutual trust and confidence; (b) there should be some agreement that all or some of the shareholders participate in the management of the business; and (c) there should be pre-emption rights over the shares. The crux of the matter is that the court will not intervene unless the agreement embodied in the articles does not properly define the parties' rights and expectations.

Colin is attempting to invoke an equitable jurisdiction and so the court will be interested in whether or not he has 'clean hands' and has delayed in seeking this remedy. Colin should also bear in mind that to have the company wound up will be to 'kill the goose that lays the golden eggs'. In view of the fact that the value of the company has increased from £900 in 1987 to £900,000 at the present day, Colin would be advised to view this remedy as a last resort.

By virtue of s461 the court has an almost unlimited discretion as to the appropriate order upon the hearing of a petition under s459 alleging unfairly prejudicial conduct. Commonly the order will be that petitioners' shares be purchased by the respondent. The range of remedies available should alone make this a more attractive choice of remedy to Colin. The paramount question is whether there has been any unfair prejudice.

In common with the remedy of the just and equitable winding up, exclusion from management can form the basis of an unfair prejudice application: *Re London School of Electronics Ltd* (1986). As before the court will require to be satisfied that the removal from the board is both unfair and prejudicial. Mere removal alone will not suffice and so much depends on the basis upon which Colin became a member of Lorry Ltd. There is no requirement that Colin come to the court with clean hands although his non attendance at board meetings may influence the court as to the relief which it is prepared to grant. There is however one further element which may make a petition under s459 the most appropriate remedy.

3) Can Colin pursue any remedy against Alan and Barry for allegedly diverting contracts to the newly formed Lorry (London) Ltd? According to the rule in *Foss* v *Harbottle* (1843) the proper plaintiff in an action in this respect would be Lorry Ltd. As malefactors and majority shareholders Barry and Alan are unlikely to procure Lorry Ltd to bring proceedings against themselves. Prima facie therefore there is a fraud on the minority of exactly the type contemplated in *Cooks* v *Deeks* (1916) which Colin may attempt to redress on behalf of Lorry Ltd in a separate derivative action. It should be noted however that under s459 CA 1985 as amended by CA 1989 conduct which is prejudicial to the interests of the 'members generally' will be actionable. Prior to this amendment conduct which affected all members equally (and therefore in reality the company itself) was not actionable. In the present case Alan and Barry's actions will ultimately diminish the value of theirs and Colin's holdings in Lorry Ltd. It is therefore open to Colin to remedy this loss to Lorry Ltd under s459. It should be noted that by virtue of s461(2)(c) the court may authorise civil proceedings to be brought in the name and on behalf of the company. This would thereby enable Colin to redress wrongs done to both himself and Lorry Ltd in a single petition under s459 by sidestepping the confusing rules governing common law derivative actions.

4 Promoters and Pre-incorporation Contracts

4.1 Introduction

4.2 Key points

4.3 Recent regulations

4.4 Analysis of questions

4.5 Questions

4.1 Introduction

The title of this chapter really encompasses two separate areas of law. The first concerns the liability of promoters for statements contained in a company prospectus issued prior to a flotation, whilst the second concerns the extent to which the company can be made liable, after incorporation, for contracts entered into, purportedly on its behalf, prior to incorporation. The two areas are covered in the same chapter because they both relate to the very early stages of a company's existence and consequently often occur together in a problem question.

4.2 Key points

a) *Flotation*

Only a public company may offer its shares to the public. Securities of a public company (principally shares and debentures) may be listed on the Stock Exchange or be unlisted.

Section 142 Financial Services Act 1986 provides that such securities may only be admitted to the Official List of the Stock Exchange if they comply with Part IV of the Act. The principal requirement (s144) is that the Stock Exchange Listing Rules (contained in what is known as the Yellow Book) be complied with.

The Listing Rules comprehensively set down conditions for admission, admission procedures, time limits and contents of the listing particulars and other offer documents issued by the company. Other offer documents include mini or abridged prospectuses. Prior Stock Exchange approval is required for publication of all such documents, and the Stock Exchange also has power to control advertisements for share offers.

Offers of unlisted securities are now controlled by the Public Offer of Securities Regulations 1995 which contains a similar regime to that envisaged in Part V Financial Services Act 1986 (never implemented). The regulations which came into force in June 1995 replace Part III Companies Act 1985. The new regime is not dissimilar to that for listed securities. Where securities are offered which are not admitted to official listing the person responsible for making the offer or invitation to make an offer must first register a prospectus with the Registrar of Companies and then make it available free to the public. Regulation 8 requires the prospectus to comply with the form and contents set out in the First Schedule, and regulation 9 imposes a general duty of disclosure. Advertisements (given a wide definition) cannot be issued unless they state that a prospectus will be (given a wide definition) cannot be issued unless they state that a prospectus will be published and give the address where it can be obtained.

Unlisted securities may nevertheless be traded. The Alternative Investment Market (AIM) is replacing the Unlisted Securities Market (USM) as the principal secondary market for securities of smaller and growing companies. These companies might not be able to satisfy the requirements for a full Stock Exchange listing, but still wish to raise capital by public issue, and sometimes a quotation on the secondary market may be a step towards full listing at a later stage. Entrance to the secondary markets is also controlled by Stock Exchange rules, although the requirements are less stringent than for a full listing. The investor in USM or AIM quoted companies accepts a higher level of risk but still has some protection.

Whether securities are listed or unlisted, liability may be incurred by the company, its directors, and other persons responsible for the content of offer documents if they fail to comply with the procedural requirements, or if there are significant omissions from particulars, or if the documents contain false or misleading particulars. Liability can be statutory – principally s150 Financial Services Act 1986 (listed securities) and the Public Offer of Securities Regulations 1995, regulation 15 (unlisted), which provide for similar liabilities and exemptions – or at common law for deceit or misrepresentation. There may be civil as well as criminal liability for offenders, affording injured investors rights to compensation or rescission. Students should be familiar with all potential offences and remedies and with the defences, particularly the statutory defences, available.

b) *Promoters*

There is no statutory defintion of the term 'promoter', but it is generally understood to mean those who take on the task of forming the company and getting it under way in its business.

Promoters owe fidcuiary duties to the company, although they cannot be treated as its agents during the period of promotion, for the company does not exist at that time. In particular they must not make a secret profit out of the process of formation. This is of particular importance if the promoters are intending to sell their own property to the company. Full disclosure of the circumstances must be made, either to the shareholders or to an independent board of directors. In many cases there will be no independent board, since it is likely that the promoters themselves will become the directors.

Promoters have a duty to account to the company for the profits of any property which they have bought for the purpose of selling it to the company. In equity the property belongs to the company, which is therefore entitled to insist on taking it over at cost price.

Promoters have a duty not to exercise undue influence over the decisions of the company.

Where promoters are in breach of their duties the company will be able to sue for any damages incurred, or claim an account of any profits made. If a contract has been improperly procured, then it is likely that the company will be able to rescind it.

In this area many of the remedies depend upon general contractual and tortious principles (including the tort of deceit). In any case it is necessary to consider the application of these principles.

c) *Pre-incorporation contracts*

When a company is in the process of formation it is common for contracts to be entered into on its behalf. This is a logical impossibility, since by definition the company does not exist at that point. After incorporation it may become necessary to consider who, if anyone, is liable on the contract.

Section 36C CA 1985 provides that a person who enters into a contract as purported agent for an unformed company is deemed to have made the contract in a personal capacity and is personally liable on it. This rule is subject to contrary agreement between the parties to the contract, but it is important to understand that the contrary agreement cannot serve to make the company liable on the contract.

The only way in which the company can become liable is if, after incorporation, it enters into a contract with the original creditor in the same terms as that of the orginal contract between the promoter and the creditor. It is not possible simply to ratify the original contract, since the principles of agency do not permit ratification of a contract made when the purported principal did not exist.

4.3 Recent regulations

The Public Offer of Securities Regulations 1995 replaces Part III CA 1985 and Part V Financial Services Act 1986 (unimplemented), significantly amending the rules relating to contents of prospectuses and liability for misstatement in relation to offers of unlisted securities.

4.4 Analysis of questions

This is a topic which has occurred on the London LLB External paper frequently since 1983, and which is popular in degree examinations more generally. It is therefore given extensive treatment in this book. On the London paper it usually appears as a problem question.

4.5 Questions

QUESTION ONE

Dee and Ellie were directors of Choc-a-holic Ltd, a successful confectionery company which supplies 'environmentally-friendly' chocolates to high class retailers. Wishing to raise additional finance for further expansion, they sought advice from Lorings, a notable merchant bank. Subsequently Choc-a-holic Ltd issued £1 million ordinary shares and converted to a public company with the new name of Choc plc. The shares were offered for sale to the public and Choc plc obtained a listing on the Stock Exchange.

The listing particulars, which were issued on 3 January 1995, explained that the company only used organically produced ingredients that were environmentally friendly and that the company's expansion plans intended to build on this and a further 30 outlets had been obtained for the increased sale of the confectionery. The profits forecast stated that the company's profits were likely to increase by 50 per cent as a result of these expansion plans.

An EEC report was 'leaked' to the directors of the company which stated that Choc plc confectionery products did not comply with the new EEC approved definition of 'environmentally friendly' and that 99 per cent of the ingredients were from sources that did not comply with a new EEC Regulation's definition of 'organic.'

The directors chose to ignore the leaked report. The sale of the shares was a success. After trading in the shares commenced the EEC report was published. As a result the price of the company's shares has fallen by 90 per cent. All retail outlets are now refusing to stock the company's products. The Stock Exchange has suspended dealings and the company is expected to go into insolvent liquidation.

Advise Caramel who agreed to take 100 Choc plc shares on flotation, and Hazel who bought 100 shares on the market after trading in the shares commenced.

University of London LLB Examination
(for External Students) Company Law June 1995 Q5

General Comment

This question concerns liability for information about a company which ought properly to be provided by listing particulars and a knowledge of the statutory and common law remedies available. It is very important to deal in some detail with those remedies which operate against persons other than the company where insolvent liquidation appears likely.

Skeleton Solution

Outline provisions in Financial Services Act 1986 about general requirement of disclosure – class of claimants – statutory defences, s151 – insolvent liquidation and recovery from directors personally – compensation and measure of damages – alternative common law remedies.

Suggested Solution

Caramel and Hazel have each acquired 100 Choc plc shares and seem to have sustained a heavy loss as a result. The listing particulars emphasised the importance of 'organic' and 'environmentally friendly' factors, but Dee and Ellie find out, apparently before the sale of shares began, about their non-compliance. There are statutory remedies for persons suffering losses by reason of defects in listing particulars and these must be considered first.

Section 150 Financial Services Act (FSA) 1986 is relevant here and subs(1) and (3) impose liability to pay compensation to persons acquiring securities and suffering loss as a result of misleading statements or omissions in the particulars (subs1), or in supplementary listing particulars (subs3). Section 146 FSA 86 imposes a general duty of disclosure in listing particulars, and this extends to such information as would normally be found to enable investors to assess 'the prospects of the issuer of the securities' (s146(1)(a) and Chapter 6, part 6 Stock Exchange Listing Rules), ie Choc plc. This information was absolutely crucial to an assessment of Choc plc's prospects. Provided there was sufficient time between the directors becoming aware of the problem and the onset of share dealing, there was a clear duty to issue supplementary particulars based on 'significant new matters' which would have needed to go into the listing particulars had they been known about earlier (s147(1)(a)).

Caramel purchased under the original flotation and Hazel bought on the open market after trading commenced, but we do not know whether this was before or after publication of the report. Caramel seems to be well within the class of persons contemplated by s150(1), as her loss was directly caused by the omission of supplementary particulars. Hazel's position is not so clear, because if she had purchased subsequent to the publication of the EEC report, the price may have begun to reflect the true situation. Certainly, this would be the case within a few days at most, but this a matter of evidence. There seems to be nothing in the legislation to prevent an open market purchaser being an 'acquirer' within the Act.

31

The next point is whether there are relevant defences against either of the investors. This seems to turn upon the chronological order of events and the defences are set out in s151 FSA:

1. Section 151(1)(a) gives a defence if the particulars, when submitted, were believed to be true and that acquisition took place before it was reasonably practicable to correct matters. This might be available if the leak was close in time to the onset of dealing. There seems to be no reason to doubt the directors' belief in the truth of the particulars although, if they had no reasonable foundation for their belief through lack of inquiry, ie 'Nelsonian' (ie deliberate) blindness, s146(3) would preclude reliance upon this defence.

2. Section 151(2) might defend had the directors relied upon a statement by an expert on the points later defined by the EEC, although this sounds unlikely.

3. Section 151(5) might defend against Hazel but not Caramel. This is that the open market purchase was made in the light of knowledge of the 'change or new matter'. This, again, is a matter of evidence.

4. Section 151(6) would defend if the directors 'reasonably believed' that supplementary particulars were not called for. Much will depend upon just what was leaked and how authentic the information seemed. If the directors had the full substance of the report they will have no defence, but a mere 'whisper' might allow this defence to work.

It sounds as if insolvent liquidation is close, so an important question is: who may be liable to the investors? Section 150(1) imposes liability upon 'the persons responsible for' the particulars. This includes the 'issuer' (s152(1)(a), and directors at the time the particulars were submitted (s152(1)(b)). This seems to catch the directors but, by the wording of s147(1) and (3) and s150(3), it is clear that for failure to issue supplementary particulars only the issuer is caught, not the persons responsible for the original particulars. All is not lost, however, because s147(3) imposes a duty upon the persons responsible for the original particulars to notify the issuer, ie Choc plc, of any 'new matter' requiring supplementary particulars. This will catch the directors quite neatly.

If Caramel and Hazel can get this far and the directors cannot find a defence, the question becomes one of what remedy is provided. The Act does not give much guidance, and merely refers to 'compensation' for loss, so damages are contemplated but nothing is said of the measure. The Companies Acts' measure of damages for untrue statements in prospectuses is usually the difference between the higher of (a) the market value at purchase (if any) and (b) the price actually paid (the flotation price in Caramel's case or the market price for Hazel), and the true value of the securities at that time when the untrue element in the prospectus is disregarded. This appears to be the approach under the FSA and the recent case of *Smith New Court Securities* v *Scrimgeour Vickers (Asset Management) Ltd* (1994) was decided on that basis.

Outside the FSA provisions, most avenues for Caramel and Hazel are based upon misrepresentation and would need, of necessity, to be pursued against the company. This seems of little use in the circumstances, although rescission would possibly be worth pursuing if circumstances changed. There could be some difficulty with this as Choc plc may not have been in being at the time of the particulars, so that the directors could not possibly have been its agents and therefore rescission would not be available (*Lynde* v *Anglo-Italian Hemp Spinning Co Ltd* (1896)). It would certainly be too late once the company was in liquidation (*Oakes* v *Turquand and Harding* (1867)). There might be a reasonable possibility of pursuing the directors personally under *Hedley Byrne* principles (*Hedley Byrne & Co* v *Heller and Partners* (1964)) for negligent misstatement, and the recent House of Lords' decisions on reliance cases indicate a favourable reception. However, the existence of statutory duties and remedies such as those in the FSA probably stands in the way of a common law action purely for damages.

The point about the various remedies is that they are not mutually exclusive but are, in fact, cumulative, so that any or all of them are available and this is not affected by rescission (*Archer* v *Brown* (1985)). It is clear that double recovery would not be possible.

QUESTION TWO

In the summer of 1993, Ann Appleby and Betty Berry decided to form a company to manufacture wine but in view of their imminent holidays, agreed to do nothing about it until the Autumn. In August 1993, without telling Betty (who was still on holiday), Ann purchased a plot of land, 'Grapeacre', located in southern England. The purchase was made at a properly conducted auction for a price of £200,000 (about half its true market value at that time) and was transferred into the sole name of Ann.

In November 1993 Ann explained to Dave Daft that she was forming a wine manufacturing company to be called 'Wino Ltd'. She arranged that he would supply a hydraulic grape press to be delivered to the factory on Grapeacre in February 1994 in return for a price of £50,000 payable within 3 months of delivery. Ann gave Dave a typewritten document setting out this arrangement, at the bottom right-hand corner of which appeared the name 'The Wino Company' and directly underneath that, also typed, 'Ann Appleby'.

In December 1993 Ann and Betty formed a company with the name 'Bokay Ltd' (having changed their minds about the desirability of the name 'Wino Ltd'). They each subscribed for 500,000 £1 fully paid shares. In January 1994 Ann sold Grapeacre to Bokay Ltd for £600,000 (its true market value at that time). In July 1994 Ann and Betty sold all their shares in Bokay Ltd to Eric Endacott who has since found out all the above facts. Dave has never been paid for the grape press he supplied.

Discuss.

University of London LLB Examination
(for External Students) Company Law June 1995 Q8

General Comment

Here, consideration must be given to the circumstances in which promoters may be held liable for breach of duty towards the company, and some analysis of the nature of the duty is called for. The position of director/shareholders who deal with their own company must be taken into account, and also the status and effects of pre-incorporation contracts upon company and promoter.

Skeleton Solution

Nature of promoters' duties – importance of chronological order of dealings – nature of breach, remedies available and purpose of damages – Ann as director/shareholder, disclosure requirement – liability of company for pre-incorporation agreements – novation possibility – personal liability for Ann.

Suggested Solution

There are three principal points raised by the question: first, the duties that are owed by promoters towards the company itself; second, Ann's profitable transaction while director or shadow director; and, third, the question of rights or obligations arising from arrangements made prior to incorporation but in contemplation of it.

a) *The duties owed by promoters*

This matter is relevant because of Eric's awareness of Ann's profit of £400,000 from Grapeacre. He may feel that as she was a promoter of Bokay Ltd that the company has some claim to this profit. Ann will be viewed as a promoter, having the aspect of one who undertakes to form a company for a given project and who does all that is necessary for that purpose (*Twycross* v *Grant* (1877)), although there is no statutory definition. The promoter is seen as owing a fiduciary duty towards the company analogous to that of an agent, but the courts have developed a particular approach towards promoters. The vice for the promoter is to make secret profits from the promotion as did many professional promoters in the last century. Everything depends upon when the initial purchase or transaction creating the potential for profit takes place. If it is after the first active steps towards promotion have taken place then disclosure to everyone else subscribing for the capital is necessary (*Re Cape Breton Co* (1885)). Conversely, if the transaction takes place before any active steps are taken, when only an intention to promote exists, he will owe no duty to account (*Erlanger* v *New Sombrero Phosphate Co* (1878)). Although there is some artificiality about this temporal distinction, it is applied. He will, however, still owe a duty to disclose, as distinct from a duty to account, even in the latter situation, ie where the purchase took place before active steps were taken (*Re Lady Forrest (Murchison) Gold Mine Co Ltd* (1901)).

Applying these principles to the Grapeacre transaction, Ann purchased before any active steps were taken so she will not owe a duty to account to the company, but she will have a duty to disclose fully to Betty in January 1994, assuming that she is the only other member and director. if there were no disclosure, the company would have had the right to rescission but, possibly, the right to rescission had been lost because of passage of time, or restitutio in integrum is neither possible nor desired. The case law indicates that damages may be sued for by the company (*Re Leeds and Hanley Theatre of Varieties* (1902)), provided that the true market value at the time of the company's purchase is ascertainable (*Re Cape Breton Co*). This raises the question of the measure of damages; will it be the difference between the purchase price of £500,000 and £200,000 or between £500,000 and the true market value of £400,000 or is there, in fact, any loss at all? This is not a case of a duty to account, it is merely for the loss caused to company by a failure to disclose, and the loss to the company appears to be nil. On this basis it is difficult to see how the company could get more than nominal damages.

Ann must have been either a director or, at least, a shadow director at the time of the purchase of Grapeacre and there will be possibilities under the director duty to account to the company for profits, unless authorised by the company, where the opportunity to profit arose through the directorship (*Regal (Hastings) Ltd* v *Gulliver* (1967)). Nevertheless the company in general meeting can consent to the retention of profits, provided full disclosure of the matter had been made in the notice convening the meeting. It sounds as if this may have occurred and, in any case, *North-West Transportation Co Ltd* v *Beatty* (1887) is authority for the proposition that a director acting in the capacity of shareholder can deal can deal with the company in his own interest, provided there is no fraud or oppression. It sounds as if it could be difficult to require Ann to account for her profits on this basis.

b)   *The supply of the grape press*

This sounds as if an agreement was concluded in November 1993, before Bokay Ltd was incorporated, and the question becomes one of whether there was a contract at all for the press and, if so, who has rights or obligations under it. Bokay had no legal existence and could not contract for itself or via an agent (*Kelner* v *Baxter* (1866)). It could not adopt or ratify the contract after it was incorporated (*Natal Land and Colonization Co Ltd* v *Pauline Colliery and Development Syndicate* (1904)). For a company to be party to an agreement concluded prior to its incorporation, that agreement must be incorporated into a new contract agreed post-incorporation when the company had become a legal person. The Natal Land case shows that mere performance of pre-incorporation agreements does not amount to evidence of a new contract, but is restrictively viewed as the 'offer' in a conventional offer/acceptance analysis in which the other party to the original agreement must then supply some 'acceptance', without which there is no contract with the company. This situation looks less like a novation than an attempted adoption of the old agreement which will not make the company a party to it (*Re Northumberland Avenue Hotel Co Ltd* (1886)). Nevertheless, if there is some evidence of fresh terms this will point towards a fresh agreement made after incorporation (*Howard* v *Patent Ivory Manufacturing Co* (1888)), and it might be argued here that as Dave originally entered into agreement with Wino Ltd but subsequently delivered, and presumably invoiced, to Bokay Ltd, that he has entered a new contract with the company. The existence and terms of such a contract would be a matter of evidence. Even if no such contract can be shown, Dave should be entitled to a quantum valebant against the company (*Rover International Ltd* v *Cannon Film Sales Ltd (No 3)* (1989)).

If there was no post-incorporation contract, and the company has not used the press or made itself liable to Dave, the question is whether Ann can be personally liable to Dave on the agreement. Both under the common law (*Kelner* v *Baxter*), and by s36C(1) CA 1985, persons who purport to act for the company, or as its agent on pre-incorporation contracts, are personally liable (*Phonogram Ltd* v *Lane* (1982)), and the level of awareness of the parties is not relevant at all, although express agreement to the contrary will protect. Ann could be personally liable.

QUESTION THREE

'The common law was unable to solve the problems created where negotiations conducted prior to the incorporation of a company were intended to result in a contract binding on that company when incorporated. The legislature eventually had to step in.'

What were these problems? Do you agree that the common law did not offer a satisfactory solution? Has the legislature now solved these problems satisfactorily?

University of London LLB Examination
(for External Students) Company Law June 1991 Q2

General Comment

Normally the topic of pre-incorporation contracts appears in a problem question; however this essay question concerns the problems of pre-incorporation contracts, namely the logical impossibility of entering into such contracts, as the company at this point does not exist. Case law in this area needs consideration and the implication of s36C CA 1985 and whether this provision adequately resolves all problems in this area.

Skeleton Solution

Pre-1985 position – consideration of case law where contract would be binding depended on the words used when the contract was signed – were common law remedies adequate? – post s36C CA 1985 where promoters held personally liable unless contrary intention can be shown – further company may ratify original contract – conclusion: has legislation solved all problems?

Suggested Solution

Until a company is incorporated it cannot contract or enter into an agreement and in turn cannot be liable or entitled under such a contract because it is not in existence. The question whether the company was liable depended on the way in which the contract was signed. If signed 'for and on behalf of the company', then the person signing purported to do so as agent. The company could not be bound as there can be no agency whilst the principal (ie, the company) is not in existence: *Kelner* v *Baxter* (1866).

Section 36C Companies Act 1985 (previously s36(4)) has clarified the position to an extent, where a promoter who enters into a pre-incorporation contract will be bound as principal and deemed to be personally liable on it (subject to any agreement to the contrary). This is by far the most important provision relating to pre-incorporation contracts, but there are other relevant statutory provisions. Section 150 Financial Services Act 1986 provides a remedy to an investor who acquires securities or an interest in them and suffers loss by reason of misleading information in listing particulars.

In the past there was some doubt as to the position of a person who signs not as an agent but merely as purporting to authenticate the signature of the company. At common law this is most unlikely to place personal liability on the signer: *Newborne* v *Sensolid* (1954). However, the distinction between signature as an agent and signature authenticating the signature of the company has now been abolished. Lord Denning has gone so far to say that 'this distinction has now been obliterated.' In *Phonogram Ltd* v *Lane* (1982), the fact that the promoter signed 'for and on behalf' of the company made no difference to his liability. The Court of Appeal held these words were not sufficient to constitute 'an agreement to the contrary' for the purposes of s36(4) and the promoter was held personally liable as the company could not later ratify a contract made prior to its incorporation.

Therefore the only way in which the company can take over the liability is by making an entirely new contract with the third party on the same terms as that made by the promoter. The company may make such a contract either expressly or impliedly, by its conduct. To be sufficient to create a contract in these circumstances however, the company's conduct must unequivocally refer to the alleged agreement and will, even then, only amount to an offer which will be converted into a contract if the third party accepts it. This was illustrated in *Natal Land and Colonization Co Ltd* v *Pauline Colliery and Development Syndicate* (1904). The problem for the other party is to prove that the company did make a new contract after incorporation and the general attitude of the courts seems to be to require clear evidence; simply acting in the mistaken belief that a pre-incorporation contract is binding is not enough: *Re Northumberland Avenue Hotel Co* (1886). However, if a company after incorporation takes possession of property transferred to it in a pre-incorporation contract, the courts may be able to infer that the only possible explanation is that a new contract was made after incorporation: *Re Patent Ivory Manufacturing Co* (1888), where the directors renegotiated the terms of the pre-incorporation contract and this was held to amount to an offer to enter into a fresh agreement and was therefore binding on the company and the third party.

A promoter may be able to protect himself from personal liability for pre-incorporation contracts in various ways. Firstly, by making the agreement with a third party 'subject to contract'. This means that there is no contract and therefore no liability on the promoter, until the company, after incorporation, enters into the contract with the third party. Secondly, the promoter can also make the contract himself and then once the company has been incorporated, assign the benefits of the contract to it, and in return, persuade the company and the third party to enter into a contract of novation whereby the liabilities will also be transferred. However, it is difficult to imagine circumstances where a third party would agree to a non-liability clause given that such an agreement does not serve to make the company liable.

Although the position has been clarified to some extent by legislation, it might be preferable if companies could simply ratify pre-incorporation contracts. A further statutory amendment to this effect may serve to make the law more tenable in this area.

QUESTION FOUR

'It may have taken over a hundred years, but the Financial Services Act 1986 has finally solved the problem of providing an adequate remedy for someone who suffers damage through an investment in a public company and who was induced to make that investment by a material misrepresentation.'

Discuss.

University of London LLB Examination
(for External Students) Company Law June 1992 Q3

General Comment

This is quite a difficult question in that it requires critical analysis of the solution offered by the Financial Services Act 1986 to the problem of compensating those misled into investing in a public company. This basic objective of investor protection is one with which company law has long been preoccupied and as capital markets become more complicated it becomes in turn more complex to fulfil. It should be noted that this question was written prior to the passing of the Public Offer of Securities Regulations 1995, but is included because a similar question in modified form could well be set in the future.

Skeleton Solution

Gaps in 'old law' – s67 Companies Act 1985 – definition of 'prospectus' – new statutory regimes for public offers of listed securities (Part IV FSA) and unlisted securities (Public Offer of Securities Regulations 1995) – new statutory remedies s150 FSA – persons liable to pay compensation – defences available to responsible persons – measure of damages – continuing common law remedies preserved.

Suggested Solution

Prior to the Financial Services Act (FSA) 1986 the Companies Act requirements relating to public issues and prospectuses did not apply at all to the listed securities markets ie those securities admitted to the Stock Exchange's official list – the tightest and most difficult to enter UK public capital market. The Companies Act 1985 (Part III ss56–79, the prospectus provisions) only applied to the Unlisted Securities Market and the 'over the counter' market for securities. This meant that there were disparities in the different regimes for public issues and defects arose such as the fact that the prospectus provisions of the Companies Act were interpreted to apply only to offers for the subscription or purchase of securities for cash. Since most takeover offers are structured for non–cash consideration they fell outside the investor protection regime. Part III CA 1985 has been replaced by the Public Offer of Securities Regulations 1995 (see below).

The Financial Services Act 1986 aims to rationalise and put on a more level footing the disclosure and compensation provisions relating to the Stock Exchange's official listed market and the other markets in which the public is induced to part with its money by way of investing in company shares. Historically investor protection in the former had been good whereas it left much to be desired in the latter.

Part IV FSA deals with the admission of securities of a public company to the official list of the Stock Exchange. It designates the Stock Exchange as the competent authority for the purposes of making listing rules, and applying them to determine whether a company fulfils the criteria contained therein. The Act talks of prescribed listing particulars rather than using the term 'prospectus', the Stock Exchange should ensure that its listing rules require in particular that listing particulars contain enough information pertaining to the financial position and prospects of the company issuing securities as well as information on rights attaching to those securities to enable an investor to make a reasonably informed assessment of those matters (s146 FSA). They must be approved by the Stock Exchange and then registered with the Registrar of Companies.

What remedies exist then if despite apparent compliance with these statutory requirements, the relevant listing particulars or prospectus contain information which adds up to a material misrepresentation of the true position, so that an investor is misled into investing his monies where he otherwise would not have done, and thereby suffers loss? The principal statutory remedies are contained in s150 FSA which governs compensation for false or misleading listing particulars and s166 which governs compensation for false or misleading prospectuses and replaces s67 Companies Act 1985. Section 150 FSA imposes civil liability on the persons responsible for any listing particulars which contain false or misleading statements or omissions which in turn cause loss to any person who has acquired the securities to which the particulars relate. It is worth noting that compensation is payable under s150 to anyone who bought the securities in question even if he bought on the secondary market and did not rely directly on the listing particulars. It might perhaps be thought that s150 would award a misled investor his loss of expectation of gain as a result of the misleading statement as a measure of damages. However the Act is not clear here; in using the words 'suffers a loss' it seems that the basic tort measure of damages, viz out of pocket expenses, is being employed. This seems strange and less than satisfactory in an investment context. The persons liable to pay compensation to a misled investor are enumerated in s152 FSA as the issuer, every director or person who has given his authority to be named as a director in the listing particulars, others who have expressly assumed responsibility for the contents of the particulars, and lastly others who authorised their contents. Section 151 FSA provides defences available in a s150 compensation action which are broadly similar to those contained in the old prospectus provisions of the Companies Act (s68 1985 Act) namely, reasonable belief in the veracity of the statement, reasonable reliance on the authority of an expert, acting in an official capacity etc. It is arguable that an investor who has suffered loss and cannot proceed against any of the persons liable under s150 could proceed against the Stock Exchange itself for breach of statutory duty. Part V FSA 1986, which applied mirror provisions to unlisted securities was never implemented. Instead, in response to the EC 'Prospectus Directive', the Public Offer of Securities Regulations 1995 were passed and implemented in June 1995. These provide in respect of all offers of unlisted securities (save those exempted in regulation 7) for a prospectus with the form and content specified (regulation 8 and Schedule 1) to be published and made freely available, and registered at the Companies Registry prior to publication. Persons responsible for the prospectus (as defined in regulation 13) may uncur liability for false or misleading prospectuses (regulation 14) and have available to them the defences in regulation 15, broadly similar to those in s151 FSA 1986 and formerly (in relation to unlisted securities) in s68 CA 1985. With unlisted securities, it may also be possible to invoke remedies enjoyed by the Securities and Investments Board (SIB) under the FSA on behalf of the investor. Of particular value are s61 (restitution orders) and ss53 and 54 (access to the SIB compensation scheme).

Finally whether the securities are listed or unlisted, the misled investor may have a common law right to rescind the contract of allotment for the securities on the basis that a material misrepresentation has been made; rights to damages which may exist under the Misrepresentation Act 1967; and an action for deceit.

In order to be able to rescind the contract of allotment the misrepresentation must be shown to be the responsibility of the company, ie made by the directors or the company's agents: *Lynde* v *Anglo-Italian Hemp Spinning Co Ltd* (1896) and the investor must not have lost his right to rescind by affirming the contract in any way, eg acting as a member, attending and voting at meetings etc. Rescission does not equal compensation although it will help the investor to avoid other possible liabilities (further calls to pay if shares part paid etc). Section 2(2) Misrepresentation Act 1967 may give the investor damages instead of rescission in the case of the material misrepresentation being an innocent one, and s2(1) affords a remedy in damages for negligent misrepresentation. The usual difficulties with the application of the Misrepresentation Act 1967 and ascertaining damages under it apply but there is nothing to indicate that the Act does not apply to public offers of shares. Regardless of an action against the company the investor can proceed against the promoters, directors, issuers and experts responsible for the prospectus if it can be shown they acted fraudulently. The difficulties of establishing fraud at common law are legendary, however.

The statutory framework provided for investor compensation by Part IV FSA and the Public Offer of Securities Regulations 1995 in the event of misleading prospectus and listing particulars statements is likely to be clearer and more certain in operation than the general common law remedies and more rational and wider in application than the pre-existing Companies Act provisions, although it is not likely to be without its own difficulties for judicial interpretation.

QUESTION FIVE

Ice Rinks plc was until recently a private company controlled by its founders, Jane and Chris. It has had an outstanding history of growth and now manages 10 ice rinks under lease from various local authorities. Jane and Chris wanted to increase the scale of their operations and on the advice of Londonbank, a leading merchant bank, they decided to raise fresh capital for the expansion by issuing 4 million £1 shares and by obtaining a listing on the Stock Exchange. Accordingly, in March 1994, Londonbank made an offer for sale of 4 million ordinary shares. This was accompanied by an application to the Stock Exchange for listing. The application was successful.

Listing Particulars were published which stated that the turnover of Ice Rinks plc was likely to increase by 50 per cent in 1994 and 1995 because of the Winter Olympics generating publicity for the sport. This statement was not referred to in the accounts and was not taken into account in the profit forecast.

The issue price was 150 pence per share and the flotation was a great success with the price of shares rising steadily to 250 pence after the first month of trading.

The Listing Particulars omitted to mention that the leases on 7 of the 10 ice rinks held on lease were due to expire in April 1994 and the respective local authorities were refusing to renew the leases.

The Winter Olympics has not resulted in the hoped-for increase in turnover for the ice rink industry and the fact that the leases were not being renewed has also come to light. It has now been learned that a proposed EC Directive with the stated aim of rendering the ice rink industry environmentally friendly will require costly changes in the ice-making plants at ice rinks. The price of shares in Ice Rinks plc has now fallen by 90 per cent.

Advise Slippy who bought shares in Ice Rinks plc on flotation by application from Londonbank, and advise Slide who purchased shares one month later when the shares were at their peak in the market.

[In answering this question, candidates are not required to display a detailed knowledge of the contents of the Stock Exchange's Listing Rules – 'The Yellow Book'.]

University of London LLB Examination
(for External Students) Company Law June 1994 Q8

General Comment

This question deals with problems which arise when listing particulars contain untrue or misleading particulars. The position under the Financial Services Act 1986 must be considered, but so too must the common law remedies. Mention could also be made of possible criminal sanctions to complete the picture.

Skeleton Solution

The flotation and the offer for sale – listing particulars – persons responsible for false or misleading particulars – defences – FSA remedies – common law remedies – criminal sanctions.

Suggested Solution

Financial Services Act 1986 provisions

Ice Rinks plc ('the company') is a listed company on the London stock exchange. Like the vast majority of listed companies, it started out as a private company and was later 'floated' on the stock exchange by means of an offer for sale. Under this procedure the company allots a block of new shares to the issuing house (Londonbank) and the latter re-sells the shares by offering them to the public. Londonbank will also have agreed to underwrite the issue, promising to buy up any unsold shares.

The law on listed issues is now contained in Part IV of the Financial Services Act (FSA) 1986, implementing a number of EC Directives. A document known as the Listing Particulars (formerly prospectuses) must be prepared and made available to the public. The content of the Listing Particulars is broadly specified in the FSA 1986, with the detailed content being supplied by the stock exchange's rule book, called the Listing Rules ('The Yellow Book').

Section 146(1) FSA 1986 contains a general duty of disclosure. The Listing Particulars ('particulars') must contain all the information that investors would reasonably require to make an informed decision on whether or not to buy the shares. The information should relate to the assets, liabilities, financial position, profits and losses and prospects of the issuer, and the rights attaching to the shares.

Section 146(2) goes on to provide that only information which is known or which would have been reasonable to obtain by making enquiries need be included. Section 146(3) gives further guidance on what needs to be included, saying that regard must be had to:

a) the nature of the issuer and of the securities;

b) the nature of the persons likely to consider acquiring the securities;

c) matters which may reasonably be within the knowledge of professional advisors.

The statement that there is a likelihood of a 50 per cent increase in turnover falls within s146(1) as it relates to the issuer's prospects. The particulars should also have included the information that the local authorities were refusing to renew the leases on seven of the ice rinks. Section 148 exempts disclosure of certain information but it does not apply here.

It is not clear if and when the proposed EC Directive came into existence.

a) If it was in existence when the particulars were being prepared, then it is submitted that it is information which could have been reasonably discovered by making enquiries under s146(2). It should therefore have been included in the particulars.

b) If it came into existence after the preparation of the particulars and before dealing commenced then supplementary listing particulars should have been submitted to the stock exchange under s147, as the proposed directive probably amounts to a 'significant new matter'.

Section 150 provides that compensation is payable by 'persons responsible' for 'untrue or misleading' statements in the particulars, which includes omissions. So the failure to mention the proposed directive and the refusal to renew seven of the leases would be covered.

The omissions are 'untrue or misleading'. Forecasts such as the turnover prediction are also likely to be considered to be untrue or misleading. In a different context, a duty of care was held to be owed to the purchaser of shares who bought on the strength of a profit forecast in a takeover document: *Morgan Crucible Co plc* v *Hill Samuel Bank Ltd* (1991). In the present case it is said that there is a 'likelihood' of an increase in turnover, which may not be strong enough to be misleading.

Section 152 says that the persons responsible for the particulars are:

a) the issuer of the securities (the company);

b) the directors;

c) every person who has accepted responsibility for all or part of the particulars;

d) any other person who has authorised the contents of the particulars or part of them.

Remedies under the FSA 1986

a) *Slippy*

Subject to the defences in s151, the company and its directors, presumably Chris and Jane, would be liable to compensate Slippy. Londonbank would also incur liability for those parts of the particulars for which they have accepted responsibility, or authorised.

The range of persons responsible is wider than the previous statutory regime (s67 Companies Act (CA) 1985), and now includes the company itself.

Exemptions from liability to pay compensation are contained in s151. In respect of the turnover prediction, 151(1) provides a defence where it was 'reasonably believed, having made such enquiries (if any) as were reasonable, that the statement was true and not misleading'. Another available defence might be contained in s151(2), where a statement is made by an expert. The turnover prediction, however, does not appear in the accounts and was not referred to in the profit forecast, which tends to suggest that is not the view of an expert.

There do not appear to be any defences available covering the omission to state the refusals by the local authorities to renew seven out of 10 leases on the ice rinks. It is unlikely that those responsible for the particulars did not know about the refusal of the local authorities to renew the leases.

As mentioned earlier, in relation to the proposed directive much depends on if and when it came into existence. The 'reasonable belief' defence might again be available under s151(1).

The onus of proof is on the person claiming to fall within one of the exemptions in s151.

The measure of damages under s150 will probably be assessed according to tortious principles, ie to restore Slippy to his original position. This is not entirely free from doubt but it is supported by Gower (*Principles of Modern Company Law*, 5th ed, p345).

b) *Slide*

Slide's position is similar to that of Slippy. He too will be able to claim compensation. Compensation is not limited to those who purchased shares from the company and extends to those who, like Slide, purchase the shares in the market after dealing has commenced. This is an improvement on the former provision in s67 CA 1985.

Slide will have to show a causal connection between the misstatement/omission and the loss. This will be difficult if there has been a lapse of time such that the particulars can be said to have had an influence on the market price. The lapse of time in Slide's case is one month and it is probably not long enough to bar a claim by Slide for compensation.

Common law remedies

Section 150(4) FSA 1986 expressly preserves existing common law remedies available to an investor who suffers loss as a result of a misrepresentation.

a) Slippy may be available to rescind his contract with Londonbank. The issue here is whether there has been a misrepresentation. An omission is not usually regarded as a misrepresentation unless it can be regarded as a positive statement. Not mentioning the EC Directive and the refusal to renew the leases might be equivalent to a positive statement that there is no proposed directive in existence and that all the leases are renewable. The difficulty with the turnover prediction is that it may be regarded as a statement of opinion rather than one of fact.

If rescission is available, Slide will be able to rescind against his vendor, as he purchased in the market.

The usual bars to rescission apply, such as lapse of time etc.

b) If the misrepresentations are fraudulent damages may be available under the tort of deceit: *Derry* v *Peek* (1889). In the present case, the facts do not really suggest fraud.

c) If the misrepresentation is negligent or innocent then there may be a claim for damages under the Misrepresentation Act 1967. It used to be the rule that the investor had to rescind his contract before a claim for damages could be made: *Houldsworth* v *City of Glasgow Bank* (1880). This is no longer necessary due to s111A CA 1985.

d) Damages may be available for negligent misstatements under the principles established in *Caparo Industries plc* v *Dickman* (1990). Under this rule those responsible for the Listing Particulars will owe a duty of care to those investors who apply for shares on the basis of the particulars, but not to subsequent purchasers in the market: *Al-Nakib Investments (Jersey) Ltd* v *Longcroft* (1990). Applying this to the present case, Slippy may have a remedy under this heading, but Slide will not as he is a subsequent purchaser in the market. This shows the advantages of claiming compensation under the FSA 1986, which does extend to subsequent purchasers.

Criminal liabilty

Under s47(1) FSA 1986 it is an offence for any person to knowingly or recklessly make a statement, promise or forecast which is misleading, false or deceptive or to dishonestly conceal any material fact. The purpose must be to induce another to enter into an investment agreement, such as to buy shares in a company.

Under s19 of the Theft Act 1968, the officers of the company (directors) will be liable for statements which to their knowledge may be false, misleading or deceptive, if made with intent to deceive a member or creditor of the company: *R* v *Lord Kylsant* (1932).

Slippy and Slide will not gain any personal compensation from these criminal prosecutions, unless the court awards them compensation as the victims of an offence under s35 of the Powers of Criminal Courts Act 1973.

5 Capital

5.1 Introduction

The word 'capital' has several meanings and students should become familiar with the various types of capital. It is a fundamental principle that a company's capital (by which is sometimes meant nominal capital, sometimes issued, sometimes both together) be maintained to provide a measure of security for creditors and investors. Thus the *nominal* capital may be increased, consolidated, subdivided or converted into stock, but may not be reduced except by following the procedure in ss135–138 CA 1985, which includes the requirement to obtain court approval.

5.2 Key points

a) *General*

Capital might be reduced indirectly by paying dividends out of capital, by the company purchasing its own shares or giving financial assistance to others to do so. All these have therefore been prohibited or tightly controlled by law. In general, public companies are more strictly constrained in this regard and, in addition, are required to have a minimum nominal capital of which a specified proportion is paid up (see chapter 6) and must call a general meeting if their net assets fall to half or less of their called-up share capital (s142 CA 1985).

b) *Dividends*

A company must not pay dividends except out of profits available for the purpose (s263 CA 1985). Profits available for the purpose are accumulated realised profits less accumulated realised losses.

Whether profits are to be treated as accumulated is decided according to the principles of good accounting practice (CA 1985, Sch 4, paras 88–91).

Part VIII of CA 1985 contains detailed rules relating to the treatment of revaluations of assets, and to the use of interim and initial accounts as the basis for a dividend.

Where an unlawful dividend is paid, a shareholder who knows of the unlawfulness may be required to repay the dividend to the company (s277 CA 1985).

Public companies are subject to a further restriction in that they may not pay a dividend if the result of doing so would be to reduce their net assets below the value of their called-up capital plus undistributable reserves (s264 CA 1985).

c) *Purchase of own shares*

It has long been established that for a company to purchase its own shares is a capital reduction and thus forbidden (*Trevor* v *Whitworth* (1887) 12 App Cas 409). This general rule is now contained in s143(1) CA 1985, but is relaxed by a number of other provisions.

By s159 company may issue redeemable shares, ie shares which are expressed on the face of them to be redeemable, and these will then be redeemable in accordance with the terms and conditions attached to them at the time of issue. However, a company must always have some shares which are not expressed to be redeemable.

Shares not issued as redeemable may also be purchased by the company (s162 CA 1985). The articles must permit the redemption or purchase, and the relevant procedure (which differs according to whether it is a 'market purchase' (s166) or 'off-market purchase' (s164)) must be followed. Any company may pay for its shares out of distributable profits or out of the proceeds of a fresh issue of shares made for that purpose. Private companies only may also use capital subject to the safeguards in ss171–177. These include a statutory declaration by the directors, supported by an auditors' report, to the effect that the company is solvent and will remain so for the coming year. Declarations without reasonable grounds give rise to an offence for which directors are personally liable.

d) *Assistance for purchase of own shares*

Sections 151–154 CA 1985 impose a general prohibition on a company providing financial assistance, whether directly or indirectly, for the purchase of its own shares.

At the same time s153 provides exemptions from the prohibition where the assistance is given as an incidental part of some larger purpose of the company and is given in good faith in the best interests of the company. The difficulty of applying this section is shown by the case of *Brady* v *Brady* [1989] AC 755.

Section 151 additionally provides exemptions from the general prohibition which apply only to private companies. This section contains the relaxation of the rules introduced by the 1985 Act. Essentially private companies are exempt from the prohibition so long as they follow certain procedures (specified in ss155–158). These involve a statutory declaration and auditors' report similar to those required for direct purchase. If the net assets of the company are to be reduced by the giving of the assistance, then the funds used must be distributable profits of the company (s155(2)).

Finally, the proposal must be approved by a special resolution of the General Meeting, except where the company proposing to give the assistance is a wholly-owned subsidiary of the company which is to receive the assistance.

5.3 Recent cases

Acatos and Hutchinson plc v *Watson* (1994) The Times 30 December – purchase of a company's entire share capital was not a breach of s143 CA 1985.

Parlett v *Guppy (Bridport) Ltd* (1996) The Times 8 February (Court of Appeal) – to be unlawful, financial assistance under s151(1) CA 1985, the company's net assets must be reduced to a material extent.

5.4 Analysis of questions

The subject of company capital has proved popular in the past, primarily in essay form but has not appeared since 1989. There is no reason why it should not come up again. It is, however, a topic of which students should be wary. Firstly, it can be presented in a number of forms. One of these concerns the rules against paying dividends except out of profits available for the purpose; another form of the question addresses itself to reductions of capital and the need to obtain the sanction of the court. The third area which may be set concerns payment for shares. Care is needed in distinguishing quite what the question is asking for. More commonly, the three areas may appear together. The second problem for students is that this is a technical area of the law, with a number of detailed rules. It is difficult to write adequtely about profit distribution without some knowledge of the accounting concepts of profit and realisations; this is a knowledge possessed by very few law students. It is also an area where a student who is ill-prepared has little hope of bluffing his way through. Proper knowledge of the technical rules is indispensable, and students who do not have it are advised to avoid this topic in the examination.

With those caveats in mind it is possible to go on and look at the questions which come up in this area.

5.5 Questions

QUESTION ONE

'Companies are forbidden to make any distribution of dividends except out of profits legally available for this purpose.' Discuss the development and interpretation of this principle, both by the courts and the legislature.

University of London LLB Examination
(for External Students) Company Law June 1985 Q2

General Comment

At first sight this looks to be a clear (if difficult) question about the modern rules on distributions contained in Part VIII of the 1985 Act. Closer reading of the question shows, however, that a further twist has been inserted. The judicial development of this doctrine occurred before the present statutory provisions were introduced in 1980. Consequently the candidate is required to discuss both the pre-1980 case law and the current legislative provisions, probably in roughly equal proportions.

Skeleton Solution

Old rule was: no dividend out of capital – new rule is: no dividend except out of available profit – new rule is more restrictive, since accounting periods are not treated in isolation – available profits are accumulated realised profits less accumulated realised losses – realisation is determined according to accounting principles – profit and loss not defined by statute – public companies subject to additional restrictions.

Suggested Solution

The principle stated in the question is clearly based very closely on the wording of s263 of the 1985 Act, and is a good statement of the general principle (there are exceptions) which applies under the present law. Before 1980, when the present rules were introduced, the rule was more accurately stated as being that dividends could not be paid out of capital since this would offend the capital maintenance doctrine: *Flitcroft's Case* (1882); *Verner* v *Commercial and General Investment Trust* (1894). This was a much narrower doctrine than that which now prevails. In particular where there was a profit on revenue account in the current year, a dividend could be paid even though losses on previous years had not been made up: *Ammonia Soda Co Ltd* v *Chamberlain* (1918). In addition, a surplus arising on a revaluation of fixed assets which were not to be sold could be distributed, since this surplus would be additional to the company's issued capital, so that the capital maintenance doctrine was not infringed – *Dimbula Valley (Ceylon) Tea Co Ltd* v *Laurie* (1961). The court was not concerned with issues as to the prudence of a distribution: *Lee* v *Neuchatel Asphalte Co* (1889). Essentially the court treated each accounting period in isolation. However, increasing difficulty was felt with these rules, partly because they were significantly at variance with good accounting practice and partly because of pressure from the EEC for the harmonisation of company law. New rules were consequently introduced in 1980, and these are now consolidated in Part VIII of the 1985 Act.

The general principle under the new provisions is that stated in the question. It is important to be aware that 'distribution' here does not cover all forms of distribution of a company's assets. Section 263 of the 1985 Act excludes from the definition the issue of bonus shares, purchase of own shares, payments in a reduction of capital and distributions of assets in a winding-up. All these are covered by separate specific provisions of the 1985 Act. All other forms of distribution are included, however, and it may be observed that distributions by way of sales at an undervalue to a member are covered, as well as declarations of dividends.

The next question to ask is what are 'profits available for the purpose'? Section 263 defines these as accumulated realised profits less accumulated realised losses. This reverses the *Dimbula Valley* rule, since one accounting period must be taken with another. Only the net profits are available for distribution, since sums previously distributed must be taken into account in making the calculation. The use of the term 'realised' in the new rule is also significant. A profit achieved by revaluing a fixed asset is not a realised profit, and therefore cannot be taken into account (subject to certain specified exceptions). Realisation is to be determined according to the notions of good accounting practice (Sch 4 Para 88) which is one further step along the path of allowing accounting notions to prevail for legal purposes.

The remaining element in the definition is that of 'profit' and 'loss'. These terms are not defined, and it appears that the earlier, rather unsatisfactory authorities, such as *Re Oxford Benefit Building and Investment Society* (1886) (which turns on the particular articles of the Society) and *Re Spanish Prospecting Co Ltd* (1911) remain good law in this context. This point may be of little importance, however; even if it can be determined that there is a profit or loss according to these rules, it will still be necesary to decide whether there has been realisation, and this, as explained above, is determined according to accountancy principles.

Public companies are subject to the additional restrictions imposed by s264. They may make distributions only to the extent that their net assets after the distribution are not less than the amount of their called-up share capital plus their undistributable reserves: the last phrase includes the share premium account and the capital redemption reserve.

The accounts used to justify a distribution are the 'relevant accounts'. These will usually be the last annual accounts, but interim accounts may sometimes be used.

Under s277 the recipient of an unlawful distribution who is a shareholder is liable to repay it to the company if he had reason to know that the distribution was unlawful. *Re Aveling Barford Ltd* (1989) confirms that the position is the same where the recipient is not a shareholder.

Further restrictions on distributions may be imposed by the memorandum or the articles, but neither may provide any exemption from the requirements of Part VIII of the Act.

It can thus be seen that the new law differs radically from the old. In particular, it is much more interventionist and restrictive. There is as yet very little authority on the new rules, and it should be clear from the above that authorities on the pre-1980 rules must now be treated with great caution.

QUESTION TWO

a) Success plc has an issued share capital of £1 million divided into 800,000 £1 ordinary shares and 200,000 £1 preference shares. The articles of association of the company provide that the holders of the preference shares 'shall be entitled to an annual dividend of 18 per cent in preference to the ordinary shareholders'. The articles further provide that 'the rights attached to any shares shall be deemed to be varied by the reduction of capital paid up on those shares'.

You are asked to advise the board of directors who feel that the company has too much capital and wish to pay off the preference shares at par in reduction of capital. The preference shares stand at £1.26 in the market.

b) York Ltd has an issued share capital of 12,000 £1 shares. Four brothers, Andrew, Bill, Colin and David are the directors of the company and each of them holds 3,000 shares. Andrew wishes to sell all his shares and is prepared to let his brothers buy 1,000 shares each. His brothers are anxious to purchase the shares since they want the ownership of the company to remain in the family. The Beano Bank plc is prepared to lend the necessary money to Bill, Colin and David, provided that the company guarantees the loans with a floating charge over its assets. However, the directors have now been told that the floating charge would infringe section 151 of the Companies Act 1985.

Advise the directors.

University of London LLB Examination
(for External Students) Company Law June 1995 Q7

General Comment

The first part of the question requires a review of the case law on the relationship between reduction of capital, cancellation of capital and variation of class rights, as well as the statutory provisions covering permitted reductions. The second part needs detailed analysis of the giving of financial assistance by a company towards transactions in its own shares, the rationale behind the general prohibition and knowledge of the exempt situations.

Skeleton Solution

a) Class rights question – whether cancellation is 'reduction' – statutory requirements for reduction – special situation of preference shares.

b) Rationale of statutory rules concerning acquisition of own shares – 'larger purpose', employees exception – private company relaxation, statutory requirements.

Suggested Solution

a) This part of the question raises points of company law which must be separately addressed:

   i) *The effect upon the class rights of the preference shareholders*

   The express provision in the articles that a reduction of capital is deemed to be a variation raises the question that has troubled the courts many times, whether a cancellation of the class amounts to a 'reduction' or 'variation'. In *Re Northern Engineering Industries plc* (1994) a very similar situation occurred and the Court of Appeal had little sympathy for the argument that a 'reduction' was different to or less than a cancellation of the class. The directors must look at the rest of the articles and consider carefully the requirements imposed there or under the Companies Act (CA) 1985 regarding class consents, or they may face a challenge on a class rights basis.

   ii) *The statutory provision for reduction of capital in public companies*

   The directors will need to bear in mind the requirements of ss135 to 141 CA 1985 concerning the circumstances and processes required for a valid reduction of share capital. The directors will, of course, have to rely upon authority in the articles to reduce capital – Table A art 34 will suffice if no other article covers the matter. The director's purpose seems to be well within s135(2)(c) as a disposal of surplus and unnecessary capital as in *Prudential Assurance Co Ltd* v *Chatterley-Whitfield Collieries Ltd* (1949). This case is also authority for the point that the directors may repay the shares at par rather than at £1.26 provided that there is nothing in the rights attached to the shares which would entitle the preference holders to share in a distribution of surplus assets of the company (*Re Saltdean Estate Co Ltd* (1968)). The reduction will have to be done by special resolution (s135(1)), and is subject to confirmation by the court (s136)), which means that other creditors may be allowed to object, (s136(3)). There really seems no problem in this and there is no danger of the capital being reduced below the authorised minimum level for a public company which would activate s139. The order and minute of reduction, and the court order in confirmation, must be delivered to the Registrar of Companies, and the resolution will only take effect upon registration and not before (s138(2)). This is, of course, a statutory exception to the general rule against company self purchase (s143(1)(b)).

b) This part of the question concerns the extent to which a company can take part in the acquisition of its own shares by way of providing financial assistance. Sections 151–158 CA 85 provide a regulatory mechanism to prevent abuses by the controller of a company which, effectively, allowed companies to provide the means of purchasing themselves as in *Re VGM Holdings* (1942) and *Belmont Finance Corporation Ltd* v *Williams Furniture Ltd* (1979). The assistance here is by way of the provision of a guarantee in the form of a floating charge. This is clearly within 'financial assistance given ... by way of security' in s152(1)(a)(ii), so the directors must proceed with care. There is an important exception in s153(1) if the transaction is such that the company's primary purpose lies not in the acquisition by the brothers or assisting the acquisition but, instead, is an 'incidental part of some larger purpose of the company' (s153(1)(a)), and the assistance is given 'in good faith in the interests of the company' (s153(1)(b)). This question of 'larger purpose' was looked at by the House of Lords in *Brady* v *Brady* (1989) and also in the case of *Plant* v *Steiner* (1988), and it does seem that this 'larger purpose' must be distinguished from the motive or reason for the transaction. The maintenance of share control within a family is much more likely to be viewed as a motive as it is difficult to see what larger purpose is served as the company acquires no new benefit, service or asset. Even a freedom from deadlock is not viewed as such on the basis of *Brady* v *Brady*. It seems that this will not help the directors here.

It may be that the directors can take advantage of s153(4)(bb) which allows for exemption for share transactions between employees. If this could not be complied with because the directors were not employees within the section, there is a general relaxation of s151 for private companies under s155 and this might be applicable here. There would be no reduction of net assets as no payment is made here (s155(2)), special resolution of the general meeting is required (s155(4)), and the directors would have to make a statutory declaration of solvency (s156). The special resolution would need to be passed within a week at the latest of the making of the statutory declaration (s157(11)). There is also a timetable given by s158 so that the assistance cannot be given before four weeks have elapsed following the special resolution. No assistance can be given later than eight weeks after the statutory declaration unless the court orders otherwise (s158(4)). A copy of the special resolution, the statutory declaration and an auditor's report must be sent to the Registrar within 15 days of the special resolution (s156(5)), but failure to observe these formalities did not breach s151 or invalidate the resolution in *Re NL Electrical Ltd* (1994).

From all of the above it is clear that the directors must fall within the employee exception or must take great care to observe the private company requirements, otherwise they will breach s151. The consequence of this is that the company would face a fine and 'every officer of it who is in default' faces imprisonment or fine or both by s151(3).

QUESTION THREE

'The legislature and the courts go to great lengths to compel a company to maintain its capital.' Discuss.

University of London LLB Examination
(for External Students) Company Law June 1987 Q2

General Comment

The question clearly asks for a general consideration of the rules relating to the maintenance of capital.

Skeleton Solution

Capital maintenance doctrine aims to protect creditors – four limits: prohibition on purchasing own shares; prohibition on giving financial assistance; restrictions on distributions; rules as to payment for shares – first two have become more lenient in recent years, whereas third has become stricter – generally, the problem of capital maintenance is well-recognised, but the legislation is somewhat piecemeal.

Suggested Solution

The core of a company is its capital, by which is meant the fund contributed by shareholders (or by creditors in the case of loan capital) which is required as a guarantee fund. In theory the creditors are able to look to this fund for the payment of their debts if the company runs into financial difficulty. This concept would obviously be undermined if the company were allowed to return that capital to the people who have provided it, and the doctrine of capital maintenance therefore lays down a general rule that returns of capital to the members are prohibited, though, as is explained below, there are certain exceptions to this rule.

There are four limbs to the doctrine of capital maintenance. The first is that a company may not buy its own shares (*Trevor* v *Whitworth* (1887)); the second is that a company may not provide financial assistance to another for the purchase of its own shares (Companies Act (CA) 1985 ss151–157); the third is that distributions of a company's assets may only be made out of profits available for the purpose (CA 1985 Part VIII); and the fourth concerns the way in which consideration for shares is provided.

Turning to the first of these rules, it should be observed that the 1981 Act (now consolidated in the 1985 Act) relaxed the prohibition somewhat. Before that time purchase of a company's own shares was almost entirely prohibited, but in 1981 companies were given the power to issue redeemable shares as well as a general power to purchase their own shares subject to safeguards aimed at protecting creditors. There are a number of situations where it is useful to allow companies to re-purchase their own shares (dealing with retiring or dissentient shareholders may be cited as examples). Such purchases must normally be financed out of distributable profits or out of the proceeds of a fresh issue of shares. In addition the nominal value of the shares purchased must be paid into an account within the company's books (the 'capital redemption reserve'). A further safeguard is that the purchase must be approved by the company in general meeting; in the case of a private company the amount which may be expended in such purchases is also strictly defined (CA 1985 s171).

Financial assistance for the purchase of shares is generally prohibited under s151, but here again the rules are more lenient than they used to be. Such assistance is permitted if approved by a special resolution of the company after the directors have made a Statutory Declaration as to the company's solvency. More contentiously, there are exceptions where the assistance was given in good faith and not for the purpose of assisting in such a purchase (as where the recipient misuses money entrusted to him) or where it was given in good faith but as an incidental part of some larger purpose. These exemptions, which are apparently necessitated by the imposition of criminal sanctions for the wrongful giving of such assistance, provide loopholes which do much to weaken the effect of the general prohibiton.

The rules as to the making of distributions (which means primarily but not exclusively dividends) date from 1980; exceptionally in the present context the new rules are stricter than the old, which merely forbade the paying of dividends out of capital. Profits available for the purpose are accumulated realised profits less accumulated realised losses, so that one accounting period must be taken with another; realisation is determined according to good accountancy practice. The new rules go a long way to ensuring that the capital of the company is not dissipated by improper dividend payments. If payments are made in breach of these rules, a member who received a payment with actual or constructive knowledge of its unlawfulness is liable to repay it to the company (s277). The same result is reached if the distribution is made to a non-member: *Re Aveling Barford Ltd* (1989).

The rules as to payment for shares also date from 1980. They relate to the way in which a company, particularly a public company, should be paid for its shares. For instance, a public company cannot accept an undertaking to perform services, nor an undertaking which may be performed more than five years after allotment: both these methods are obviously open to abuse. A public company must receive at least 25 per cent of the nominal value of the share (as well as the whole of any premium) on allotment; before it can accept any non-cash consideration an expert's report on the value of that consideration must be obtained and copies must be served on the company and the proposed allottee. The issuing of shares at a discount is now prohibited for all companies. There is criminal liability for the breach of these provisions.

In summary it may be said that the importance of capital maintenance is well recognised, though certain exceptions have been introduced in recent years, subject to the safeguards necessary to protect creditors. Reductions of capital may also be sanctioned by the court, but again permission will not be given unless creditors' interests are adequately protected.

QUESTION FOUR

In 1979 Excelsior plc made a net trading loss of £1,500,000 and in 1980 another loss of £1,000,000. In 1981, however, it made a profit of £1,000,000 and entered into negotiations to purchase a factory from Henry. The price was eventually agreed at £500,000 despite the fact that valuers appointed by Excelsior assessed the factory's value at £400,000. The directors of Excelsior decided to pay the price asked by Henry because they considered that the factory would considerably increase the company's profitability over the next few years. The purchase price was paid partly in cash (£200,000) and partly by the issue to Henry of 300,000 £1 shares, which issue was made concurrently with a rights issue made by the company to its existing shareholders of 1 share at par for each share held. James, one of the directors of Excelsior, who held 100,000 shares wanted to take up the rights issue, but was unable to raise the cash. He therefore negotiated with the company to defer payment in respect of his acceptance of the rights issue pending the declaration by the company of a dividend. At the end of 1982 the company in fact declared a dividend in respect of the entire profit made in 1981 and this enabled James to pay the company the amount owing in respect of the rights issue. In 1983, the company was compulsorily wound up.

Advise the liquidator.

University of London LLB Examination
(for External Students) Company Law June 1984 Q8

General Comment

This question is something of a rarity – a problem question on the maintenance of capital.

Skeleton Solution

Purchase of factory – valuation rules – consequences of breach – duty to pay in cash.

Dividends – losses of previous years must be made good before dividend can be paid – this has not been done – liquidator can require repayment from any shareholder who was aware of this.

Financial assistance – disguised return of capital prohibited – there has probably been a breach here – liquidator should be advised to sue James.

Suggested Solution

Three issues arise in this problem: the provision of financial assistance for the purchase of a company's shares, the declaration of dividends and payment for shares.

The factory has been purchased from Henry in cash and through the issue of 300,000 £1 shares. Under s103 Companies Act 1985 a company is forbidden to allot shares as fully or partly paid-up for non-cash consideration unless the consideration has been valued by an independent expert within the past six months and a copy of the report has been served on the company and the proposed allottee. If this requirement is contravened the allottee is liable to the company for an amount equal to the nominal value of the shares plus any premium thereon (a subsequent holder of the shares will be similarly liable unless he is a bona fide purchaser for value without notice of the contravention of s103). The fact that the directors paid an extra £100,000 for the factory in the belief that it would be a profitable acquisition does not necessarily involve them in liability – this may have been a perfectly proper decision – but the expert's report must state the extent to which the par value of the shares and any premium are to be treated as paid up (a) by the consideration and (b) in cash (s108(4)).

The second problem concerns the declaration of dividends at the end of 1982. Before 1980 the only significant rule was that dividends must not be paid out of capital (*Flitcroft's Case* (1882)), and this allowed the payment of a divdend where there was a surplus on revenue account for the current year even though losses of previous years had not been made good. An unrealised profit generated by a revaluation of fixed assets could also be used to fund a dividend or a bonus issue: *Dimbula Valley (Ceylon) Tea Co Ltd* v *Laurie* (1961). New rules were introduced in 1980 (see now CA 1985 Part VIII). Dividends may be paid only out of profits available for the purpose, and the profits available for the purpose are accumulated realised profits less accumulated realised losses so far as not previously written off in a reduction or reorganisation of capital duly made. One very important consequence of this is that accounting periods are no longer treated in isolation – thus losses of previous years must be made good before any dividend can be paid. In the case of public companies such as this one there are further restrictions under s264. Plcs may not make distributions if the result would be to reduce the net assets below the sum of the called-up capital and the undistributable reserves (share premium account, capital redemption reserve).

In the present case it is clear that previous losses have not been made good, so that the distribution is unlawful. Under s277 a member who receives a wrongful distribution with actual or constructive knowledge that it is unlawful is liable to repay it to the company. Thus the liquidator could sue for repayment of the dividend.

The third point is the provision of financial assistance to James in respect of the rights issue. It should be observed that the financial assistance here consists not of declaring a dividend but of agreeing to defer the payment for shares. The rules in this area were relaxed somewhat by the 1981 Act (see now CA 1985 ss151–157) but there are still restrictions on what is effectively a disguised return of capital. The general rule is still that it is unlawful for a company or any of its subsidiaries to give assistance for the purchase of that company's shares. There are exceptions (if the assistance was not given for the purpose of assisting in the purchase or if it was merely incidental to some broader purpose), but these exceptions, which are couched in regrettably vague and subjective terms, do not appear to apply here. Other exceptions allow the giving of assistance where the directors have made a statutory declaration as to the company's solvency and the transaction has been approved by the General Meeting, but these also are not relevant here.

Breach of s151 is a criminal offence, but there will also be civil liability on James (*Steen* v *Law* (1964)), and the liquidator should therefore be advised that it may be worthwhile bringing an action against James.

QUESTION FIVE

To what extent, if at all, is the law on financial assistance [contained in ss151–158 of the Companies Act 1985] still destructive of genuine commercial transactions? Is there any rational policy running through the legislation or case law? How could the law in this area be improved?

University of London LLB Examination
(for External Students) Company Law June 1994 Q2

General Comment

This is a demanding question in that it requires a critical analysis of the provisions dealing with the prohibition against a company giving financial assistance for the acquisition of its shares. It also requires a fairly detailed knowledge and understanding of the case law, especially the complex case of *Brady* v *Brady*. Consideration also needs to be given to recent proposals for reform. Students generally find this a difficult area, as indeed it is, and the question should only be attempted if you fully understand the topic and have read around it.

Skeleton Solution

Capital maintenance doctrine – prohibition against financial assistance – examples of financial assistance with reference to case law – the destruction of genuine commercial transactions – *Brady* v *Brady* – reform proposals – consideration of DTI's suggested two-tier structure.

Suggested Solution

Under the capital maintenance doctrine, a company's share capital must be kept intact for the benefit of the creditors. While it cannot be guaranteed that the fund will be intact when the creditors come to rely on it, case law has established that the share capital cannot be paid out of the company except in the legitimate course of its business or under a recognised procedure in the legislation: *Trevor* v *Whitworth* (1887).

One way in which the capital of a company may be reduced is where the company gives financial assistance to another person for the purchase of its shares. Section 151 of the Companies Act (CA) 1985 lays down a general prohibition against this and it implements Article 23 of the Second Company Law Directive which contains a similar prohibition, but only in relation to public companies.

Financial assistance is prohibited if given before, at the same time as, or after the acquisition of a company's shares and covers gifts, guarantees, securities, indemnities, loans etc: s151(2) CA 1985. The courts will not try to strain the meaning of the term 'financial assistance' in order to bring an arrangement within the meaning of the section. Instead, they will look at the commercial realities of the case: *Charterhouse Investment Trust Ltd* v *Tempest Diesels Ltd* (1986).

A number of exceptions to the prohibition are contained in s153 CA 1985, and there is a total relaxation of the prohibition for private companies, provided they comply with the procedure laid down in ss155–158 CA 1985.

The original prohibition was contained in s45 CA 1929. This became s54 CA 1948 which was reworded in CA 1981 due to problems of interpretation. The current provisions are now contained in ss151–158 CA 1985. The policy running through the legislation has always been to stop abuses by the giving of financial assistance but, at the same time, trying to ensure that genuine commercial transactions are not caught. So, if company A lends money to company

B so that B can purchase shares in A, this will clearly be in breach of s151 CA: *Steen* v *Law* (1964).

The original provisions were enacted to stop a common abuse, whereby a takeover bidder would borrow money from a bank and then repay the bank out of the company's funds after the takeover was complete: *Selangor United Rubber Estates* v *Cradock (No 3)* (1968).

While the previous and current legislation on financial assistance may be said to have a rational policy, it appears that the courts have struggled to interpret and apply it in such a way as to allow genuine commercial transactions. A good example, although decided under the old provisions, is *Belmont Finance Corporation Ltd* v *Williams Furniture Ltd (No 2)* (1980). Here, company A purchased an asset from company B. Company B then purchased shares in company A. Had company A provided financial assistance? The Court of Appeal held that it was an artificial transaction designed to put company B in funds so that it could purchase A's shares. The directors of A had to account for the assistance, amounting to £500,000, as constructive trustees. The directors of company A argued, unsuccessfully, that the asset was purchased at a fair price and that it was a genuine commercial transaction in the company's interests.

In *Belmont*, Buckley LJ left open the position where a company puts a third party in funds, partly to allow it to purchase its shares, and partly as a result of a bona fide commercial transaction.

The uncertainty which the *Belmont* decision caused led to the introduction of rules allowing private companies to give financial assistance within ss155–158 CA 1985 and also to allow financial assistance, under s153(1) and (2) CA 1985, for the acquisition of shares where:

'a) ... the company's principal purpose in giving that assistance is not to give it for the purpose of any such acquisition, or the giving of the assistance for that purpose is but an incidental part of some larger purpose of the company, and

b) the assistance is given in good faith in the interests of the company.'

This 'principal purpose' exemption was considered by the House of Lords in *Brady* v *Brady* (1988). The facts are extremely complex, but in outline the business of Brady was that of a soft drinks' manufacturer and road haulier. It was run by two brothers, Bob and Jack. The company began to make losses as a result of the breakdown in the relationship between Bob and Jack. A plan was devised whereby the business would be split up, with Jack taking the haulage side, and Bob the drinks side of the business. To off set the difference in value between the two sides of the business, it was agreed that Jack's new company, M Ltd, would receive assets from Brady Ltd to help pay for the shares in Brady Ltd.

It was accepted that this amounted to financial assistance by Brady Ltd and this was relied on by Bob when he was sued by Jack, who wanted specific performance of their agreement. Jack claimed the transaction fell within the larger purpose exemption in s153 CA 1985.

The House of Lords held that the transaction did not fall within s153, but granted specific performance on the ground that it fell within the private company exemption in ss155–158.

Despite finding that the scheme was in good faith and in the interests of the company, Lord Oliver was unable to find some larger purpose to which the financial assistance was merely incidental. He said that it was necessary to distinguish between the purpose and the reason for giving the assistance. In this case the only *purpose* of the assistance was to enable Jack to acquire the shares in Brady. The *reason* was to promote the re-organisation of the family business so that it could be split between Jack and Bob and allow them to go their separate ways. Their Lordships felt that the advantages which the scheme produced were mere 'by-products'.

Lord Oliver justified this approach by saying that any other result would deprive s151 of 'any useful application'. However, most commentators agree that this is a very narrow interpretation of the wording in s153, as it failed to take into account the wider commercial considerations of the scheme. It is now very difficult to think of a clear example of when the larger purpose exemption would apply and its scope is very uncertain.

The result of *Brady* is that genuine commercial transactions will probably continue to be caught by the financial assistance provisions.

It is suggested that the law in this area could be improved along the following lines.

a) The 'larger purpose' exemption could be amended so that financial assistance would not be prohibited where the 'predominant reason' for the transaction is for the benefit of the company. If this test is adopted then the problems in *Brady* would be overcome.

b) It is difficult to understand why the penalties contained in s151(3) make the company itself liable to a fine, for this will reduce a company's capital still further. Consideration should be given to repealing this sanction.

c) The procedure allowing private companies to give financial assistance could be simplified. For example, the requirement to pass a special resolution could be replaced by the requirement simply to pass an ordinary resolution.

d) It is arguable that financial assistance which does not materially reduce the net assets of the company should be allowed by way of a 'de minimis' exemption. This would help clear up a doubt about whether or not a company has provided financial assistance when it pays the expenses and costs incurred by a person who has subscribed for its shares.

e) Some commentators have suggested the complete abolition of the financial assistance rules in relation to private companies. They have done so arguing that companies can guarantee another's debt without any formality, but that if the guarantee relates to the acquisition of its shares, then it has to comply with the procedure in ss155–158. They argue that it is arbitrary to have no formalities for the first type of guarantee, while imposing a strict procedure on the second type. Complete abolition is, however, only a remote possibility.

Reform of the law on financial assistance is currently being considered by the Department of Trade and Industry (DTI), which has issued a consultative document, 'Company Law Review: Proposals for Reform of Sections 151–158 of the Companies Act' (October 1993). In it, three approaches to reform are suggested:

a) To amend the existing ss151–154.

b) To reproduce Article 23 of the Second EC Directive.

c) To completely re-structure ss151–154.

The DTI favours the third option and has proposed a two-tier structure. The first tier would implement Article 23 of the directive. It would therefore only apply to public companies and the private company exemption would not apply. The second tier would cover financial assistance outside the directive and would therefore apply to some public companies and all private companies. The private company exemption would apply and would be extended to those public companies in the second tier. The current exemptions contained in ss152(3) and

(4) (such as the larger purpose and employee share scheme exemptions etc) would apply to both tiers.

The DTI feels that its two-tier structure would 'prohibit objectionable financial assistance while permitting innocent financial assistance'. If this is correct, then it is to be commended.

It is unlikely, however, that any changes in the law in this area will be made in the near future.

Finally, mention should be made of *Arab Bank plc* v *Mercantile Holdings Ltd and Another* (1993). In this case, Millet J has cleared up an uncertainty in the law by holding that s151 does not apply if financial assistance is given by a foreign subsidiary of an English parent company, for the purpose of purchasing the parent company's shares. Presumably, any reform will not now have to consider the question of whether or not a foreign subsidiary is within the financial assistance provisions.

QUESTION SIX

a) 'Every major Companies Act, beginning with the Act of 1867, has required that reduction of share capital ... should be confirmed by the court[s] [which] have a discretion to confirm or not to confirm ... and ... this discretion fell to be exercised by reference to ... whether the scheme would be 'fair and equitable'. *Per* Lord Cooper in *Scottish Insurance Corporation Ltd* v *Wilsons & Clyde Coal Co Ltd* (1949).

Explain and discuss this statement.

b) Willow Ltd was formed in 1986, at which time it issued 50,000 £1 ordinary shares. In 1988 the company issued 50,000 £1 'A' preference shares, the terms of issue of which stated merely that the shares carried a 10 per cent preference dividend.

In 1990 the company issued 30,000 £1 'B' preference shares, the terms of issue of which stated that the shares carried an 11 per cent preference dividend and preference as to a return of capital on a winding up, but no right to vote.

As a result of bad luck, the company has recently lost assets and the directors now wish to cancel £30,000 of share capital which is not represented by available assets. They intend to cancel the 'B' preference shares.

Advise the directors as to whether this might be done, and if so, how.

University of London LLB Examination
(for External Students) Company Law June 1994 Q6

General Comment

A very straightforward question provided the student is familiar with this area of law. Frequently, students will avoid questions relating to maintenance of capital and variation of rights. This is unfortunate because the area is not very difficult once the rationale behind the rules is understood.

Skeleton Solution

Reduction of capital – discretion of court to confirm – order of repayment to shareholders on winding up – order in which losses are to be borne.

Procedure for reduction – whether reduction amounts to variation of rights.

Suggested Solution

a) The question sets out part of the dissenting opinion of Lord Cooper. In *Scottish Insurance Corporation Ltd* v *Wilsons & Clyde Coal Co Ltd* (1949) Lord Cooper held that a proposed reduction of capital directed at repaying expensive preference share capital (expensive because the preference shareholders had a cumulative right to a fixed-rate preferential dividend) was unfair and ought not to be confirmed. In order to confirm a reduction, the court has always insisted that shareholders of equal standing be affected in a similar manner, or at least consent to being treated differently. But there is absolutely no rule that a reduction be borne equally upon all shares of the company. The rule is that where classes of share have different rights (expressed in the articles) to a return of capital on a winding up, a reduction of capital should be framed so as to conform with those rights: see *Prudential Assurance Co Ltd* v *Chatterley-Whitfield Collieries Ltd* (1949).

Lord Cooper was troubled by the effect of a reduction which had the effect of 'expelling' from membership of the company those to whom capital was to be repaid. More recently, the House of Lords pointed out in *House of Fraser plc* v *AGCE Investments Ltd* (1987) that preference shareholders who are given a preferential right to a return of capital could (as an alternative to complaining about expulsion) in fact bring proceedings if they were not the first to be repaid in a reduction of capital.

Lord Cooper also protested against the generally non-interventionist policy of the courts when confirming reductions, pointing out that Parliament had delegated the discretion of whether or not to confirm reductions of capital to the courts and not to an administrative official, eg the Registrar of Companies. For that reason, Parliament must have intended that the role of the courts would be an active one, as opposed to a 'rubber-stamping' exercise. However, since 1993, petitions seeking confirmation of a reduction of capital are generally no longer heard by a High Court judge but by a registrar of the Companies Court.

b) The directors of Willow Limited should be advised that the court will only confirm the reduction if it is satisfied on the following points: (i) that all shareholders of equal standing are treated equally, or have consented to unequal treatment; (ii) that the shareholders have had the reduction and the reasons underpinning it properly explained to them; and (iii) that no creditors are prejudiced by the reduction.

The creditors of Willow Ltd will suffer no prejudice because the assets representing the reduced capital have already been lost. It is extremely likely, however, that the 'B' preference shareholders will challenge the reduction on the ground that it is not in accordance with their rights under the articles, and therefore amounts to a variation of their class rights. If this is correct, the reduction cannot be approved without an extraordinary resolution at a separate class meeting of the preference shareholders.

The 'B' preference shareholders are unique in the sense that they have a preferential right to a return of capital on a winding up. Thus, in a liquidation, losses would be borne first by the ordinary and 'A' preference shareholders (which have no preferential right to a return of capital), see *Poole* v *National Bank of China* (1907). The same principle will apply on a reduction. While the courts have not developed any comprehensive definition of what will amount to a 'variation' of class rights, it is likely that the cancellation of the 'B' shares would amount to a variation. Section 125(3) of the Companies Act 1985 provides that where a variation of rights is connected with a reduction of capital, and the articles or memorandum of association contains a variation procedure, the rights shall not be varied unless the procedure is followed.

It may be concluded therefore that the proposed reduction will not be confirmed by the court unless it has been approved by the holders of the 'B' preference shares at a separate class meeting.

6 Shares

6.1 Introduction

6.2 Key points

6.3 Recent cases

6.4 Analysis of questions

6.5 Questions

6.1 Introduction

The subject of shares is a large one, which is in many ways fundamental to the structure and theory of company law; as appears below, some matters related to it are in this book dealt with in other chapters. Students therefore need to be aware that it is not sufficient to be familiar with the material in this chapter, for questions commonly overlap with chapters 5: *Capital* and 10: *Meetings*, as well as occasionally with chapters 11: *Directors* and 12: *Minorities*.

6.2 Key points

a) *Issuing shares*

Every company must have an authorised capital, and shares may not be issued beyond the limits of that capital. A public company must have the minimum authorised capital prescribed by s118(1) CA 1985.

No shares may be allotted unless the directors have been authorised to allot (s80 CA 1985). Such authority may be given in the articles or may be conferred by an ordinary resolution of the General Meeting. In the latter event it may be valid for a period not exceeding five years. A private company may only take advantage of the elective resolution procedure under s379A CA 1985. This substitutes the provisions of s80A for those of subsections 80(4) and (5), and authority may be given for any fixed period or indefinitely, although it is revocable at any time. On an elective resolution ceasing to have effect, the authority takes effect as if for a fixed period of five years or, if it has already run for five years, it ceases immediately.

It is a criminal offence to make an allotment without s80 authority, but this does not affect the validity of the allotment.

Section 89 CA 1985 provides that in private companies shares issued for cash must initially be offered to existing members in proportion to their shareholdings. A shareholder who suffers loss as a result of a breach of this rule can claim compensation from the company (s95 CA 1985) but the violation does not appear to affect the validity of the allotment.

In all cases the power to issue shares must be exercised bona fide in the best interests of the company. Thus it is not proper to issue shares solely in order to defeat a motion for the removal of a director, nor to defeat an attempted takeover. Where it appears that an issue of shares has been made for an improper purpose, the issue can still be ratified by the general meeting (GM). In such cases the court will order the matter to be referred to the

GM for a decision, on the basis that the shares whose issue is disputed may not be voted at that GM.

In addition to the above, the issue of shares for an improper purpose may in some cases be evidence of a course of conduct unfairly oppressive to the minority, so as to bring s459 CA 1985 into consideration. As to this section see chapter 12: *Minorities*.

b) *Class rights*

Where there are different classes of shares further special problems arise. A modification of the rights attaching to that class of shares normally requires the consent of the holders of the shares of that class at a special meeting as well as a resolution of the GM of the company.

Such resolutions are in any event open to challenge as not having been made in good faith. It is not wholly clear what test is to be applied, but the better view seems to be that the resolution must be for the benefit of holders of that class of shares as a whole. This can cause difficulties where some (but not all) holders of eg preference shares are also holders of ordinary shares, and it is desired to reduce the privileges attaching to the preference shares, thereby benefitting holders of ordinary shares). There have been judicial suggestions that it must be for the benefit of all members of that class including the objectors, but it is thought that this would give too much veto power to a small minority (see, eg, *Re Holders Investment Trust* [1971] 1 WLR 583).

c) *Rules as to payment for shares*

Shares may not be issued at a discount (s100 CA 1985) but may be issued at a premium subject to s130. A non-cash consideration may be accepted although, in the case of public companies, subject to special rules concerning acceptance of undertakings and valuation of non-cash consideration. Furthermore, a public company cannot commence business unless it has allotted shares to a nominal value not less than the authorised minimum (see above) and those shares are paid up as to at least one-quarter and the whole of any premium. Public companies which do not satisfy these requirements may have to re-register as private.

d) *Voting rights*

This topic is dealt with in chapter 10: *Meetings*.

e) *Transfer of shares*

It is common in small private companies for the articles of association to contain restrictions on the freedom to transfer shares. These are considered desirable because of the need to control who becomes a member.

The provisions come in a number of common forms. One form gives the directors an absolute discretion to refuse to register any transfer of shares. A modified version of this removes the discretion where the transfer is to a member of the transferor's family. Another version allows the directors rights of pre-emption on any shares which are to be offered for sale.

Such restrictions are in principle valid, but the power given to the directors must in all cases be exercised bona fide in the best interests of the company.

f) *Maintenance of capital*

Important topics which overlap with those discussed in this chapter include the rules as to payment for shares, reductions in capital, purchase by a company of, or giving financial assistance for the purchase of, its own shares, and dividend rules, are all dealt with in chapter 5: *Capital.*

6.3 Recent cases

Re Thundercrest [1995] 1 BCLC 117 – a company was not entitled to allot shares in a rights issue to another when they knew the original allottee wanted the shares but had not received the offer letter.

6.4 Analysis of questions

This topic appears quite commonly on London LLB External papers, but often in conjunction with other subjects. This chapter consequently contains a number of cross-references to other chapters. The problem of varying class rights has been popular in recent years.

On the London LLB External Paper these topics have almost always arisen in the form of problem questions. However, some essay questions are also included.

6.5 Questions

QUESTION ONE

Violet, Red and Blue are shareholders/directors of Rainbow Ltd, each holding 250 of the issued £1 ordinary shares in the company. Green, who is not a director and has a rival business, holds the other 250 shares, and there is a further £1,000 of nominal capital unissued. The articles of Rainbow Ltd contain a provision that any member wishing to transfer his shares must first offer them to the other members.

Violet and Red are approached by Black, who offers them a very good price for their shares in Rainbow Ltd. Without telling Blue or Green about this, at a directors' meeting Violet and Red propose issuing all the unissued capital to the directors, telling Blue it would be useful to have more shares in case they ever had to fight off a takeover bid. Blue objects that they do not have the authority to issue the shares and, after a heated argument leaves the meeting. Violet and Red then go ahead with issuing the remaining capital to themselves. They then propose calling a general meeting to pass a resolution removing the pre-emption clause from the company's articles.

Before the meeting can be held, Blue dies, leaving his shares to Green. Although his executor executes a share transfer in favour of Green, Violet and Red refuse to register it, saying that, because of the pre-emption clause, Blue's shares now belong to them. They then decide that since they now hold all but 12.5 per cent of the issued share capital, they can change the articles without holding a meeting and so they write to Green saying that as they have inserted a clause in the articles which says that competitors are not allowed to be members of the company, he must transfer his shares to them. They then execute a contract to sell all the issued shares in the company, including Green's and Blue's to Black.

Advise Green

Written by the Editor

General Comment

This is a complex question which centres on directors' powers in connection with the issue and transfer of shares, although other topics are touched on. The first thing to do in any question of this nature is to work out in what proportions the shares are held and how the proposed changes affect these proportions. Only then is it possible to evaluate whether resolutions effecting the changes will be valid.

Skeleton Solution

No duty to disclose self-interest – authority to allot: s80 – proper purpose rule. Transmission of shares on death – director's power to refuse to register – reasons. Alteration to articles – special resolution – whether meeting can be dispensed with. Remedies open to minority shareholder.

Suggested Solution

It is usual and acceptable for articles of small private companies to contain a pre-emption clause of the type in this question, since it is reasonable in a small company for the members to wish to restrict membership. There seems no reason why Violet and Red should feel obliged to tell the other shareholders about the approach from Black, even though they are also directors, since they owe no duty to them as individuals (*Percival* v *Wright* (1902)). Directors must be given specific authority by the general meeting, or by the articles, to allot shares (s80 Companies Act (CA) 1985). From Blue's reaction, it does not seem that the directors have the appropriate authority. Even if they did have the authority, Blue would be right to be concerned about the purpose of the issue since the 'proper purpose rule' states that directors may only use their powers for the purpose for which they are granted. The true reason – to make a profit for the directors – would certainly be an improper purpose, and even their given reason was considered to be an improper purpose in *Hogg* v *Cramphorn* (1967).

Furthermore, s89 CA 1985 provides that companies proposing to allot shares must first offer them on the same or more favourable terms to existing members. Private companies may exclude these statutory pre-emption rights by a provision in the articles disapplying the relevant sections, but Table A does not provide such a disapplication. Unless the articles of Rainbow specifically disapply s89, it may be that these rights apply and Green and Blue are entitled to part of the newly allotted shareholding in proportion to their existing holdings.

Contravention of s80 does not affect the validity of any allotment made, but any director who 'knowingly and wilfully' permits it is liable to a fine (s80(9)). Under the proper purpose rule, the directors concerned would be in breach of their fiduciary duties and the allotment would be invalid unless ratified by the general meeting (*Bamford* v *Bamford* (1970)). The new shares would not be counted in the votes at the general meeting and, since Violet and Red validly hold only 50 per cent of the issued capital, they could be outvoted by the combined efforts of Blue and Green. It would then be a matter of whether one of them was chairman with a casting vote which would either sanction or invalidate the allotment. Contravention of s89 gives rise to a joint and several liability on the company and every officer who knowingly authorised or permitted the contravention to compensate any person to whom an offer should have been made.

Assuming, however, that the allotment was valid, the additional shares give Violet and Red 75 per cent of the voting power at a general meeting which would be sufficient for them to pass a resolution removing the pre-emption clause from the articles. Section 9 CA 1985 provides that the articles may always be altered by special resolution (a 75 per cent majority at a general meeting of which 21 days' notice has been given). The only objection that a dissenting minority shareholder can raise is that the alteration is not in the interests of the company as a whole. However, case law suggests that the court will not interfere unless fraud can be proved (*Shuttleworth* v *Cox Bros & Co (Maidenhead) Ltd* (1927)). Possibly the court may consider it sufficiently 'fraudulent' if the majority has not considered the effect on the minority (under the extended definition of 'fraud' to be found in *Estmanco (Kilner House) Ltd* v *Greater London Council* (1982) and *Clemens* v *Clemens* (1976).

The directors' right to refuse to register a transfer depends on the articles. A right of refusal is often contained in the articles of small private companies for the same reason as they contain pre-emption rights. If the articles do not require the directors to give their reasons, they do not have to do so (*Re Smith & Fawcett Ltd* (1942)), but if the directors do give their reasons, the court is allowed to examine them and decide whether they are in fact reasonable. A refusal by Red and Violet to register on the ground that Blue's shares belong to them is, it is submitted, unreasonable. They cannot simply appropriate Blue's shares since even when there is transmission on death, a proper instrument of transfer is required (*Re Greene* (1949)) and the proper procedures for pre-emption must be followed, ie offering the shares to all the members.

Green is doing nothing wrong by being involved in a rival company as a shareholder owes no duties to a company in this regard. Even a director may be involved in a competing business (*Bell* v *Lever Bros* (1933)). However, alterations to the articles which have the effect of expelling a member who is competing have been permitted by the court in the past (*Dafen Tinplate Co* v *Llanelly Steel Co* ((1920)). Nevertheless, even if Violet and Red do validly hold 87.5 per cent of the voting capital, as they claim, there is still a need formally to pass a special resolution at a properly convened general meeting. A written resolution is only valid if all the members entitled to attend and vote at the general meeting consent to it.

Green is luckier than his predecessors in earlier decades since s459 CA 1985 provides a remedy in respect of conduct unfairly prejudicial to members of a company. This is considerably wider and more satisfactory than the remedy provided by the 'fraud on the minority' exception to the rule in *Foss* v *Harbottle* (1843) on which he would formerly have had to rely. Provided that he can show a case for unfairly prejudicial conduct, the court is able to afford him almost unlimited remedies and, in this particular case, orders for rectification of the register to perfect the transfer to him of Blue's shares, for compensation for loss of s89 pre-emption righs (if applicable) and for the purchase of his shares at a fair price, would be the remedies he should seek.

QUESTION TWO

The share capital of Valhalla Limited ('the company') consists of 60,000 £1 shares which are held as to 15,000 by Alan, 12,500 each by Barry, Colin and Donald (all four of whom are directors) and 7,500 spread among five different investors who take no interest in the affairs of the company but who may be relied upon to vote as instructed by Barry. Originally the company was carried on by Barry, Colin and Donald, but when they arranged for the company to buy Alan's business, this was paid for by the issue to Alan of 15,000 shares. On this occasion as part of the agreement under which Alan's business was purchased, the articles of association of the company were altered so as to include the following clause:

'No resolution by the board of directors of the company, or by the company itself, which concerns the acquisition or disposition of property for a price in excess of £100,000, shall be valid unless agreed to by any shareholder holding more than 20 per cent of the issued share capital of the company.'

Barry, Colin and Donald are now anxious to expand the property development operations of the company and recently proposed the purchase of a corner site for £1m for redevelopment. Alan voted against this proposal. Barry, Colin and Donald are concerned that Alan will veto the proposed expansion of the company's business and have been searching for ways in which Alan's entrenched veto might be eliminated.

Advise them.

University of London LLB Examination
(for External Students) Company Law June 1992 Q8

General Comment

A question involving the position of minority shareholders is always a strong candidate for inclusion in the paper. Whether the question is set in the guise of to what extent the majority can lawfully make life uncomfortable for the minority, or advising the minority how fair the position is, the basic legal material requiring discussion is still the same.

Skeleton Solution

Division of share capital – votes and resolutions – clause in articles – alterability of articles – restraints on alterability – terms of contract for sale of business – possible claim for breach of contract – class rights – variation of class rights.

Suggested Solution

Alan holds one quarter of the issued shares, the other directors between them hold over 60 per cent, and the remaining shareholders will vote as instructed by Barry. Hence (assuming each share holds only one vote as appears to be the case) the other directors will not only be able to carry a resolution voted on by a show of hands at a general meeting but can also do so on a poll (where there is one vote per share held), which Alan as holder of one tenth of the voting rights would, under Companies Act s373, be able to demand. An ordinary resolution will suffice (subject to the power of veto) to authorise the purchase.

A resolution to acquire the site could instead be passed at a meeting of the board of directors, where Alan is a minority. Despite the resolutions Alan would (as a holder of more than 20 per cent of the shares) exercise his veto under the articles; the veto is effective despite a resolution passed in general meeting approving the acquisition: *Quin & Axtens* v *Salmon* (1909).

The other directors may seek to alter the articles and delete the veto by special resolution in general meeting under s9. They (plus the small shareholders who would support them) command the 75 per cent of the votes which is the minimum necessary for its passing (see s378). At least 21 days' notice specifying the intention to propose the resolution as a special resolution must first have been given to the members. Neither waiver of notice nor written resolution procedure are plausible here.

There are, however, certain constraints upon a company's ability to alter its articles. The most relevant is that the alteration must not constitute a fraud on the minority and must be bona fide intended to benefit the company as a whole. Otherwise the fact that the alteration is productive of hardship to the minority appears to be unimportant: *Allen* v *Gold Reefs of West Africa* (1900). 'Intended to benefit the company as a whole' seems here to relate to the intended benefit of the shareholders as a collective body: *Greenhalgh* v *Arderne Cinemas Ltd* (1951). There appears to be no evidence of malice towards Alan, the majority do not appear to be acting other than in the general interest, and their view is not obviously unreasonable. The resolution should therefore be valid.

We are not, however, informed of the precise terms of the contract for sale of Alan's business; did the contract itself provide that Alan, as any shareholder with at least 20 per cent of the shares, should have the right of veto? If so, mere alteration of the articles would not of itself be effective to eliminate a right contained in a contract itself quite separate from the articles. In *Baily* v *British Equitable Assurance Co* (1904) the Court of Appeal stated that it would be dangerous to hold that a company had any greater power to breach contracts than a private individual would have. But it is not clear what remedies can successfully be invoked to protect the contract right. In *British Murac Syndicate* v *Alperton Rubber Co* (1915) the court granted an injunction to restrain the company from altering its articles to insert provisions inconsistent with the separate contract, while in *Punt* v *Symons and Co* (1903) it was suggested that it might be appropriate to enjoin the company from breaking the separate contract rather than from altering its articles. Or the remedy might be damages only, a position seemingly supported by a dictum of Lord Porter in *Southern Foundries Ltd* v *Shirlaw* (1940). However, any agreement by a company to fetter its right to alter its articles is void (*Russell* v *Northern Bank Development Corporation* (1992)).

It could further be argued that the rights of each holder of 20 per cent or more of the shares are, under the present articles, different from each shareholder with less than that quantity, and thus constitute a separate class of shares. In *Cumbrian Newspapers Group Ltd* v *Cumberland and Westmorland Herald Newspaper and Printing Co Ltd* (1986) it was held that rights conferred on a shareholder as such by the company's constitution are class rights even though not attached to any particular class of shares. This, if correct, would appear to be the case here. If so, it is suggested that it is far from clear that the variation of class rights provisions in s125 would apply, since these refer to variations where the rights attach to a class of shares. But if s125 did apply, a holder of at least 15 per cent of the shares could apply to the court within 21 days to disallow a variation, on the basis that the variation would be unfairly prejudicial; such a plea would, however, be very likely to fail on the merits.

QUESTION THREE

'The restrictions on the issue of new shares by a private company are an unjustified fetter on the freedom to raise capital.' Discuss.

Written by the Editor

General Comment

This question is not taken from a London LLB External paper, but is included to provide an example of an essay question on the issue of new shares. It may be noted that this question is the only one in this chapter to deal with the rather neglected question of the effect of exceeding authorised capital, a point which could easily be raised in a problem question.

Skeleton Solution

Three restrictions: authorised capital, directors' authority, pre-emption rights.

Authorised capital: easily increased, no authority on effect of accidentally exceeding it. Issue possibly void.

Directors' authority: gives shareholders some control, issue without authority valid, but criminal offence by directors.

Pre-emption rights: protects existing shareholders, damages for breach, unclear whether allotment invalid.

Rules try to balance power between directors and shareholders: they impose some constraints on a company's freedom, but these are basically justified.

Suggested Solution

A private company which wishes to issue new shares must be careful to comply with three major requirements, two of which did not exist before 1980. These are the limit of authorised capital, the requirement that the directors be authorised to issue new shares, and the pre-emption rights of existing shareholders.

Authorised capital: A company is required to have an authorised capital, which must be stated in the memorandum (Companies Act (CA) 1985 s2). This capital can be increased by ordinary resolution, which must be filed with the Registrar within 15 days (s121). The Act is silent on the question of what happens where shares are issued in excess of the authorised capital. There is of course no good reason why this should happen, since authority for an increase can so easily be obtained, but it might occur by oversight. It is generally thought that such an issue would be void since the shares do not properly exist, but there is no authority on the point, and it is not impossible that a court would seek to avoid this very awkward conclusion.

Directors' authority: CA 1985 s80 requires directors to have authority before allotting any shares in the company. Such authority may be contained in the articles, or may be given by ordinary resolution of the company. An issue of shares made in violation of this requirement is a criminal offence by the directors and anyone else who is knowingly a party to it, but this does not affect the validity of the allotment.

Pre-emption rights: CA 1985 s89 requires shares issued for cash to be offered to existing shareholders pro rata to their existing holdings before being offered elsewhere. Section 92 allows a shareholder whose pre-emption rights are ignored to claim damages from the company, but there is no provision which expressly invalidates the allotment, and it is thought (again in the absence of any authority) that it would be valid.

In addition to the above directors need to be aware that an allotment which is made for an improper purpose, such as to benefit the directors personally, or to defeat a take-over bid, is liable to be set aside, or at least referred to a General Meeting of the company: *Hogg* v *Cramphorn* (1967); *Howard Smith Ltd* v *Ampol Petroleum Ltd* (1974).

It is fair to say that the legal restrictions, especially the s80 authority and the pre-emption rights, were introduced to protect existing shareholders from having their shareholdings diluted or the value of them weakened by an unnecessary issue of shares. Of course it may be argued that the 'proper purposes' doctrine serves much the same purpose, so that the statutory rules are unnecessary. However, it is to be observed that the test of what is a proper purpose is inevitably imprecise. The statutory rules have the merit of clarity and certainty. At the same time it must be admitted that they do add some additional bureaucracy to the process of issuing shares; it is nevertheless submitted that they are on balance to be welcomed as a useful protection for minority shareholders.

QUESTION FOUR

'Although the class rights concept has important consequences in many different areas of company law the reality is that it is more likely to lead to confusion and to obstruct desirable change than to provide any real measure of protection for shareholders or creditors.'

Discuss.

University of London LLB Examination
(for External Students) Company Law June 1995 Q2

General Comment

The question involves consideration of the difficulties surrounding the source and nature of class rights, both for the member and for the courts. These problems must be set against whatever perceived protection can arise for members and creditors, followed by a conclusion as to whether the protection is real or illusory.

Skeleton Solution

Outline problem of ascertaining nature and source of rights – indicate possible sources of the rights – methods and difficulties of altering class rights according to source – class consents for certain types of alteration – changes that do or do not amount to variation of rights – protection of creditors – conclusion.

Suggested Solution

The class rights concept does, indeed, provide some safeguards for both members and creditors but it does seem that some of the protection is more illusory than real. This is illustrated by considering the position of members and creditors separately.

a) *The position of shareholders*

The essence of the class rights concept is that a member holding shares of a particular class is entitled to the rights and priorities (or lack of them) that attach to his shares, and to be treated by the company and its controllers in strict accordance with those rights. That is the basis upon which he acquired those shares and the degree of protection given to the member is dictated by his ability to prevent changes to the rights against his wishes. The problem that most commonly presents itself for the member is to ascertain, with certainty, just what his rights are, from where they arise and who or what may change them. This is a major problem because the rights might derive from one or any combination of the company's memorandum, the articles, the shareholders in general meeting, the board of directors or even from statements made in listing particulars for new share issues. When one adds to this problem of source the fact that the method required to alter the rights will vary according to their source, the complexity becomes great.

Theoretically, it should always be possible to find out the source and nature of class rights by reference to the Registrar of Companies. Any rights set out in the memorandum or the articles will be able to be seen but it may be that shares have been issued under the power in, or similar to, Table A art 2, which allows the issue of shares with such rights as the Board attaches when deciding to issue them. Here, the class member will need to look at the particular resolution of the Board or the General Meeting, as the case may be, to ascertain his rights. Even then, he may not be sure of the position because if there is any conflict between the rights given by resolution and any rights in that or any other class of shares given by the memorandum, or the articles, the resolution is, to that extent, ineffective: *Hogg* v *Cramphorn Ltd* (1967). Section 128 Companies Act (CA) 1985 provides some help in that upon any allotment of shares with rights that are not set out in either memorandum or articles or in any special resolution of the general meeting and which differ from the rights attaching to previously issued shares, a statement of the share class rights must be sent to the Registrar within one month of the allotment: s128(1) CA 1985. This also applies to any naming of the new class created by the differential rights attached to the new allotment. Despite this, there is still a possibility of missing additional rights which might attach to the rights by reason of being set out in listing particulars or similar documents, as happened in *Jacobs* v *Batavia & General Plantation Trust Ltd* (1924).

The next problem for the prospective or actual class member is to establish just how his rights would need to be altered procedurally. This is often a complex matter as everything depends upon the source of the rights. If given by the memorandum, they can only be altered if the memorandum so provides (s267 CA 1985), or if the memorandum itself contemplates alterations in a way set out in the articles so that the article becomes incorporated by reference into the memorandum (*Re Welsbach Incandescent Gas Light Co Ltd* (1904)), or by the consent of all the members of the company (s125(5) CA 1985). If, on the other hand, the rights are given by the articles or by the resolution of the Board or the General Meeting, the method of alteration and conditions for validity of the alteration depend upon whatever provision, if any, is made in the articles themselves. With the exception of an article providing for alteration of rights by resolution of the General Meeting, CA 1985 requires class consents to the alteration. If there is no provision in the articles for alteration the rights may only be altered with the consent of 3/4 in nominal value of the issued shares in the class or by an extraordinary resolution having a majority of 3/4 of the votes cast at a separate class meeting: s125(2) CA 1985. These last consents also apply where there is provision in the articles or memorandum for alteration of rights but where the purpose of the alteration is in any way connected to directors' authority to issue shares or to reduce share capital: s125(3) CA 1985.

If the class member gets through the maze outlined above he may then face the further problem of trying to ascertain just what it is that amounts to an alteration of his rights. The law on this point makes a strong distinction between changes that materially affect the rights of a class and changes which have no effect beyond altering the value of the shares. In the latter case, the position of the class member is greatly changed but it will not amount to an alteration by which rights are 'affected, modified, dealt with or abrogated': *White* v *Bristol Aeroplane Co Ltd* (1953). Here existing preference shareholders who could have exercised voting rights to prevent such alterations were held by the court to have been properly prevented from voting against the issue of new fully-paid preference shares to ordinary shareholders. The result was a serious dilution of the existing preference class so that their prospects on a repayment of capital and their limited voting powers in General Meetings or class meetings were both greatly reduced. The court concluded that what was altered was not the class rights but the enjoyment of those rights in the sense of the capacity to turn them to personal advantage.

Similar difficulties are to be seen in the question of whether the cancellation of a class of shares, usually preference, amounts to an alteration of class rights. There are cases that point both ways in this area and much depends upon whether there is an ultimate right to participation in surplus assets after repayment of all shares of every class, as in *Re Old Silkstone Collieries Ltd* (1954) and *House of Fraser plc* v *ACGE Investments Ltd* (1987). In *Re Northern Engineering Industries plc* (1994), the Court of Appeal held that the complete cancellation of a class of preference shares would equate to a reduction of capital which, by the articles of association, constituted a deemed variation of class rights, but the case only serves to illustrate the difficulties where such express deeming provisions are absent.

b) *The position of creditors*

The position of creditors of the company is as full of uncertainty as that of the shareholder. They can be no more sure of the continuation of the existing capital structure, share classes and control of the company than anyone else. The creditor might, in certain circumstances, be allowed by the court to object to an alteration of class rights which consisted of a reduction in capital (s136 CA 1985), but objections will not be heard in most alteration situations.

In summary, it is submitted that the unwieldy and obscure position on class rights is such that any perceived protection offered to either member or creditor is likely to be outweighed by the difficulties in ascertaining the true extent of the rights in question.

7 Debentures

7.1 Introduction

This chapter examines the problems which arise in connection with the taking of loans by the company in return for a debenture (any document which acknowledges a company's indebtedness). Debentures may be unsecured but are more often secured by a charge on the company's assets.

7.2 Key points

a) *Fixed charges*

A fixed charge attaches to specific assets of the company. If the asset includes land, it may be referred to as a mortgage, and the charge may need to be registered at the Land Registry (registered land) or Land Charges Registry (unregistered).

b) *Floating charges*

A floating charge (which can only be given by a company) attaches to present and future assets which by their nature are changing all the time, eg stock, but it is inherent in the nature of a floating charge that the company can deal freely with the assets until 'crystallisation' (see below) (*Re Yorkshire Woolcombers Association Ltd* [1903] 2 Ch 284). Thus, if the company is prevented by the charge from doing so, the charge must be fixed even though the assets are 'floating' (*Siebe Gorman & Co Ltd* v *Barclays Bank Ltd* [1979] 2 Lloyd's Rep 142).

c) *Crystallisation of floating charges*

'Crystallisation' means that the charge becomes fixed and attaches to specific assets. It occurs on the happening of certain events – at common law, default or liquidation – which are often specified in the debenture. 'Automatic crystallisation' is sometimes attempted by a clause in the debenture which is triggered when a fixed charge is created ranking in priority to the floating charge. As this type of clause subverts the principle that fixed charges take precedence over floating charges, there is some doubt as to its validity, although there are dicta in support (see *Davey* v *Williamson* [1898] 2 QB 194, *Evans* v *Rival Granite Quarries Ltd* [1910] 2 KB 979 and *Re Brightlife Ltd* [1986] BCLC 418), and such a clause has been upheld in New Zealand (*Re Manurewa* [1971] NZLR 909).

d) *Registration*

Any charge or debenture must be registered at Companies House within 21 days of its creation. Failure to comply with this requirement renders the security void, though it does not invalidate the loan. The court may permit registration after the 21-day period has expired and the charge takes effect subject to any charges registered in the meantime. A certificate of registration is conclusive evidence of the date of registration.

e) *Priority of charges*

Fixed charges take priority over floating charges for repayment, and legal over equitable charges. Where there is more than one charge of the same rank, the first in time of creation prevails provided it is properly registered. The chargees themselves may agree to alter the order of priority (*Re Automatic Bottlemakers Ltd* [1926] Ch 421). A clause may be included prohibiting the creation of a later charge having priority (a 'negative pledge' clause). The present position is that this is effective only if the later chargee has actual knowledge both of the existence of the earlier charge and the negative pledge clause. Constructive notice, by mere registration of the earlier charge alone is insufficient (*Wilson* v *Kelland* [1910] 2 Ch 30).

f) *Receivership*

A debenture or charge usually contains a power for the debenture holder to appoint a receiver in the case of default. If it does not, application may be made to the court to make an appointment. An administrative receiver, appointed under a floating charge, must be a qualified insolvency practitioner. The receiver takes over the management of the business for a time in order to obtain payment for his own debenture-holder, but he has first to pay the costs of the receivership and holders of charges having priority to his own. Section 44 Insolvency Act (IA) 1986 makes him an agent of the company. The administrative receiver has extensive powers to manage the company.

7.3 Recent cases and statutes

Re Pearl Maintenance Services [1995] 1 BCLC 449 – whether a charge over book debts was fixed or floating.

Re Real Meat Co Ltd (In Receivership) [1996] BCC 254 – priority of charges.

The Companies Act 1985 made important changes to the law relating to registration and registration procedures. However, these provisions have never come into force.

7.4 Analysis of questions

Debentures have been a consistently popular topic on the London LLB External paper, and consequently represent a sensible choice of subject for students preparing for that examination. Debentures commonly occur in connection with liquidation (since it is usually only then that questions about the validity of the debenture come to the fore). Consequently, the subject-matter of this chapter overlaps to some extent with that of chapter 9: *Liquidations* to which reference should also be made. However, this chapter contains a good deal of material which is relevant to the procedure to be followed in liquidations where the company has granted debentures. Generally it may be said that the major points raised in these questions are: priorities between charges (especially where one charge is fixed and another floating), clauses restricting the power to create later charges, and automatic crystallisation clauses. The position of preferential creditors in a liquidation is often thrown in as a minor point.

7.5 Questions

QUESTION ONE

Henry is the majority shareholder and managing director of Bat and Ball Ltd ('the company'), whose business consists of selling sports equipment. Owing to the recession, Henry lent the company £50,000 on 1 January 1989, but by the middle of 1989 business had hardly improved and Henry, worried about his loan, caused the company to grant him a fixed charge over its shop and book debts as security for a further loan of £50,000. In November 1989 the Midwest bank, where the company's overdraft was £75,000, threatened to petition for the winding up of the company unless it was given some form of security. As a result, Henry caused the company to grant a floating charge to the bank over all the company's assets.

Although the position looked increasingly hopeless, Henry, on the advice of his accountant, continued trading because an end to the recession was widely forecast. In fact, this turned out to be too optimistic a forecast and in November 1990, a petition was presented for the winding up of the company and a winding up order was granted in March 1991. For the six months prior to the grant of the winding up order, Henry only drew half his agreed salary (ie £1,500 per month instead of £3,000).

The company's fixed assets and book debts are valued at £50,000 and the company's other assets would yield £10,000.

Advise the liquidator.

University of London LLB Examination
(for External Students) Company Law June 1991 Q5

General Comment

Debentures is a fairly popular topic; however there is a twist to the question in that Henry, the main shareholder in Bat and Ball Ltd has been granted a fixed charge. Essentially the principles remain the same. Distinction has to be made between fixed and floating charges. The concept of crystallisation, registration of charges and priority of charges. Fraudulent and wrongful trading are also relevant though fraud maybe difficult to prove.

Skeleton Solution

Liquidation retrospective to date of petition – distinguish between fixed and floating charges and registration of charges – concept of crystallisation – fixed charge takes priority unless caught by automatic crystallisation clause, only happens if later chargee has actual notice of earlier clauses – IA 1986 s245 may invalidate floating charge, not applicable to fixed charges – fraudulent and wrongful trading relevant – order of payment.

Suggested Solution

In a liquidation money must be paid out in a strict order of priority. The first payment is the costs and expenses of liquidation, then the fixed chargees, followed by preferential creditors and lastly floating chargees and any payment due to unsecured creditors. The liquidation is deemed to have commenced on the date of the petition ie November 1990. The liquidator will be concerned to establish the priority of payment to be made in the liquidation.

It is clear that Henry has a fixed charge since this charge was created in the middle of 1989. This fixed charge created by the company is registrable under Companies Act 1985 s396, and it is valid if duly registered within 21 days. However, in so far as the charge relates to land it also requires to be registered under the Land Charges Act 1972. Failure to comply with this requirement will render the charge void against the liquidator and a subsequent purchaser for value of the legal estate. If this criterion is not met both the company and any officer in default is liable to a fine. This is because most companies obtain much of their finance from debentures secured by charges and it is important that people dealing with the company are able to find out which assets are subject to charges.

There is a possibility that Henry's fixed charge has priority over Midwest Bank's floating charge which would only have become a fixed charge on the date of the petition. However, in causing the company to grant him a fixed charge, Henry is clearly infringing Insolvency Act 1986 s239, by giving a preference to one creditor of the company (ie himself) ahead of other creditors. Such a preference will accordingly be void, and Henry may be required to repay the money to the company.

The liquidator should also be advised to bear in mind ss213 and 214 IA 1986 where a director of a company incurs personal liability for 'fraudulent trading' ie trading in such a way as fraudulently to prefer one creditor over another. The provisions also deal with 'wrongful trading' ie continuing to trade knowing that the company is insolvent. There is sufficient evidence to indicate that Henry will find himself liable under both these provisions. Under the statutory predecessors of these provisions, a narrow view was taken of the concepts of 'defrauding' and 'fraudulent purpose': *Re Patrick and Lyon* (1933), but it should not be assumed that the same approach would be taken at the present day, as the courts' attitude seems to have hardened somewhat with regard to such indiscretions. A misfeasance summons may be taken through the company by the liquidator under s212 IA 1986 against the accountant as he has a contractual relationship with the company and owes it a duty of care and was negligent in advising Henry to continue trading, when there was clear evidence that Bat and Ball Ltd was tottering on insolvency. However, success as to the outcome of such an action is debatable.

The floating charge granted in favour of Midwest Bank requires consideration. The general concept of a floating charge was explained in *Re Yorkshire Woolcombers Association Ltd* (1903) as a charge over assets present and future. Because these assets would in the ordinary course of business change, the charge to remain floating until some event occurs which causes crystallisation. The events which are normally regarded as causing crystallisation are the appointment of a receiver and the commencement of a winding up: *Re Victoria Steamboats Co* (1897). The difficulty is to decide on the validity of express clauses which make crystallisation happen on the occurrence of certain specified events, ie automatic crystallisation clauses. The point does not seem to be settled in English law, but the decision of Hoffmann J in *Re Brightlife* (1987) gives some support for the recognition of these clauses in English law.

In any event there is a possibility that Midwest Bank's charge is invalidated by IA 1986 s245. This provides that where in the twelve months before the commencement of a winding up, a floating charge is created and the company was insolvent immediately after the creation, the charge will be invalid except to the extent that fresh consideration was given for it. In other words such a charge cannot be used to secure pre-existing borrowing. It is arguable that no fresh consideration was provided by Midwest Bank as the floating charge was merely the re-financing of the company's debts to the bank. If this argument is accepted, then s245 will apply, and the charge will be invalidated.

Thus the payout in the liquidation are (in order): costs and expenses of the liquidation, the

74

preferential creditors (including Henry's wages in the previous four months preceding the liquidation, the Inland Revenue, DSS and others), then the floating charge to Midwest Bank, followed by Henry's charge to the extent that they have not been invalidated.

QUESTION TWO

Sam Sandcastle was the sole director and shareholder (apart from one share held by his wife) of Grand Illusions Limited ('the company'), a company which specialised in the manufacture and sale of jewellery. Some of this jewellery was manufactured by Sam himself under an agreement between himself and the company, some was manufactured by jewellers who sold their items to the company and some was imported by the company from abroad. The company had also entered into agreements with Denis Diamond and Pearl Pond to take their entire output of manufactured jewellery.

The company has been badly hit by the recession and the overdraft with the Bank of Cash and Credit ('the bank') climbed to £300,000 by the end of 1991. The bank demanded security and in February Sam caused the company to grant a floating charge over all its undertaking to the bank as well as a fixed charge over all its book debts. Despite hectic trading in the period from February to May, the company's fortunes continued to decline.

In May, the Bank undertook an investigation of the company's affairs and discovered:

a) that the company had a substantial amount of manufactured jewellery which when the economy improves will probably be saleable at substantial profits;

b) that the company had taken delivery of large quantities of the raw material necessary for the manufacture of jewellery, but that much of this had been supplied under contracts with retention of title provisions;

c) that Sam had caused the company to pay him £50,000 in part reduction of a loan made by Sam to the company in 1990 and in part payment for jewellery made by Sam and sold to the company;

d) that the company owed Pearl and Denis each about £10,000;

e) that the Inland Revenue was pressing for payment of Corporation Tax arrears of some £50,000;

f) that in 1991 the company entered into an agreement with the Easy Financing Company, in terms of which all sales abroad by the company were to go through the Finance Company in exchange for 90 per cent of the invoiced price and that all payments made to the company in respect of such sales were to be received by the company as agent for the Finance Company.

A petition has now been presented for the appointment of an administrator to the Company. The company's total assets are probably not worth more than £100,000 but there are signs of considerable improvement in the economy. Advise the bank whether:

i)   to accede to this petition, or

ii) to appoint an administrative receiver, or

iii) to oppose the petition in favour of a winding up petition.

University of London LLB Examination
(for External Students) Company Law June 1992 Q5

General Comment

The question poses a good many issues concerning priority of claims to the assets of an insolvent company and the validity of its recent transactions, coupled with some comparison of administration, receivership and liquidation. Thus it could not be answered satisfactorily without insolvency as a whole having been studied.

Skeleton Solution

Assets of insolvent company – avoidance of certain transactions – *Romalpa* – priority of claimants – aspects of administration, administrative receivership and liquidation compared.

Suggested Solution

The validity of the charges to the bank should first be checked. There is unlikely to have been any failure to register under the Companies Act 1985 s398, nor is there any likelihood of a preference under s239 Insolvency Act (IA) 1986. But if the company were to commence liquidation, or a petition on which an administration order was made were to be presented, within 12 months of the creation of the floating charge, and had been unable to pay its debts at the date the charge was created, the charge would be invalidated except for money paid, or the value of goods and services supplied, at or after creation of the charge (IA s245). Although the decision in *Re Yeovil Glove Co Ltd* (1965) could reduce the impact of s245 upon the floating charge to the bank, yet insofar as s245 poses a threat to the bank's position it would obviously benefit the bank to avert liquidation or the appointment of an administrator at present.

As regards the raw material supplied under the *Romalpa*-type reservation of title clauses, such clauses usually succeed insofar as the raw material is still clearly identifiable and unused; the clause may also be so worded as to succeed if the raw material has been incorporated into a larger article, provided the raw material is still readily identifiable and can be physically identified (*Hendy Lennox (Industrial Engines) Ltd v Graham Puttick Ltd* (1984), but not if they have been blended into other goods in such a manner as to lose their identity (*Borden (UK) Ltd v Scottish Timber Products Ltd* (1981)). The raw material, therefore, may well not be an asset of the company, but much will turn on the facts and the precise wording of the *Romalpa*-type clauses.

With regard to the payment of £50,000 made by the company to Sam, this may be a preference under s239. If a company has at a relevant time given a person a preference, the administrator or liquidator may apply to the court for an order restoring the position prior to the preference. The court is also given wide powers under s241. A creditor such as Sam is preferred if the company does anything which has the effect of putting the creditor in a better position should the company go into insolvent liquidation, but only if, also, the company was, when deciding to give the preference, influenced by a desire to better his position. Since Sam is, by virtue of his being a director of the company, a person 'connected' with it, the time of the preference will not be a 'relevant time' unless given within two years of the commencement of liquidation or the presentation of the petition on which an administration order was made, as the case may be.

The Revenue is no longer a preferential creditor, and Sam, Pearl and Denis are also ordinary creditors as to the sums listed as still owed to them. Hence the bank, insofar as it is a valid secured creditor, ranks in priority to them. A liquidator or administrative receiver must however pay any preferential creditors in priority to the holder of a floating charge.

The arrangement with Easy Financing Company appears to be neither a preference nor a security. The assignment would appear to be absolute. If so, the company could presumably only assign to Easy Financing such interest in the book debts as the company then had.

As indicated, the appointment of a liquidator or administrator may invalidate the floating charge to the bank wholly or in part; conversely a liquidator or administrator could seek court orders setting aside preferences. Appointment of an administrative receiver would not endanger the security conferred by the floating charge, but an administrative receiver is not empowered to have preferences set aside. The bank must choose its course according to the relative sums, dates and risks involved.

QUESTION THREE

Pip Ltd is a manufacturing company which has in recent years run into financial difficulties. On 1 January 1992 the company borrowed £100,000 from Quinn (who is not connected with the company) and issued a debenture to him for that amount. The debenture was expressed to be secured by a floating charge over all the property and undertaking of the company and the company was prohibited from creating any other charge ranking in priority to or *pari passu* with the floating charge. The debenture also provided that the floating charge was to crystallise automatically without necessity for the appointment of a receiver or other intervention by the chargee if the amount of its liabilities should at any time in fact become greater than the value of its assets. On 15 August 1992 the company's liabilities, for the first time ever, exceeded the value of its assets and it did not become solvent again for three weeks.

On 6 September 1992 the company borrowed £100,000 from Rob (who is not connected with the company) and issued a debenture to him for that amount. This debenture was expressed to be secured by a 'fixed charge over all book debts and other debts now or at any time during the continuance of this security due or owing to Pip Ltd'.

On 1 March 1994 a petition for the winding up of Pip Ltd was presented by a creditor and a winding-up order was made on 2 May 1994. The liabilities of the company exceed its assets.

Advise the liquidator as to the order of priority of the above charges, on the assumption that each was duly registered.

University of London LLB Examination
(for External Students) Company Law June 1994 Q5

General Comment

This question is a fairly standard one. The authorities on automatic crystallisation of floating charges are sparse. The candidate is therefore required to give some critical analysis of the relevant principles/doctrine.

Skeleton Solution

Floating charges – characteristics – negative pledge clauses – validity of, notice/knowledge of.

Automatic crystallisation clauses – validity of – desirability of – failure to intervene upon crystallisation – estoppel.

Suggested Solution

But for the 'negative pledge' and 'automatic crystallisation' clauses contained in the charge granted to Quinn, Rob's fixed charge would have priority. This consequence flows from the very nature of a floating charge. Of the three (non-exhaustive) criteria set out by Romer LJ in *Re Yorkshire Woolcombers' Association Ltd* (1903) (where he explained the nature of a floating charge), perhaps the most significant is the management autonomy that is afforded to the company pending crystallisation. The company retains authority to deal with the property subject to a floating charge 'in the ordinary course of business'. This involves the consequence that a floating charge will not generally take priority over a fixed charge created subsequent to it: see *Re Castell & Brown* (1898). The creation of fixed charges is part of the ordinary course of business.

'Crystallisation' is the metaphor used to describe the transition from floating charge into fixed charge. Once crystallisation has taken place, the company must have the consent of the debentureholder if it is to deal with the property subject to the charge.

To shore up the relatively poor priority of floating charges, it has become common for companies to insert negative pledge clauses, similar to that given in favour of Quinn. The validity of negative pledge clauses has been largely assumed in the decided authorities. It is worth pointing out, however, that negative pledge clauses should always be strictly construed because they limit the company's actual authority to deal with the charged asset/s. For that reason they are arguably inconsistent with the management autonomy which is one of the hallmarks of a floating charge (above). The question is whether or not Rob is bound by the negative pledge clause.

To be bound by the clause, Rob must have knowledge or notice of it. The simple fact that the debenture was duly registered does not suffice. Since there is no requirement to register particulars of any negative pledge clause when registering the charge (see s397 Companies Act (CA) 1985), there can be no constructive notice of it: see *Wilson* v *Kelland* (1910). To be bound by the negative pledge clause, Rob must have actual knowledge of it or have been wilfully blind as to its existence, eg he may have been put on notice as to the existence of the negative pledge but failed to ascertain its precise effect. We are given no information as to the state of Rob's knowledge and so will assume that he did not, in fact, know of the negative pledge in favour of Quinn. (It is worth mentioning that the 1989 amendments to the 1985 Act, see s416(2)(c), which are yet to be enacted, provide for the registration of negative pledge clauses.)

What about the purported automatic crystallisation of the floating charge? There is no decided appellate authority in which the validity of automatic crystallisation clauses has been upheld. Such clauses are of doubtful validity because it is possible that a charge will crystallise upon the occurrence of a particular event, without either the company or the chargee knowing that crystallisation has taken place. Prejudice might therefore occur to a subsequent fixed chargee who thinks that his fixed charge has priority over the earlier floating charge, which he does not know has, in fact, become a fixed charge. This is exactly the problem faced by Rob. The Cork Committee (1982) were against the introduction of automatic crystallisation clauses.

The validity of such clauses has been upheld in New Zealand in *Re Manuwera Transport Ltd* (1971) but doubted in the Canadian case of *R* v *Consolidated Churchill Copper Corporation Ltd* (1978). More recently, Hoffmann J in *Re Brightlife Ltd* (1987) remarked obiter that such clauses should, in his view, be upheld on the policy ground of general freedom to contract. Rob might argue with force that the clause is not valid for the above reasons. In addition, he might argue that both Quinn and Pip Ltd are estopped from denying the priority of his charge, on the basis that neither took any steps upon crystallisation occurring in August 1992. It is arguable that this failure constitutes an implied representation by Quinn and Pip Ltd that the floating charge had not crystallised.

Whether or not the court would be prepared to uphold the validity of the automatic crystallisation clause, it is submitted that Rob's charge would have priority on the basis of estoppel by representation.

QUESTION FOUR

Bill and Bob are the directors of Bank Finances plc ('the company') which is a long established merchant bank which trades globally. In order to finance margin calls required by their Singapore office they agreed on 1st January 1994 to create a floating charge over the company's entire undertaking (in England) in favour of Ratfink Bank Ltd in return for a loan of £1,000,000,000. The floating charge contained a clause providing that it would crystallise in the event of any default or enforcement proceedings being taken against the company. This charge was registered on 21st January 1994.

On 14th January 1994 the company refurbished their head office in London. In order to finance the interior design project Bill and Bob withheld money due to the Government in the form of VAT and PAYE and also obtained a loan from Beckley's Bank for £1,000,000. This loan was secured over the book debts of the company. The charge was registered on the 17th of January 1994.

On 15th February, John demanded payment for the office furniture that his firm had supplied to the company. Following advice from the company's finance director the board secured the amount outstanding to John by a fixed charge over the company's factory. The finance director also advised the board 'that the company is in a position whereby it is unlikely to pay all its creditors and this financial situation is unlikely to be resolved.'

The company continued to trade until November 1994 when it went into liquidation.

Advise the liquidator.

University of London LLB Examination
(for External Students) Company Law June 1995 Q6

General Comment

It is necessary here to consider the characteristics of fixed and floating charges, and the factors which establish priority both between such charges and also as against other company creditors, unsecured or preferential. The question of voidable preferences is also significant here, and detailed knowledge of statute and common law is necessary in such a question.

Skeleton Solution

Ratfink's charge, outline of floating charges – Beckley's charge, analysis – registration and priorities – John's preferences – priority between fixed and floating charges – voidable preferences – priority between floating charges and automatic crystallisation – avoidance of floating charges by liquidator – final order of priority for liquidator.

Suggested Solution

The liquidator will need to consider the order of priorities created by the transactions entered into by the company during 1994. This requires consideration of the nature of the particular charges and the respective circumstances of their creation and registration.

a) *The Ratfink Bank Ltd charge*

This is expressed to be a floating charge and, as it is over the company's entire undertaking in England and contains express provision for crystallising events, this seems to be a true floating charge, applying the tests in *Illingworth* v *Houldsworth* (1904). A charge on the company's 'undertaking' was held to be a floating charge in *Re Panama, New Zealand and Australian Royal Mail Co* (1870). The charge was properly registered and the particulars delivered within the 21 days allowed by s398(1) Companies Act (CA) 1985. Provided that this charge was also entered into the company's own register of charges, all that was necessary seems to have been done.

b) *The Beckley's Bank charge*

This is secured on the book debts of the company, but it is not expressed to be either floating or fixed so it is vital to ascertain which it is. The nature of book debts is to change rapidly and there is necessity for the company to have freedom to deal with its book debts within the normal course of business, like any other asset. The general rule about book debts charges is that they exhibit the characteristics of floating charges as explained by Romer LJ in *Re Yorkshire Woolcombers Association Ltd* (1903) and also in *Re Brightlife Ltd* (1986). There seems to be nothing of the specific and exceptional circumstances seen in *Siebe Gorman* v *Barclays Bank Ltd* (1979), which pointed towards a fixed charge, although *Re New Bullas Trading Ltd* (1994) indicates that if the true intention of the parties is of a fixed charge, the courts will uphold this position, particularly if the charge is expressed to be fixed. This charge, in the absence of good evidence to the contrary, seems to be intended to be a floating charge. This charge also seems to have been properly registered.

As between these two charges, both properly registered, it becomes necessary to consider the effect of registration. Prima facie, the first created of these equally valid charges will take preference (*Re Benjamin Cope & Co Ltd* (1914)), but the problem is that the taking of a floating charge over the entire undertaking of the company in England necessarily contemplates a freedom for the company to deal with its assets within the course of business, and a later floating charge over a substantially narrower range of assets, such as book debts, may achieve priority as happened in *Re Automatic Bottle Makers* (1926). Much will depend upon whether the earlier charge contains any prohibition upon the creation of subsequent charges having parity or priority, whether the later one was expressed to be subordinate to the earlier one and, if there was no reference to priorities in the later charge, whether Beckleys could be in the position of 'equity's darling' having no actual or constructive knowledge of the earlier prohibition. The registration of the earlier charge gives constructive notice of its existence to Beckleys, but not of any prohibition on creation of later charges ranking in priority, (*Siebe Gorman* v *Barclays Bank Ltd*). There is provision in ss414, 415 CA 1985, as inserted by s103 CA 1989, for the Secretary of State for Trade and Industry to make rules requiring such prohibiting clauses to be a necessary particular for registration, so as to cause a later chargee to have constructive notice of them, but at present this is not the case. Unless Beckleys have actual notice, they will not be bound by such a clause, if one exists. On balance, as between these two charges it seems that Beckleys may have priority. The question of priority between the floating charges and the preferential creditors is considered below.

c) *John's fixed charge*

This charge, over the factory, must observe the general rules of formality for creating such a charge over land, and there seems to be no obstacle to creating a fixed charge subsequent to the floating ones. Even an express prohibition in the earlier charges would not make the fixed charge invalid, it would be merely a breach of contract (*Griffiths* v *Yorkshire Bank plc* (1994)). Provided that neither of the earlier charges had crystallised by the time of creation, John would seem to get priority over both as only crystallisation can convert them into a fixed charge having priority. The difficulty for John is that the security was created at a time when the company was heading into trouble, and it does not seem to have been registered. Lack of registration within the statutory 21 days would cause the charge to become void as against a liquidator of the company (s399(1) CA 1985) and, provided the 'relevant event' of the beginning of insolvency proceedings took place after the creation of the charge, as seems to be the case here (s399(2)(a)), he would simply be an unsecured creditor. If, in fact the charge was registered, John should be entitled to priority against any other creditor, preferential or not. A possible difficulty for John is that the company seemed already to be in trouble at the time of his charge being given. He might be seen as having been given a 'preference' within s239 Insolvency Act (IA) 1986 if the charge was created within the 'relevant time' under s240 IA. This means within two years of the onset of insolvency if he is 'connected', or six months otherwise. He may just escape this on the given facts but, even if he was within a relevant period, if the company did not intend to create a preference and the charge was granted for good commercial reasons it will not be a preference (*Re Paragaussu Steam Tramway Co, Adamson's Case* (1874)).

The next question for the liquidator is the priority between the floating charges and the preferential creditors. It seems, in the absence of further information, that both charges are likely to be crystallised into fixed charges by the events leading up to the liquidation. Probably what it is that constitutes the express crystallisation event seems to depend upon the established law on automatic crystallisation, under which the 'going into liquidation' will be the event. It may be, of course, that Beckleys had put in a common form of clause providing automatic crystallisation immediately before any act by the company entitling Beckleys to enforce its security (*Re ELS Ltd* (1994)).

Assuming that the priority between the two charges is established by their crystallising events, the question is whether these charges will bind the liquidator. Section 245 IA 1986 makes such floating charges void if created within 12 months before the onset of insolvency. Both charges were within this period but there is statutory validity, provided that the moneys were paid as consideration for the charge and paid at the same time or after the creation of the charge (s245(2) IA). This seems to be the situation here so the charges will bind the liquidator.

The final priority to decide is that of the preferential creditors for VAT and PAYE. By s40 IA these will get priority over the floating charges, even though these will have been crystallised into fixed charges (s40(1)). Thus, the order of priority for the liquidator will be first, John's fixed charge over the factory, which seems to be created too early to be caught as a voidable preference, and will take precedence over the liquidator, next the preferential creditors and, finally, the floating charges. These will be in order of crystallisation or, if at the same time, rank equally.

8 Corporate Rescue

8.1 Introduction

The concept of corporate rescue is a relatively modern one. Prior to the Insolvency Act of 1985 the emphasis when dealing with companies in financial difficulties was on winding up as a means of protecting creditors. The more modern notion is that greater efforts should be made to rescue the company so that it can continue in business. The Insolvency Act 1986 introduced into English law the concept of the administration order, which lies at the heart of the scheme of corporate rescue which is considered in this chapter.

8.2 Key points

a) *Context*

The notion of corporate rescue arises in cases where companies are in some financial difficulty, but it is thought that there is still a reasonable prospect of saving them from total collapse. The introduction of the administration order regime reflects a change in attitude in the direction of saving companies wherever possible.

b) *Obtaining an order*

Directors, creditors or the company may petition for an administration order. The order will be made if it appears that the company is unable to pay its debts and the court is of opinion that the purpose of the order, namely securing the continuance of the business as a going concern, can be achieved.

Alternatively an order may be made for the purpose of enabling a voluntary composition with creditors or in order to effect a more advantageous realisation of the company's assets than could be achieved on a winding-up.

c) *The effect of the order*

Once an order has been made no winding-up petition may be presented (and any existing petition will be dismissed). No security may be enforced against the company without the leave of the court.

d) *The administrator*

The administrator must be a qualified insolvency practitioner. He is appointed by the court and is at all times under the direction of the court.

The administrator has extensive powers, including the removal of directors and the conduct of the company's business. He is the agent of the company.

The administrator has three months from the date of his appointment in which to formulate proposals for ensuring the survival of the company. These proposals will be sent to the Registrar of Companies, and must also be laid before a meeting of the creditors. Before any scheme can be implemented it must be approved both by the creditors and by the administrator.

One possible defect in the administration order regime is that chargees are still entitled to appoint their own receivers, and chargees will retain their existing place in the order of creditors. So far as the unsecured creditors are concerned this may well mean that the success of the new system will depend upon the co-operation and goodwill of those holding fixed or floating charges.

8.3 Analysis of questions

This topic has appeared twice on the London LLB External examination, in 1987 and 1991. For the moment it seems likely that essay questions will predominate, not least since there is not enough case law to allow a sensible discussion in problem form.

8.4 Question

'The regime of Administration was introduced on the recommendations of the Cork Committee to enable an insolvent company with the potential for partial or total recovery to avoid the destructive effects of liquidation.'

Assess the effectiveness of the means by which the legislation empowers the regime of Administration to achieve this end. To the extent that you believe that the regime fails in its purpose, what changes would you recommend?

University of London LLB Examination
(for External Students) Company Law June 1991 Q3

General Comment

This question deals with the concept of corporate rescue due to changes introduced by the Insolvency Act 1986. A general review of this new system of administration orders should be made and reference has to be made to previous law. There is however little authority and case law in this area and it is necessary therefore to concentrate on statutory provisions.

Skeleton Solution

Provisions under Insolvency Act 1986 force a company to consider insolvency earlier in order to try and rescue the company and keep it as a going concern. The role of the administrator to try and achieve this – application made by company, director or creditor – other proceedings stayed to allow administrator to make proposals – procedure relatively untested, success dependent on goodwill of creditors and chargees.

Suggested Solution

Administration is a relatively new procedure recommended by the Cork Report 'The Report of the Review Committee on Insolvency and Practice 1982'. It was introduced as an alternative to receivership. The basic purpose of an administrative order is to freeze the debts of the company in financial difficulty in order to assist an administrator to save the company or at least achieve a better realisation of its assets. It is not a procedure designed for creditors to try to enforce their security. In *Re Consumer and Industrial Press Ltd* (1988), Peter Gibson J said that the court had to be satisfied that it was more probable than not that one of the specified purposes would be achieved. This test was adopted in *Re Manlon Trading Ltd* (1988), where on balance the courts refused to make an administration order.

The new Act therefore forces directors to assess the company's financial situation much earlier in order to benefit from this form of corporate rescue, as it may bring about a more satisfactory result for members and creditors alike. The Insolvency Act 1986 also introduced other provisions to ensure that directors do assess the company's financial position in good time under ss213 and 214 IA 1986, which deals with fraudulent and wrongful trading and imposes personal liability on directors contravening these provisions. Moreover, the Company Directors Disqualification Act 1986 provides further statutory provisions for mandatory disqualification of directors by the courts if these provisions are contravened.

A receiver on the other hand will take a charge over all the company's assets and will concentrate on paying off the company's debts, firstly to preferential creditors and he is not under a duty to rescue the company, whereas an administrator will try to salvage the company's business as a going concern.

Before making an order the court must be satisfied that the company is unlikely to be able to pay its debts and such an order will be likely to achieve the survival of the whole or part of the business as a going concern, as this order would provide a more advantageous realisation of the assets than would be effected on a winding up order. The other possible purpose for an order would be the approving of a voluntary arrangement under Part I of the Insolvency Act or sanctioning of a compromise or arrangement under Companies Act s425.

If satisfied that a realisation can be achieved the court will grant the order under IA 1986 s123. The company, directors or creditors can make an application for such an order under IA 1986 s9. Notice of this petition must be given to any person entitled to appoint a receiver as he must consent to such an order. The effect of the application is that the company cannot be wound up, no charge, hire purchase or retention of title clauses can be enforced against the company, without consent of the court and this also applies to any proceedings commenced against the company.

The making of such an order will automatically dismiss any outstanding winding up petition and any existing administrative receiver will have to vacate his office.

The administrator must be a qualified insolvency practitioner and his powers include management of the affairs, property and business of the company. He can deal with charged property, remove directors and require information from the officers and employees of the company, and, in exercising his powers, the administrator is deemed to be an agent of the company.

Within three months of the order, he must send to the registrar, the creditors and members a statement of his proposals for achieving the purpose of the administration. A meeting of creditors is then convened to approve these proposals: s23 IA 1986.

This meeting is an important feature of administration, as these proposals must be approved before implementation: *Re Consumer and Industrial Press Ltd (No 2)* (1987). However, this committee is much weaker than the committee of creditors in a liquidation, since it has no powers to give directions to administrators, and its consent is not necessary in his discharging his duties as administrator.

However, where there is a receiver in place, the person who appointed the receiver must consent to the appointment of the administrator. This is the main failing of corporate rescue as any creditor or member may apply to the court for an order that the company is or has been managed by the administrator in a manner unfairly prejudicial to him, and the court can then make any order it thinks fit: s27 IA 1986. This provision is very similar to s459 CA 1985, and unsatisfied creditors have the opportunity to veto the appointment of an administrator.

The Cork Committee made its recommendations after studying various procedures in a number of countries including France, Australia and United States. Its observations were twofold. Firstly, whether administration will work depends on the goodwill of chargees as they can block the procedure by appointing a receiver and then vetoing the appointment of the administrator. This is because it takes a long time between applying for an order and obtaining it and this leaves time for chargees to appoint a receiver. Secondly, when a company is in financial difficulties and an administrator is appointed, the company's business may continue to suffer in that people may be reluctant to trade with the company, as they will be worried that the company may not be able to meet its financial obligations.

Therefore, although the administrator's role is geared towards rescuing a company, his task can be hindered, and his success is very much dependent on the goodwill of chargees.

9 Liquidations

9.1 Introduction

9.2 Key points

9.3 Recent cases

9.4 Analysis of questions

9.5 Questions

9.1 Introduction

This chapter deals with some of the problems which arise when a company goes into liquidation. As these problems can be spread over a wide spectrum of company law, there is a certain amount of cross-referencing.

9.2 Key points

a) *Types of liquidation*

If a company is solvent it may commence a members' voluntary liquidation (winding-up) by special resolution passed at a general meeting and the directors must make a statutory declaration of solvency. If the company is insolvent, it must pass an extraordinary resolution and call a creditors' meeting and the liquidation will be a creditors' voluntary winding up. In each case the date of commencement of the winding up (which is an important calculation date for a number of statutory sections) will be the date the resolution was passed.

Application may also be made to the court on one of seven grounds in s122 Insolvency Act 1986, the most usual of which is that the company is unable to pay its debts (s122(1)(f)). This may be proved by showing that notice has been served on the company requiring repayment of a debt of £750 or more and the company has for 21 days neglected to pay. If the petition is granted, the date of commencement of the winding up is the date of the petition (not the date of the order).

b) *Role of liquidator*

When a company goes into liquidation, whether voluntary or compulsory, it is the duty of the liquidator to collect in all debts due to the company and to settle, in so far as the assets permit, all debts owed by the company. Three major types of problem arise. The first is that of establishing which claims on the company are valid. The second is establishing the priority of valid claims. It is likely that some creditors will seek to have their claim classified in a higher category than that to which it properly belongs. The liquidator will have to deal with attempts of this kind. The third type of problem concerns the examination of the conduct of directors and other officers and employees of the company. If there has been misconduct, then it may become the duty of the liquidator to take action against the individuals who are in default.

c) *Validity of claims*

The major area of difficulty here arises in connection with retention of title clauses. These are clauses contained in contracts for the sale of goods which purport to reserve title in the goods to the seller until the goods are paid for in full. A more extreme variant of these clauses is found where the parties deal on the basis of a rolling account. In such cases the clause may provide that no title to any goods supplied is to pass unless the account is entirely clear. The effect of this can be to prevent the passage of title even to goods which have been fully paid for.

The validity in principle of retention of title clauses was accepted by the Court of Appeal in *Aluminium Industrie Vaassen BV* v *Romalpa Aluminium Ltd* [1976] 2 All ER 552. Subsequent cases have, however, severely restricted the ambit of the principle, holding that the right to reclaim the goods can be lost if they are irretrievably mixed with other goods, and that in any event the right created in favour of the seller may well amount to a charge on the goods such as requires to be registered under s395 CA 1985 and is void in the absence of such registration: *Borden (UK) Ltd* v *Scottish Timber Products Ltd* [1981] Ch 25, *Re Bond Worth Ltd* [1980] Ch 228, *Re Peachdart Ltd* [1984] Ch 131 and *Re Weldtech Equipment* [1991] BCC 16. At the present day it is fair to say that the courts look with disfavour on retention of title clauses, and will often find some way of rendering them ineffective if not actually void.

d) *Order of priority*

The Companies Act 1985 provides that the first charge in a liquidation is the costs and expenses of the liquidation, followed by satisfaction of the fixed charges, then preferential creditors (including employees up to four months wages or £800, the Inland Revenue and the Customs and Excise for one year's arrears). Next come the holders of floating charges, then the unsecured creditors. The final creditors are the deferred creditors, after which any surplus is distributed to the members.

Because of the above order of priorities it may be important to know whether a particular charge is valid. This may depend upon whether it has been duly registered at the Companies Registry under s398 CA 1985. There may also be questions about the date at which a charge crystallised.

e) *Misconduct*

As a general rule shareholders and officers of a company are not liable for the company's losses beyond, in the case of the shareholders, the paid-up amount of the share capital. This principle may not apply where there has been misconduct. The most blatant form of this arises where the company's funds have been fraudulently misappropriated. In such cases it may be necessary to consider criminal as well as civil proceedings. Misconduct may also take the form of wrongfully authorising payments to a director or to a person or company connected with a director, and here there may be civil proceedings for the recovery of the money. Finally, the questions of wrongful and/or fraudulent trading under ss213–214 IA 1986 may arise. Wrongful trading occurs where the directors carry on business knowing that the company is unable to meet its debts. Fraudulent trading means carrying on business for the purpose of defrauding creditors. It is a criminal offence and liability may be incurred by anyone who is party to it, not just by the directors of the company.

9.3 Recent cases

Re Arrows Ltd (No 4) [1994] BCC 641 – admission of private examinations under s236 IA 1986 in criminal proceedings.

Re Cranley Mansions Ltd [1994] 1 WLR 1610 – meaning of 'agrees' in r1.17(3) of Insolvency Rules – voluntary arrangements.

Re Sherborne Associates Ltd [1995] BCC 40 – wrongful trading, survival of claim after death of director.

9.4 Analysis of questions

This is a topic which is closely connected with that of debentures, since it is for the most part only when a company goes into liquidation that questions about the validity and priority of debentures come to the fore. Students will appreciate that in view of this it is wise to prepare either both topics or neither. These aspects of liquidation have been considered at length in chapter 7: *Debentures* and will not be repeated here. There are, though, a number of other important points arising in connection with liquidations, and these are examined in this chapter.

9.5 Questions

QUESTION ONE

In May 1989 Pop Ltd agreed to buy Cherry's shares in Orange Ltd for £250,000. The following events then happened in the order listed.

Orange Ltd sold machinery parts, surplus to its requirements, to Pop Ltd for £40,000. Pop Ltd re-sold them for £60,000.

Pop Ltd borrowed £70,000 from a bank.

Cherry transferred her shares in Orange Ltd to Pop Ltd for £150,000 in cash; she also resigned as a director of Orange Ltd. At the same time she was paid by Orange Ltd £40,000 in 'compensation for loss of office' and was appointed a consultant to the company for two years at £30,000 per annum.

Orange Ltd paid £70,000 from its distributable profits to the bank in discharge of Pop Ltd's indebtedness.

Orange Ltd has just gone into insolvent liquidation. Advise the liquidator.

Written by the Editor

General Comment

This is a very mixed question, containing a number of different points which are likely to concern the liquidator.

Skeleton Solution

Sale of machinery may be misfeasance – £40,000 compensation recoverable from Cherry unless approved by company in General Meeting – consultancy fee proper only if Cherry actually works for the company – payment of £70,000 almost certainly improper – may be recovered from directors or payee.

Note generally IA ss213, 214 on fraudulent/wrongful trading.

Suggested Solution

The question suggests that the machinery parts may have been sold at an undervalue of some £20,000. This could possibly amount to misfeasance by the directors of Orange Ltd, and is a matter which the liquidator ought to investigate. In the absence of a proper explanation, he should consider taking action against the directors. In this context Cherry's position is particularly open to question. One interpretation of the facts given would be that Cherry was seeking to benefit Pop Ltd in return for their agreement to buy her shares. It is also to be observed that Pop Ltd ultimately does not pay in full the agreed purchase price of the shares. Although this is not directly relevant to the liquidation, since it is a matter between Cherry and Pop Ltd, it may be seen as further evidence of wrongdoing by Cherry.

On resigning her directorship Cherry received £40,000 compensation. Companies Act 1985 s312 requires that details of such compensation be disclosed to the company and approved by it. It is unclear whether this was done in the present case. If not, it is suggested that the liquidator may be able to recover the money from Cherry.

As regards the appointment as consultant, this does not appear to be subject to the s319 requirement of approval by the general meeting, since it is not an appointment to a directorship. Nevertheless, the liquidator would do well to investigate the circumstances of the appointment, and in particular to check whether Cherry has in fact been working as a consultant.

The payment of the £70,000 in discharge of Pop Ltd's indebtedness also looks extremely suspicious. It is very hard to understand how the making of this payment can have been in the best interests of Orange Ltd, and the liquidator should certainly investigate the circumstances in which it came to be made. There is a distinct possibility that the directors of Orange Ltd can be made personally liable for this wrongful dissipation of the company's assets, or that the money can be recovered from Pop Ltd: *Aveling Barford Ltd* v *Perion Ltd* (1989).

A more general question which arises from any insolvent liquidation is whether the directors have carried on business knowing that the company was unable to meet its debts (in which case they can be made personally liable for wrongful trading – Insolvency Act (IA) 1986 s213) or whether they have sought to defraud any of the creditors by carrying on business knowing of the insolvency, in which case they may be criminally liable for fraudulent trading – IA 1986 s214.

In summary, the liquidator should be advised to investigate very carefully the circumstances of and justification for all these transactions. If not satisfied by the explanations which he receives, he should consider taking action against the directors of Orange Ltd (especially Cherry) and/or against Pop Ltd for recovery of sums wrongfully paid.

QUESTION TWO

In 1986, Helen, then aged 24, qualified as a chartered accountant. In 1987 she formed Pear Ltd and its wholly-owned subsidiary, Sub Ltd. Helen holds all the shares in Pear Ltd except one, which is held by a nominee for her. Pear Ltd holds all the shares in Sub Ltd, except one, which is similarly held by a nominee for Pear Ltd. Helen is the only director of both companies and neither company has filed any accounts with the Registrar for the last three years. Other than her shares in Pear Ltd, Helen has virtually no assets.

Since 1987 Pear Ltd has made telephone answering machines and has flourished so that it

Since 1987 Pear Ltd has made telephone answering machines and has flourished so that it now has assets of over £1 million and employs 40 people. Sub Ltd however, is mainly engaged in supplying Pear Ltd with components and is not run primarily with a view to making a profit on its own, although for the first two years, 1988 and 1989, Sub Ltd made profits of £8,000 and £3,000 respectively. However in 1990 it made a loss of £38,000; in 1991 a loss of £23,000 and in 1992 a loss of £11,000.

In September 1991 Big Bank plc was pressing for a reduction of Sub Ltd's overdraft of £40,000. Helen then paid £20,000 of her own money into the account, taking in return a debenture from Sub Ltd for £20,000 and a floating charge to secure both that £20,000 and an earlier loan by her to the company of £15,000.

On 2 April 1993 a creditor presented a petition for the winding up of Sub Ltd and a winding up order was made on 14 May 1993. The assets of Sub Ltd fall short of its liabilities by £60,000.

Advise Helen as to her potential liabilities, if any, and her position generally.

University of London LLB Examination
(for External Students) Company Law June 1993 Q5

General Comment

A fairly straightforward question requiring an understanding of the remedies available to liquidators of insolvent companies.

Skeleton Solution

Avoidance of floating charges – 'connected persons'.

Wrongful trading – parent companies as shadow directors – relevance of Helen's qualification as an accountant.

Company Directors Disqualification Act 1986.

Suggested Solution

The issues are: (1) is the floating charge taken by Helen totally or partially void? (2) could Helen have incurred liability for wrongful trading? and (3) is Helen likely to be disqualified as a director?

1) Section 245(2)(a) IA 1986 enables the liquidator of an insolvent company in certain circumstances to avoid floating charges. It provides in essence that a floating charge created at the relevant time will be invalid except to the extent of the aggregate of the fresh consideration supplied to the company at the same time as or after the creation of the charge. The relevant time for the above purposes is defined in s245(3)(a) as being two years in the case of a charge created in favour of a person connected with the company, beginning with the onset of the insolvency.

    From the facts of the instant case it can be seen that in September 1991, Helen in return for her cash injection of £20,000 took a debenture secured by a floating charge to the value of £35,000. As a director of Sub Ltd, Helen is a connected person and so the floating charge (since it was created less than two years before the winding up order made in May 1993) is potentially liable to challenge from the liquidator. The question is whether Helen has provided fresh consideration. Section 245 IA 1986 aims to prevent the substitution of a secured debt for an unsecured debt. Provided the payment is for the benefit of the company the court will treat it as fresh consideration, *Re Matthew Ellis Ltd* (1933). As per the wording of the statute the consideration provided in return for the charge is £20,000. Helen's security is therefore likely to be valid only to the value of £20,000. She may seek to prove as an ordinary unsecured creditor for the balance of £15,000 but in view of the £60,000 shortfall of assets over liabilities will receive nothing.

2) Is Helen liable for wrongful trading? In order to hold a director liable for wrongful trading the court must be satisfied that at some time before the commencement of the winding up, the director knew or ought to have concluded that there was no reasonable prospect of the company avoiding going into insolvent liquidation: s214 IA 1986. Section 214(4) IA 1986 provides that the facts of which the director will be taken to know will be judged according to: the general knowledge, skill and experience that may reasonably be expected of a person carrying out the same functions of that director, and the general knowledge, skill and experience that that director has. Helen's conduct will therefore be judged according to both objective and subjective standards. It should be noted that the standard is almost certainly therefore higher than that required to be exhibited by directors in the discharge of their common law duties of care and skill: per Romer J in *Re City Equitable Fire Insurance Co Ltd* (1925). It is significant therefore that Helen is a qualified accountant, as a consequence of which her decision to continue to trade will be measured against the likely decision of a similarly qualified 'reasonable' accountant.

We are told that Helen has not caused Sub Ltd to produce any annually audited accounts for the last three years. Helen's failure mirrors that of the directors in *Re Produce Marketing Consortium (No 2)* (1989). In this case Knox J found that the directors could not rely on their own failure to keep proper accounts as a defence to the contention that they knew or ought to have known that the company would enter an insolvent liquidation. The only defence available to Helen is that once the inevitability of an insolvent liquidation occurred to her, she took every step with a view to minimising loss to creditors that she ought reasonably to have taken: s214(3) IA 1986. Thus far Helen is prima facie liable for wrongful trading.

Helen might seek to take solace in the fact that Pear Ltd, whilst the parent of Sub Ltd, is a different company and accordingly should logically remain unaffected by the demise of its subsidiary. She should be advised however that liability for wrongful trading applies to 'shadow directors' as it does to formally appointed directors. The term is defined in s251 as 'a person in accordance with whose directions or instructions the directors of the company are accustomed to act'. We are told that Sub Ltd exists mainly for the purpose of supplying Pear Ltd with components. It is not inconceivable (although there is no authority directly in point) that because of the high degree of connection between the two companies, Pear Ltd may be regarded by the court as a shadow director of Sub Ltd. Thus the assets of Pear Ltd may ultimately be used to satisfy the £60,000 shortfall.

3) Is Helen likely to be disqualified as a director pursuant to the CDDA 1986? The 1986 Act provides numerous grounds upon which Helen may be disqualified. By virtue of ss3, 6, and 11 she may be disqualified on the following grounds respectively; for persistent breach of companies legislation (failure to deliver accounts and annual return); duty of court to disqualify unfit directors of insolvent companies; disqualification for participation in wrongful trading. In relation to 'unfitness', Parts I and II of Schedule 1 to the Act list the factors that are to be considered by the court in determining fitness. As to the behaviour

warranting disqualification it will require at the very least a lack of commercial probity as opposed to ordinary misjudgment: *Re Lino Electric Motors Ltd* (1988).

QUESTION THREE

Ace Ltd manufacturers and distributes Zapgrow, a combination of insecticide and fertiliser for use in crop spraying. Zapgrow has two ingredients, a highly toxic and volatile insecticide called Lethol and a powerful fertiliser called Ferti.

In 1991 Ace Ltd purchased a factory in order to ensure an adequate supply of Lethol for its manufacturing processes. In 1992, acting on advice from its legal department as to possible liability in the event of accidents at the factory, the board of directors of Ace Ltd decided to 'devolve' the manufacture of Lethol. In pursuance of this policy the factory was sold to Fay, a cousin of Cal. Cal is a director of Ace Ltd. Fay then sold it to Greed Ltd which had an issued share capital of two £1 shares which were vested in her brother Harry. Greed Ltd then entered into an agreement with Act Ltd whereby it undertook to supply to Ace Ltd, 500 gallons of Lethol per month. On 20 February 1994 when the factory was shut down for the weekend, chemicals stored there exploded, severely injuring 20 people living in houses nearby. Experts' reports put it beyond doubt that Greed Ltd was negligent in the manner in which the chemicals were stored. On its latest balance sheet Greed Ltd is shown to have a surplus of assets over liabilities of £1,500.

Sub Ltd is a subsidiary of Ace Ltd and has been manufacturing Ferti which it has then supplied to Ace Ltd. Ann and Bob are directors of Ace Ltd and Den and Ern are directors of Sub Ltd. Ern was appointed managing director of Sub Ltd last year. As well as being a director of Ace Ltd, Cal is also a director of Sub Ltd. The two boards have been meeting together once a year to co-ordinate group policy. On 25 March 1994, after receiving an order form signed by Ern 'on behalf of Sub', Ian supplied 200 tons of nitrates to Sub Ltd at a price of £25 per ton. On 9 May 1994 Sub Ltd went into insolvent liquidation with substantial liabilities and virtually no assets and without having paid Ian. It now transpires that it had been in financial difficulties for several years.

Advise Ian and advise Jon (who was one of those injured in the explosion).

University of London LLB Examination
(for External Students) Company Law June 1994 Q4

General Comment

This is a fairly difficult question. Attention to detail is an absolute necessity if students are to distil the legal issues from the morass of factual detail.

Skeleton Solution

Personal liability of directors for improper use of company name and for wrongful trading pursuant to s214 Insolvency Act 1986 – lifting the veil

Suggested Solution

Ian is an unpaid creditor of Sub Ltd which has gone into an insolvent liquidation. Sub Ltd has no assets and it is therefore unlikely that Ian will ever receive payment from Sub Ltd. It is significant that the contract was made by Ern 'on behalf of Sub'.

Pursuant to s349(1) Companies Act (CA) 1985, every company is obliged to have its name mentioned in all business letters and orders for goods purportedly made on behalf of the company. Pursuant to s349(4) of the Act, any director who orders goods on behalf of the company but who fails to mention the company's name pursuant to subs(1) (above) will be liable to a fine. More importantly, he will be personally liable to the creditor unless the creditor is paid by the company. Can Ian use s349 to his advantage and hold Ern personally liable for payment in respect of the 200 tons of nitrates supplied to Sub Ltd?

Ern might argue that Ian cannot have been misled simply by the omission of the word 'Ltd' from the written order and/or that the company's name (ie Sub Ltd's) name was correctly given, notwithstanding this omission. Ern will almost certainly fail on both counts. In *Atkins v Wardle* (1889) it was held that directors were personally liable even though the word 'Ltd' appeared at one place in the document but not in another. Where a director omits the word 'Ltd' he has no locus standi to seek rectification of the document so as to escape liability: see *Blum* v *OCP Repartition SA* (1988). It matters not whether or not Ian was misled by the omission of the word 'Ltd' unless Ian was himself responsible for the error: see *Scottish and Newcastle Breweries Ltd* v *Blair* (1967).

Ian therefore has no options. He may attempt to prove in the insolvent liquidation of Sub Ltd, or alternatively, he may sue Ern directly. It is worth mentioning briefly that the liquidator of Sub Ltd may seek to impose personal liability on the directors of Sub Ltd for wrongful trading, pursuant to s214 Insolvency Act 1986. There is insufficient information to advise confidently that liability will be imposed. However, in view of that fact that Sub Ltd has been in financial difficulties for years, it may possibly be worthy of investigation by the liquidator.

Jon will probably be less fortunate that Ian. We are told that Greed limited has an excess of assets over liabilities amounting to £1,500. This may or may not be sufficient to satisfy any judgment that he obtains against Greed Ltd. In the event that it is not, Jon may ask whether there are any other potential defendants that might be sued. In view of the fact that Greed Ltd manufactured 'Lethol' for use by Ace Ltd, he may ask whether Ace Ltd can be made liable. Any such argument will very likely fail.

Ace Ltd disposed of the 'Lethol' factory precisely to avoid liability for the type of accident which has, in fact, occurred. Crucially, there is no proprietary relationship between Greed Ltd and Ace Ltd, in the sense that Ace Ltd does not own any shares in Greed Limited. The relationship between the companies is tenuous. Greed Limited is owned by Harry, who happens to be a cousin of Cal, who is a director of Ace Ltd. If the facts were different in that Greed Limited was a subsidiary of Ace Limited, or both companies had common owners, Jon might have argued that the 'veil of incorporation' could be lifted so as to make Ace Ltd liable. This would be an 'uphill struggle' for Jon, following the decision of the Court of Appeal in *Adams* v *Cape Industries plc* (1990). In *Adams*, the Court of Appeal expressly recognised that it was a proper use of the corporate structure for groups to organise their affairs so that liability fell upon one company in the group rather than another. Such a scenario is to be distinguished from those cases where the veil is lifted to prevent evasion of a pre-existing obligation.

10 Meetings

10.1 Introduction

This chapter examines the problems which may arise in connection with the conduct of a company's general meeting. Questions usually concern the validity of a resolution passed at a general meeting. (The related topic of a member's standing to challenge an invalid resolution is dealt with in chapter 12: *Minorities*, and the two topics should be learned together as problems typically feature both.) A resolution may be invalid because the majority by which it was passed was insufficient, the procedure under which it was passed was defective, or the meeting at which it was passed was invalid. Annual General Meetings (AGMs) must be held, the first within 18 months of incorporation, and subsequent AGMs within 15 months of the last (s366 CA 1985), unless the company is a private company which has elected to dispense with the requirement (s366A). A general meeting which is not an AGM is an EGM (Extraordinary General Meeting).

10.2 Key points

a) *Notice of meetings*

A meeting will be invalid if proper notice is not given. This will be 21 days in the case of an AGM, and 14 days in the case of an EGM (Extraordinary General Meeting) (unless a special resolution is proposed, in which case the notice must be 21 days also). All the members entitled to attend and vote may agree in writing to accept shorter notice of an AGM (95 per cent of the membership for an EGM) (s369).

Notice must be given to all those entitled to attend and failure to do this will invalidate the meeting, but there is usually a saving in the articles for accidental omissions. Notice will be invalid unless it contains certain information (including the date and place and the fact that the member is entitled to appoint a proxy to attend and vote in his stead) and states the business to be transacted with sufficient particularity to enable members to decide whether or not to attend. The full text or substance of special, extraordinary or elective resolutions must be included (*Re Moorgate Mercantile Holdings Ltd* [1980] 1 WLR 227, 242). If directors are to benefit personally from the resolution, this should also be clear (*Baillie* v *Oriental Telephone Co* [1915] 1 Ch 503).

While the board usually calls a meeting, holders of 10 per cent of the voting capital may require the board to call an EGM (s368), and the court has power to call a meeting if the directors at any time wrongfully fail to do so (s371).

b) *Quorum*

A meeting will be invalid if it is not quorate. A quorum is the minimum number of persons who must be present in person or by proxy. The articles usually specify a quorum (Table A states two members or proxies). Sometimes one person may be a valid quorum (see eg s370A CA 1985 – single member companies, and the court's power to call meetings). An inquorate meeting may be adjourned. (As to adjournment generally, see *Byng* v *London Life Association Ltd* [1990] Ch 170.)

c) *Procedure*

Statute says very little about the conduct and procedure at meetings. Table A, however, lays down fairly comprehensive rules and most companies adopt these. Except where noted, the rules which follow are those in Table A, but the relevant articles of association must always be consulted to see whether these rules have been varied.

The meeting will have a chairman who is specified in the articles or elected by the meeting (s370(5) CA 1985). Table A says the chairman of the board or, in his absence, another director is to chair the meeting. The chairman has considerable power in deciding whom to allow to speak and for how long, ruling on amendments to resolutions, deciding whether a poll may be taken, often exercising proxy votes and deciding whether to adjourn the meeting. He will usually have a casting vote and it is important to check how and when it is to be exercised.

The initial vote is usually taken on a show of hands in which the members will have one vote each. In a poll, voting rights will normally be based on the number of shares held so there may be advantage to demanding a poll. Additionally, proxy votes which are not taken into consideration on a show of hands may be included in a poll. The chairman is entitled to insist on a poll and a valid demand may also be made by the holders of at least 10 per cent of the votes, or by any five members of the company present in person.

d) *Resolutions*

Resolutions are usually proposed by the directors, but members holding at least one-twentieth of the total voting rights, or 100 members holding shares on which there has been paid up an average sum per member of not less than £100, may propose a resolution and require the board to give notice of it (s376).

An ordinary resolution is passed by a simple majority of votes at a meeting of which at least 14 days' notice is usually required. A special resolution requires 75 per cent and 21 days' notice (s378(2)), while an extraordinary resolution, which also requires 75 per cent of the votes, requires no minimum notice. It should be noted that the majorities are of those voting in person or by proxy (in the case of a poll), not a majority of all the members. Students should familiarise themselves with the occasions on which a special or extrordinary resolution is required.

Certain resolutions (eg a resolution to remove a director) requires 'special notice', even though only a simple majority of votes is needed to pass the resolution. Special notice is a minimum of 28 days.

The CA 1989 introduced two new kinds of resolution for private companies only:

i) Elective resolution

This is available where specified in the 1985 Act to dispense with certain requirements (the most important perhaps being the duration of directors' authority to allot shares under s80A CA 1985 – see chapter 6: *Shares*). It requires 21 days' notice and agreement at the meeting by all members entitled to vote in person or by proxy.

ii) Written resolution

This is an agreement in writing by all the members entitled to attend and vote at a general meeting. It is available for any matter which can be effected by any kind of resolution at a general meeting, save only removal of a director or auditor before expiration of office, and is as effective as a resolution passed at the meeting.

The scope of amendment to resolutions is narrow: amendments proposed prior to a meeting must be given the same notice as the original resolution. At the meeting itself only limited amendments (and none of substance) may be accepted (*Re Moorgate Mercantile Holdings Ltd* above).

10.3 Recent cases

Harman & Anor v *BML Group Ltd* [1994] 1 WLR 893 – exercise of court's power to order a meeting under s371 CA 1985.

Re British Union for the Abolition of Vivisection (1995) The Times 3 March – the court exercised its power under s371 CA 1985 to direct the company to hold an EGM in such a way as to avoid potential disruption.

10.4 Analysis of questions

This has not proved a popular area for questions on the London LLB External paper in recent years, although it is more popular elsewhere. Where analysis of resolutions has appeared the questions have generally been heavily slanted towards minority protection and some of these appear in chapter 12: *Minorities*. There appears to be no particular reason why questions should not be set on meetings alone, however. This chapter contains two purpose-written questions, one problem, one essay, which demonstrate how this might be done.

10.5 Questions

QUESTION ONE

Mace Ltd has articles of association in the form of Table A. It has a nominal and issued share capital of £10,000 divided into 10,000 shares of £1 each. Ginger holds 300 shares, Saffron 200 and Coriander 2,600. None of them are directors but Coriander's husband, Chilli, who owns no shares, is. The balance of the shares are held as to 1,000 by Clove, 1,000 between the chairman and the other directors and 4,900 between a number of small shareholders, most of whom do not attend general meetings.

The board of Mace Ltd gives notice of an EGM on 1 November 1995. It states that the meeting is to take place at the company's registered office on 21 November 1995. The business to be discussed is stated as follows:

'The following resolutions are to be discussed and passed if considered appropriate:

1. A special resolution that the name of the company be changed to Allspice Limited

2. An ordinary resolution to increase the capital of the company to £15,000 and subdivide the shares into 30,000 shares of 75p each.'

The Secretary fails to send notice to Clove whom he believes to have sold his shares. Clove is, however, told about the meeting by his friend Chilli and attends. Ginger and Saffron write to the Chairman of Mace Ltd proposing a resolution to remove Chilli as a director. As the Chairman does not like Chilli, he instructs the Secretary to send an amended notice adding a resolution to this effect which goes out on 5 November.

At the meeting, Coriander proposes that resolution 1 be amended to substitute 'Spicerack Limited' for 'Allspice Limited'. The Chairman decides to put both alternatives to the meeting and 'Allspice Limited' is chosen by all but Coriander. Ginger then points out that 30,000 75p shares do not total £15,000. The Chairman blames the Secretary who he says is bad at arithmetic and the corrected resolution (30,000 50p shares) is passed, Coriander voting against. The removal of Chilli is then put to the meeting and, although Coriander and sufficient others present give a majority against, the Chairman says that the resolution is carried by the proxies he holds and his own casting vote.

Advise Coriander who wishes to challenge the resolutions passed at the meeting.

Written by the Editor

General Comment

This question is typical of the kind of problem which might be set on the topic. Candidates need to grasp the provisions of both Companies Act 1985 and Table A, and be able to apply them to the situation. They must also be aware of the importance of the value of shareholdings given in calculating the necessary majorities and qualifying percentage holdings.

Skeleton Solution

Two areas: validity of notices and resolutions.

Notices – notice period – to whom to be given – contents.

Resolutions – majorities and notices required – right of minority to propose – amendments – use of proxies and Chairman's casting vote

Suggested Solution

For a resolution to be valid it must, first of all, have been passed at a valid meeting. Notice of general meetings must be given to all entitled to attend and vote, otherwise the meeting is invalid (s370(2) CA 1985). Notice was not given to Clove, which might have invalidated the meeting, but there is a saving in the articles for accidental omissions (Table A, art.39). There may be some doubt as to whether this was an 'accidental omission', however. But, when a member attends a meeting, it is assumed that he received notice of it (Table A, art.113).

The notice itself must conform to certain requirements. It must contain the date, place and time of the meeting and a statement that a proxy (agent) may be appointed to attend and vote in the member's stead. It is not clear whether the notice in this case conforms to the rules in all respects and, if it does not, this might be a ground for challenge.

The notice must also state the business to be transacted sufficiently that members can decide whether or not to attend and set out the text or substance of any special, extraordinary or elective resolution to be proposed (s378 and *Re Moorgate Mercantile Holdings Ltd* (1980)). The notice appears to conform with this requirement.

The required notice in this case is 21 days because a special resolution is to be proposed, while 14 days would have been sufficient if only ordinary resolutions were on the agenda (s369). Again the notice appears satisfactory in this respect.

As regards the resolutions themselves, changing a company's name requires a special resolution (a 75 per cent majority of votes of members present in person or by proxy at a general meeting of which at least 21 days' notice has been given (s378(2)). Coriander proposes an amendment. Amendments may be proposed, accepted and voted upon at a general meeting, but not amendments of substance (*Re Moorgate Mercantile Holdings Ltd* above). The name is clearly fundamental and this would have been a substantial amendment, so the Chairman was wrong to put it to the meeting. However, the resolution to change the name to 'Allspice' was not validly passed since with Coriander voting against a 75 per cent majority could not have been obtained.

As regards resolution 2, the amendment here may fall within the definition of 'clerical error' and might thus be acceptable. As only an ordinary resolution is needed (s121) to alter the capital (provided a reduction is not proposed), Coriander's 26 per cent would not be sufficient to block it. Thus, it would appear to have been validly passed.

Turning to the resolution to remove Chilli, an ordinary resolution is always sufficient to remove a director (s303(1)). However, although Ginger and Saffron together hold one-twentieth of voting shares and are accordingly able to propose a resolution (s376(1)), their resolution can only be put to an AGM, and in any case a resolution to remove a director is invalid if at least 28 days' notice (special notice) of its proposal are not given. This is required under s303(2) to enable the director to make representations. Possibly it was also wrongly notified, since it appears to have been the Chairman's personal decision to give notice rather than a decision of the board. Finally, for the resolution to be passed on a majority of proxy votes, all of the proxies would need to have been valid and properly lodged in accordance with the articles. If the Chairman's casting vote was needed to attain a majority, it should have been exercised in accordance with the articles, ie there must have been an equality of votes for him to exercise a second vote (Table A, art. 50).

It therefore seems that Coriander can challenge resolution 1. Passing a resolution by the wrong majority is an exception to the rule in *Foss* v *Harbottle* (1843) but this would not mean that her choice of name would take precedence. A separate meeting would have to be requisitioned by Coriander to put this forward. She has sufficient voting capital under s368 to requisition a meeting (only 10 per cent is required) but it seems would have to lobby some support for her resolution.

Coriander apparently has no ground for challenging resolution 2, although this resolution dilutes her voting capital below the 26 per cent required for her to block a special resolution. Although *Clemens* v *Clemens Ltd* (1976) suggests that such dilution is inequitable, it may be confined to the particular facts of a quasi-partnership company, and *Greenhalgh* v *Arderne Cinemas Ltd* (1946) might support the view that it is generally acceptable for the majority to use their voting rights in this way. At best, she might try to argue that it is conduct unfairly prejudicial under s459 CA 1985, but such an argument seems unlikely to succeed.

The resolution to remove Chilli would seem to be invalid. However, if it seems likely that were the proper procedure to have been followed (28 days' notice, representations, etc) the resolution would still have been passed, the court may refuse to cancel it.

QUESTION TWO

Outline the formalities required for the calling of a company general meeting. Are the existing requirements sufficient to protect the interests of all concerned?

Written by the Editor

General Comment

For the most part this is a straightforward essay question, which merely requires a through knowledge of the relevant statutory provisions. The final part of the question does, however, call for some critical comment on the present rules, and it is no doubt on this part of the answer that the good student's ability will become apparent.

Skeleton Solution

Distinguish AGMs and EGMs: AGM each year – 21 days' notice required, unless short notice procedure followed.

EGM when called by directors or requisitioned by 10 per cent of members. 14 days' notice needed.

Notice of meeting must specify business to be transacted.

Rules provide reasonable balance between too many GMs and too few, though creditors are entirely unprotected.

Suggested Solution

Company general meetings fall into two types, the Annual General Meeting (AGM) and Extraordinary General Meetings (EGMs). All meetings other than the AGM are EGMs.

An AGM must be held at least once in every calendar year, and no more than 15 months may elapse between AGMs. However, so long as a company holds its first AGM within 18 months of incorporation, it need not hold an AGM in the year of incorporation or in the following year (s366). Twenty-one days' notice is required for the AGM, unless the articles provide for a longer period. Short notice is acceptable if consented to by all the members entitled to attend and vote at the AGM (s369(3)). The method of giving notice is specified in the articles, but will normally by by post to all members. However CA 1985 s366A provides that a private company may dispense with AGMs.

Holders of 10 per cent of the votes may require the board to call an EGM (s368) and the court has power to call a meeting if the directors at any time wrongfully fail to do so (s371).

The notice of the meeting must specify the business to be transacted with sufficient particularity to enable members to decide whether or not to attend.

EGMs by definition do not happen at regular intervals. Normally the calling of them is at the discretion of the board, but attention is drawn to s368 (mentioned above). Only 14 days' notice is required for an EGM.

The question also asks about the protection of relevant interests. This is a difficult issue, since it is not clear that the rules really aim to protect any particular interest. As usual in company law it is possible to identify the shareholders, the directors and the creditors as three groups whose interests must be balanced. The GM is the residual authority within the company, retaining any powers which have not been delegated to the directors. From the directors' point of view it is important not to have too many GMs, since they are liable to interfere with the smooth running of the company. This may explain the rule that the calling of EGMs is normally to be left to me directors. At the same time it is necessary to have some GMs, so that the shareholders can be kept informed and can have the chance to express their views on important matters of company policy. Thus, there must be at least one GM in each year. The s368 power to requisition a meeting is also relevant in this context, since it provides a way in which a disaffected minority can air some of their grievances. In terms of controlling the directors the requirement of giving details of the business may also be mentioned. This operates to prevent unannounced resolutions from being slipped through a GM.

In general, therefore, the conclusion seems to be that the rules provide a reasonable balance between the directors and the shareholders. It is to be observed, though, that the interests of the creditors do not seem to be treated as being of any relevance here. Admittedly, it is hard to see what can be done about this, particularly since creditors have no right to attend the meeting anyway.

11 Directors

11.1 Introduction

11.2 Key points

11.3 Recent cases

11.4 Analysis of questions

11.5 Questions

11.1 Introduction

Many of the other topics considered elsewhere involve directors since they are a fundamental part of the company structure. This chapter focuses mainly on the important area of directors' duties and abuse of position. Directors owe their duties to the company (*Percival* v *Wright* [1902] 2 Ch 421), and it is only when there is an exception to the rule in *Foss* v *Harbottle* (see chapter 12: *Minorities*) that individual members are entitled to sue them. The company may, however, sue for breach of duty if the majority of members so decide. Further controls include criminal sanctions for a director's failure to comply with statutory obligations, disqualification under the Company Directors Disqualification Act (CDDA) 1986 and the inalienable right of the company to remove a director from office at any time by ordinary resolution (s303 CA 1985), subject to any compensation rights he may have acquired under his contract of service.

11.2 Key points

a) *Fiduciary duties*

Directors were originally regarded as trustees (*Aberdeen Railway Co* v *Blaikie Bros* (1854) 1 Macq 461) and, although it is accepted that they cannot be trustees in the fullest sense, they are still agents and quasi-trustees. As such they have some of the fiduciary duties of trustees, in particular the following:

i) Not to make a secret profit

Directors are not entitled to remuneration from the company (unless specified in the articles or under their service contract) and must not otherwise profit from their office or from information or opportunities obtained by virtue of their office. Such profits must be disclosed and approved. Otherwise they must be accounted for, even if the directors acted honestly (*Regal (Hastings) Ltd* v *Gulliver* [1942] 1 All ER 378) or the company could not itself have profited (*Industrial Development Consultants* v *Cooley* [1972] 1 WLR 443). It seems that an opportunity properly considered and rejected by the company can be taken up by a director (*Peso Silver Mines* v *Cropper* (1966) 58 DLR (2d) 1) and, strangely, there is no blanket prohibition against competing with the company (*Bell* v *Lever Brothers* [1933] AC 161). In connection with secret profits, students should note the requirement under s317 CA 1985 for directors to disclose to the board their interest in contracts made by the company, and its relationship with the common law rule against secret profits as discussed in *Guinness plc* v *Saunders* [1990] 2 AC 663.

101

ii) The 'proper purpose' rule

Directors have a duty to use their powers only for the purpose for which they were given and not for some collateral purpose (*Hogg* v *Cramphorn* [1967] Ch 254), even though they believe it to be for the benefit of the company (*Howard Smith Ltd* v *Ampol Petroleum Ltd* [1974] AC 821). In both of these cases directors used their power to allot unissued capital for the purpose of defeating a takeover bid and were held to have breached their fiduciary duties. Acts in breach of the proper purpose rule can, however, be ratified by the general meeting (*Bamford* v *Bamford* [1970] Ch 212). For a more modern consideration of the rule, see *Lee Panavision Ltd* v *Lee Lighting Ltd* [1991] BCC 620.

b) *Duties of care and skill*

Like anyone else, directors must not act negligently in the performance of their duties. The problem, however, has always been the standard of care, which was fixed artificially low by Romer J in *Re City Equitable Fire Insurance Co Ltd* [1925] Ch 407 when the following rules were formulated:

i) no greater skill is required of a director than may reasonably be expected from someone of his knowledge and experience;

ii) a director is not bound to give continuous attention to the affairs of his company, nor bound to attend meetings;

iii) in the absence of grounds for suspicion, directors are jusitified in trusting those to whom duties are delegated to perform them honestly.

These principles have been affected by contracts of service, which generally provide for a higher standard. Cases have been few and indecisive, but more recently it has been suggested that a higher standard is required at least from executive directors and professionals such as accountants (*Morgan Crucible Co plc* v *Hill Samuel Bank Ltd* [1991] 1 All ER 148). The Cadbury Report (see chapter 15: *Insider Dealing*) may have affected the situation in relation to non-executive directors also. The attitude of the courts in some of the disqualification cases also suggests that more stringent standards apply nowadays.

c) *Contractual duties*

For the most part, the modern director will have a service contract which will regulate his obligations to the company and vice versa. These duties subsist notwithstanding anything in the company's constitution (*Southern Foundries Ltd* v *Shirlaw* [1940] AC 701). However, directors have a duty to manage the affairs of the company in accordance with the memorandum and articles of association (*Salmon* v *Quin & Axtens* [1909] AC 442).

d) *Statutory duties*

The statutory requirements to file accounts and other documentation at the Companies Registry, and otherwise to comply with the provisions of the Companies Acts, fall on the directors. Failure to perform these duties can attract personal liability for fines and even imprisonment, or disqualification under the Company Directors Disqualification Act 1986. Particular note should be taken of s309 Companies Act 1985, which provides that directors must have regard in the performance of their functions to the interests of employees as well as members. Questions are also very often set on on wrongful or fraudulent trading (ss213–214 Insolvency Act 1986), which may be seen in terms of directors' duties, (ss213–214 Insolvency Act 1986), which may be seen in terms of directors' duties, particularly towards creditors, and are dealt with in chapter 9: *Liquidations*.

e) *Types of director*

The law makes no distinction between executive and non-executive directors, although such distinction is of considerable practical importance (see chapter 14: *External Influences: the EC and Corporate Governance*). In the 1980s, statute introduced the concept of 'shadow directors' (persons 'in accordance with whose directions or instructions the directors of the company are accustomed to act') as an anti-avoidance device, to prevent directors evading their obligations by appointing others in their stead to hold the title but not the power or responsibility.

f) *Property transactions with directors*

The scope for directors to abuse their position by using company assets for personal gain is considerable. The fiduciary duties being somewhat limited, statute has forbidden certain transactions (subject to specified exceptions) such as loans by the company to its directors, shadow directors or persons connected with its directors (students should become familiar with the relevant definitions), and imposes stringent requirements regarding disclosure and valuation of others.

g) *Directors' powers*

Abuse or excess of power is another important aspect of this topic which has already been dealt with in some detail in chapter 2: *The Memorandum of Association and Legal Capacity*. The powers of managing the company are given to the directors' collectively (the board), although the board may delegate to individual directors. Usually, a company's articles will give the board all the management powers and, despite an early decision to the contrary (*Isle of Wight* v *Tahourdin* (1883) 25 Ch D 320), the shareholders cannot purport to exercise any of those powers themselves (*Quin & Axtens* v *Salmon* [1909] 1 Ch 311; *Shaw & Sons (Salford) Ltd* v *Shaw* [1935] 2 KB 113), unless the board cannot or will not exercise its powers, eg because of deadlock or where there are no directors able to act.

h) *Disqualification*

Disqualification of a person from acting as a director for some specified period may be obtained on one of three grounds under the Company Directors Disqualification Act 1986.

i) The most serious is misconduct in relation to a company, which includes such matters as conviction of an indictable offence (s2), persistent breaches of companies legislation (s3), and fraudulent trading or other fraud or breach of duty in connection with a winding up (s4).

ii) The second category is 'unfitness'. This is a broader category which attracts a period of disqualification between two and 15 years depending on the seriousness of the case (*Re Sevenoaks Stationers (Retail) Ltd* [1991] Ch 164). The court must make an order if satisfied that the person concerned has been a director of a company which has at any time become insolvent and his conduct was such as to make him unfit to be concerned in the management of a company (s6). Schedule 1 to the Act lists matters for determining unfitness but these are not exhaustive.

iii) The residual category includes wrongful trading (s10), being a director while an undischarged bankrupt (s11) and failure to pay under an administration order (s12).

The considerable body of case law deals mainly with the types of conduct which may lead to disqualification and the appropriate periods.

11.3 Recent cases

Duckwani v *Offerventure* [1994] NPC 109 – a company entering into an arrangement with a director for acquisition of non-cash assets without obtaining the approval of the general meeting, contrary to s320(1)(d) CA 1985.

Neptune (Vehicle Washing Equipment) v *Fitzgerald* [1995] 3 WLR 108 – a sole director must still declare any interest in a company's contracts under s317 at a directors' meeting and have it minuted.

Re Continental Assurance Co of London plc (1996) The Times 2 July – serious incompetence, such as failing to read the company's accounts, may justify a disqualification order.

Re Gibson Davies Ltd [1995] BCC 11 – application under s17 CDDA 1986 for leave to act as a director while disqualified under s6 CDDA 1986.

Re Grayan Building Services Limited (In Liquidation) [1995] 3 WLR 1 (Court of Appeal) – in a case of disqualification the court cannot take into account conduct subsequent to that relied on to obtain the order.

Re Living Images (1995) The Times 7 August – a director of an insolvent company who authorised a preferential transaction could not be disqualified unless he knew the company desired to benefit the creditor and was influenced by that desire.

Re Moorgate Metals [1995] 1 BCLC 503; *Re Richborough Furniture* (1995) The Independent 21 August – a de facto director may be disqualified, but it must be clearly shown he was the sole person, or acted with other shadow directors, who directed the affairs of the company, or acted with validly appointed directors.

Re Working Project Ltd [1995] BCC 197 – disqualification proceedings may be brought after winding up concluded.

Secretary of State for Trade and Industry v *McTigue* (1996) The Times 10 July – the court may consider specific examples of unfitness.

11.4 Analysis of questions

The topic of directors is one of considerable importance in company law, and can reliably be expected to occur frequently on examination papers.

11.5 Questions

QUESTION ONE

Freedom Publishers Ltd ('the company') is a private limited company with articles in the Form of Table A, with the addition of the following clause:

'In the event of there being a resolution before a general meeting to dismiss a director, that director's shares shall carry 3 times the normal number of votes.'

The company has issued 10,000 shares, which are held as to 2,000 each by the three directors, Karl, Fred and Rosa. The remaining 4,000 are distributed amongst ten or so shareholders. Karl and Fred have become disturbed by the fact that recently Rosa has taken up with a new boyfriend who is a member of a Fascist political party and they feel that Rosa might not be able to continue to support the progressive publishing policies of the company. They consult you to consider whether Rosa might be dismissed as a director, telling you that they are likely to be able to command the support of all the other shareholders (apart, obviously, from Rosa).

Advise Karl and Fred as to what course or courses of action they should follow.

University of London LLB Examination
(for External Students) Company Law June 1987 Q6

General Comment

This apparently formidable question in fact provides an excellent opportunity for a student who is familiar with the procedures for removing directors, since it asks for a display of exactly that knowledge in the context of the particular facts presented. Mention of other matters, such as changes to the articles (chapter 3) and the rules relating to share issues (chapter 6) is also required. The question as originally set contains a particular oddity, in that the weighted voting clause is apparently insufficient to prevent the removal of a director. Confronted with what looks suspiciously like a mistake on the part of the examiner, students would be well advised to deal also with the situation which would arise if the weighted voting clause were effective.

Skeleton Solution

Weighted voting clauses are permitted, but this one seems ineffective on arithmetical grounds.

If it were effective, the majority might seek to change the articles, but R could challenge this as not being bona fide. Excluding R from board meetings would be improper. On issue of further shares, consider authority to allot and pre-emption provisions.

Suggested Solution

Companies Act (CA) 1985 s303 allows a company to remove a director from its board by means of an ordinary resolution of the company in general meeting, and at first sight this may seem the obvious course of action. However, the articles contain a weighted voting clause, such as was approved by the House of Lords in *Bushell* v *Faith* (1970). Such clauses appear to contravene the principle that a director is always removable by Ordinary Resolution, but in *Bushell* v *Faith* (1970) the House of Lords said that the clause merely affected the way in which the votes were counted on such a resolution, and therefore the likelihood of its being passed – this did not infringe the rule that such a resolution would be effective if passed. This is at best a tenuous distinction, but the decision is still regarded as good law. Although *Bushell* v *Faith* was a case of a quasi-partnership, the principle does not appear to be limited to such companies.

However, some attention to arithmetic may resolve the problem. There are 10,000 issued shares, of which Rosa holds 2,000. Fred and Karl expect to be able to obtain the support of all the other shareholders, which will be a total of 8,000. This will outvote Rosa's 6,000 (2,000 x 3). It therefore appears that a s303 resolution will succeed.

As an alternative to the solution presented above, it is worth considering what the position would be if the *Bushell* v *Faith* clause allowed, say, quintuple votes, so that Rosa could defeat the s303 resolution by 10,000 votes to 8,000. One possible approach would be to seek to remove the *Bushell* v *Faith* clause. CA 1985 s9 allows a company to alter its articles by special resolution

resolution and Karl and Fred could command the necessary majority. Rosa, as a shareholder, will presumably challenge the alteration as not being made bona fide in the best interests of the company. It has been suggested (*Greenhalgh* v *Arderne Cinemas Ltd* (1946)) that such an alteration must be for the benefit of the hypothetical individual member (a very difficult test to apply, since no such person exists) or that the alteration must not discriminate between the majority of shareholders and the disaffected minority. In *Clemens* v *Clemens* (1976) the former test was modified to ask whether the change benefitted the aggrieved member. This may, however, be too generous to the minority, since it would effectively give them a veto over any change in the articles. Nevertheless, *Clemens* v *Clemens* does show the need, at least in a small company, for the majority to have due regard to the interests of the minority. Here it would be necessary to show that it is in the company's interests to be able to remove 'rogue' directors. On the face of it this is a convincing argument, but the difficulty is that the company was set up on the basis that directors would be protected from removal. The point is thought to be a finely balanced one, and Fred and Karl are by no means certain to succeed.

An alternative strategy for Fred and Karl would be to exclude Rosa from Board Meetings. However, this is improper (*Pulbrook* v *Richmond Consolidated Mining Co* (1878)) – and Rosa could restrain such conduct by injunction.

The last possibility is an issue of further shares so as to reduce Rosa's holding to a level where the *Bushell* v *Faith* clause would no longer protect her. Section 80 authority for such an allotment is needed. If the articles do not already provide this, an Ordinary Resolution must be passed. Even then ss89–96 must be considered. These provide pre-emption rights for existing shareholders on an allotment of new shares for cash. If Rosa is able to exercise her pre-emption rights this will defeat any scheme to dilute her shareholding. Karl and Fred may try allotting for non-cash consideration, or may choose to ignore the pre-emption rights. The effect of the latter course is unclear. Section 92 would give Rosa the right to compensation for any loss, damage or expenses resulting from the breach (which might perhaps include the loss of her directorship) but it is thought that the validity of the allotment probably cannot be challenged. A more serious difficulty is that Rosa may challenge the allotment as having been made for an improper purpose. *Hogg* v *Cramphorn* (1967) and *Howard Smith Ltd* v *Ampol Petroleum Ltd* (1973) show that in such cases the court is likely to refer the matter to a general meeting to decide whether the shares (which cannot be voted at the meeting in question) have been properly allotted. It appears from the statement of facts that Karl and Fred will command a majority at this meeting, so the allotment will be ratified. Rosa's only remaining hope would then be to argue that the issue was a fraud on the minority or a disregard of the equitable obligations upon which the company was founded, which would raise the issues discussed above in connection with changes to the articles of association.

QUESTION TWO

The main business of Elite Properties plc is the acquisition, development, and disposition of property. There are 8 directors who own 15m of the company's 25m issued £1 shares. At a meeting of the board of directors about a year ago, a proposal was presented for the purchase of a site adjoining a rubbish dump. Although the price asked was low (£3m for 7 acres), it was felt that the situation might make it difficult to develop the site and sell any houses.

The site in question was, in fact, bought by Speculative Enterprises Ltd, whose share capital is held as to 25 per cent by Donald, Edward and Fred all of whom are directors of Elite Properties. Speculative Enterprises paid £2.5m for the site and a few weeks later sold it for £5m.

At a shareholders' meeting of Elite Properties called to discuss the failure by Elite to purchase the site, the directors used their votes to prevent the passing of a resolution (a) calling on the directors to compensate the company for any loss caused by the failure to purchase the site and (b) calling on Donald, Edward and Fred to account for all profit made as shareholders and directors of Speculative Enterprises Ltd.

Discuss.

University of London LLB Examination
(for External Students) Company Law June 1991 Q6

General Comment

The question involves consideration of several areas and covers directors' fiduciary duties. This includes directors avoiding situations of conflict of interest and duty to the company. *Percival* v *Wright* (1) needs mentioning and contravention of s317 CA 1985 and accountability of profits made by Donald, Edward and Fred.

Skeleton Solution

Directors duties owed to company only – consider implications of *Percival* v *Wright* – accountability for personal profit by Donald, Edward and Fred – breach of s317 – breach of fiduciary duty to act for the benefit of the company.

Suggested Solution

The fiduciary duties owed by directors are basically similar to those applying to any other fiduciary relationship, eg, between agent and principal or trustee and beneficiary. They are based upon the principle that since the company places its trust with the directors, they must display the utmost good faith towards the company they are dealing with or on its behalf.

Such fiduciary duties are owed to the company alone, in particular he owes no such duty to the shareholder: this was set out in *Percival* v *Wright* (1902). This general principle has been somewhat modified by subsequent authority. Where the shares are held by only a few people as in *Coleman* v *Myers* (1977), or where there is a special situation such as a takeover (*Briess* v *Woolley* (1954)), directors may be held to owe a limited duty of care to the shareholder. There is a possibility this approach will be taken in modern law today.

However, the content of this duty must not be such as to create a conflict with the directors' fiduciary duties to the company. Section 309 CA 1985 states that the directors when performing their functions must have regard to the interests of the members as well as the employees. The members may therefore wish to object to an act which may not be beneficial to them. Nevertheless, the directors may be able to refute this objection as they may consider it as good industrial practice and more advantageous to the company in the long run.

Hence, the resolution passed by the directors of Elite Properties plc preventing the passing of a resolution by the shareholders to discuss the company's failure to purchase the site is within their discretion, as they were concerned that the acquisition of this site might pose long term problems for the company. The directors of Elite do not have to maximise economic benefit to the company, as they felt they were acting for the benefit of the company as a whole. Moreover, the rule in *Foss* v *Harbottle* (1843) would prevent the shareholders from bringing an action, as the wrong is done to the company and it is for the company to decide what action to take. The company would be the proper plaintiff in such an action.

A director who is anyway interested in a contract with the company must declare the nature of his interest at a board meeting: s317 CA 1985. Donald, Edward and Fred would have clearly contravened this requirement and are personally liable to a fine as they made no mention of their interests in the acquisition of the site rejected by Elite Properties plc.

Further, directors have a fiduciary duty not to use either corporate information or opportunity to make an undisclosed personal profit. In *Industrial Development Consultants* v *Cooley* (1972), the managing director of IDC feigned illness in order to secure the termination of his contract. He then took out a contract in his own name which he had unsuccessfully tried to obtain for the company. Courts held he had to account to IDC for his profits. This was also illustrated in the case of *Boston Deep Sea Fishing Co* v *Ansell* (1888).

There is however a Commonwealth authority supporting the proposition that a director may retain a profit derived from an opportunity that the company has considered and rejected. In the Canadian case of *Peso Silver Mines* v *Cropper* (1966), Peso's board considered and rejected the chance to purchase prospecting claims near the company's land. One of Peso's directors bought shares in a new company which was subsequently formed to purchasese the claims. Courts held he did not have to account for his profits. This decision has been widely criticised by academics and has been described by Professor Gower as 'unsatisfactory and undesirable'.

The outcome of the call made on Donald, Edward and Fred to account for all the profit made as shareholders and directors of Speculative Enterprises Ltd would be influenced by several factors in light of *Peso*'s case. This would include the percentage of shares held by Donald, Edward and Fred in Speculative Enterprises Ltd respectively. Other factors would be the part played by all three in the Board's decision to reject the site and whether there is any link between the two transactions.

It is submitted, however, that Elite Properties plc will have a good cause of action to make Donald, Edward and Fred personally accountable for the percentage of profits made as shareholders cum directors of Speculative Enterprises Ltd. They have clearly taken advantage of a commercial opportunity as a result of being directors of Elite Properties plc.

QUESTION THREE

Basil and Brenda have for many years been active in the business of property development. They are the directors of Alpha Limited and own about 65 per cent of the shares. The remainder of the shares are spread among some 7 or 8 shareholders who take little or no part in the running of the company. Basil and Brenda were also directors of Delta Limited, a company in which they held all the shares but which was recently placed in creditors' voluntary winding up and in which there is a substantial deficit such that creditors can expect no more than 15 pence in the pound.

The main business of both companies was (and is) the purchase of suitable property, its redevelopment for either commercial or residential use and then its sale. Despite the downturn in the economy, Basil and Brenda continued throughout 1990 and 1991 with an aggressive purchasing policy. They were advised on several occasions by the companies' auditors to slow down, but they rejected this advice. This policy led directly to the insolvent liquidation of Delta Limited and, although it seems that this will be avoided in the case of Alpha Limited, that company has suffered huge losses. There will be no dividends for years to come.

These problems were increased by the huge donations of £50,000 which Basil and Brenda caused Alpha Limited to make to the Conservative Party in 1989 and again in 1990. Basil and

Brenda have considerable private means and the following transaction has also recently come to light. In the middle of 1991, before the liquidation of Delta Limited, Basil and Brenda learned of the sale of a property in North London for £150,000. As it would have been difficult to raise the finance through either Alpha or Delta, Basil and Brenda bought this property in their own names. It now turns out that this property is much more valuable than anticipated since the Local Authority has unexpectedly allowed redevelopment of this property without any restrictions. As a result Basil and Brenda are planning to sell this property for £350,000.

Advise the liquidator of Delta Limited and the minority shareholders of Alpha Limited. (Ignore the statutory remedies under section 459 of the Companies Act 1985 and section 122(1)(g) of the Insolvency Act 1986.)

University of London LLB Examination
(for External Students) Company Law June 1992 Q4

General Comment

Although this question is concerned with the duties of directors it also embraces aspects which are only marginally within that topic. The wholly separate issue of the rule in *Foss* v *Harbottle* is also raised. The candidate's ability to summon up material gleaned from quite distinct parts of company law is also tested.

Skeleton Solution

Delta Ltd – possible negligence claim against directors – fraudulent trading – wrongful trading – Alpha Ltd – negligence – ultra vires – fiduciary duty – rule in *Foss* v *Harbottle*.

Suggested Solution

As to Delta Ltd, it is possible that the directors have handled the company's affairs negligently. But the approach taken by the law in determining whether directors have been negligent could be regarded as somewhat lenient. It must first be ascertained what knowledge and experience the individual director has concerning the activity in question; having found what the knowledge and experience is, the director is then expected by law to have made a reasonable exercise of it: *Re Brazilian Rubber Plantations and Estates Ltd* (1911); *Re City Equitable Fire Insurance Co Ltd* (1925). It is therefore possible that one director or both directors would incur liability under this head. If a claim were to be made under this head, the liquidator would sue in the name of and on behalf of the company (s165 and Schedule 4 Part II Insolvency Act 1986).

If the company is in liquidation as is the case here and it appears that its business has been carried on with intent to defraud creditors or for any fraudulent purpose, the court may on the liquidator's application order anyone who was knowingly party to the fraudulent trading to make such contribution to the company's assets as the court thinks proper (s213 Insolvency Act 1986). The mental element in fraudulent trading requires '... real dishonesty involving, according to current notions of fair trading among commercial men at the present day, real moral blame': per Maughan J, in *Re Patrick and Lyon* (1933). Claims under this head are difficult to prove and therefore infrequent.

The liquidator is much more likely to make an application under s214 alleging wrongful trading by the directors; if established, the court may order such contribution to company assets as it thinks proper. Wrongful trading is committed, if the company has gone into insolvent

insolvent liquidation, by any person who at some point in time before the liquidation commenced either knew or ought to have known that there was no reasonable prospect of the company avoiding insolvent liquidation, and who was a director of the company at that time. But it is a defence to the director to show that, from the time he knew or should have known of the pending insolvency, he thereafter took every step he ought to minimise loss to the company's creditors. Moreover the facts which he ought to have known, the conclusions he should have reached and the steps he should have taken are those attributable to a reasonable diligent person having the knowledge and experience which could reasonably be expected of a person carrying on the functions of that director, plus any knowledge and experience which he in fact possessed. It should be noted that, in contrast with a common law negligence action, s214 in effect requires the director to show, as a minimum, the knowledge and experience which could reasonably be expected of a holder of that post, and irrespective of whether he in fact has such knowledge and experience.

As to the principle governing assessment of the amount of the contribution should the wrongful trading claim succeed, *Re Produce Marketing Consortium Ltd* (1989) should be cited and discussed.

As to Alpha Ltd, the possibility that the directors have been negligent is as it was in respect of Beta Ltd but there will be no claim for fraudulent trading or wrongful trading, since the company is not insolvent. As to the huge donations to a political party, the company may act within the objects clause (whose precise terms we do not know) of its memorandum, and is also by implication entitled to do things which are incidental or conducive thereto. Here the company might have express authority from its objects clause to make political gifts, but it is more probable that reliance will have to be placed on implication; in the former case the gift cannot be ultra vires (*Re Horsley & Weight Ltd* (1982)), but otherwise the payment must have been for the benefit of the company, reasonably incidental to its business, and made bona fide in the interests of the company: *Re Lee, Behrens & Co Ltd* (1932). Companies not infrequently make gifts to political parties whose programmes the directors regard as favourable to the commercial interests of the company.

The directors hold all their powers as fiduciaries, and must exercise them bona fide for the benefit of the company and for the purposes for which they were conferred, and must not without company authority profit from their position as directors. This will be particularly relevant to the North London land purchase; if the directors learned of the opportunity in their capacity as directors, they have profited from their position without authority to do so and should account to the company for the gains: *Regal (Hastings) Ltd* v *Gulliver* (1942). Difficulties remain as to which company or companies the directors are accountable to for the gain – it would seem both are in the relevant area of activity – and in what proportion if liable to both, and whether ratification of what has been done in general meeting would be valid, as a dictum in *Regal* suggests.

Should the directors be liable for negligence or accountable for the profit, or both, the wrong is to a corporate body or bodies, hence under the rule in *Foss* v *Harbottle* (1843) the company is the proper plaintiff, and prima facie the only person whom the court will hear as to the merits; since in this case the directors control the company through their shareholdings the company obviously will not resolve to sue. There are exceptions to the rule; these do not extend to claims for negligence (*Pavlides* v *Jensen* (1956)) though it may be different where the directors have personally profited from the negligence at the company's expense (*Daniels* v *Daniels* (1978)). An exception is also made when the alleged wrongdoers control the company and are alleged to have acted fraudulently; 'fraud' here is used in a wider sense than common law fraud and includes seriously oppressive conduct: *Estmanco (Kilner House) Ltd* v *Greater London Council* (1982).

Where the wrong is to the company but, under an exception to *Foss* v *Harbottle*, a shareholder is permitted to sue, he does so in what is termed a derivative action; he must also make the company a party to the suit as co-defendant, since the right of action is in truth that of the company and the court is thereby enabled to award damages or other relief, should he succeed, to the company. He must also bring a representative action, suing on behalf of himself and all other shareholders except the defendants, with the consequence that all persons involved are bound by the judgment.

QUESTION FOUR

Robber plc has two wholly owned subsidiaries, Sud Ltd and Tot Ltd. Although all three companies satisfactorily function independently of each other, Robber plc is to some extent reliant on the factories of the subsidiaries for supplies of electronic circuitry for its missile factory.

The board of directors of Tot Ltd have decided that it is virtually essential for Tot Ltd to acquire a more powerful computer system for its factory. Tot Ltd can only afford to raise £150,000 for this, but the system needed, the 'Biggerbyte 601' normally costs around £250,000. The board have recently heard, however, that Ven is prepared to supply the 'Biggerbyte 601' for £180,000, and that Sud Ltd would be prepared to lend £30,000 to Tot Ltd to help with this. Ven holds 15 per cent of the shares in Robber plc and is hoping to use the proceeds of sale of the 'Biggerbyte 601' to acquire a further 3 per cent.

At their board meeting last week, the directors of Tot Ltd decided to go ahead with the purchase of the 'Biggerbyte 601' from Ven, partly because of the low price he is offering and also because they would be happy to see him acquire more shares in Robber plc since they believe that Ven's large stake acts as a deterrent to foreign takeover bidders. The directors of Tot Ltd are anxious to go ahead but have heard that there may be legal problems.

Advise the board of directors of Tot Ltd.

University of London LLB Examination
(for External Students) Company Law June 1993 Q8

General Comment

A fairly difficult question requiring the candidate to contemplate precisely the crux of the problem. Not to be undertaken without a very careful reading of and reflection upon the problem.

Skeleton Solution

Financial assistance – definition of – purpose of prohibition.

Fiduciary duties of directors – duty to act bona fide – duty not to act for any collateral purpose – principal and subsidiary purposes.

Suggested Solution

The directors of Tot Ltd must consider in depth two matters before purchasing the 'Biggerbyte 601'. In view of the fact that Ven intends to acquire further shares in Robber Plc the directors must question whether: (1) the purchase might fall foul of the financial assistance provisions in s151 CA 1985; and (2) whether in deciding whether or not to purchase the computer it is proper for them to have regard to Ven's proposed acquisition of shares in Robber Plc.

Dealing with the question of financial assistance, s151(1) CA 1985 prohibits the provision of financial assistance by a company or its subsidiary where a person is proposing to acquire shares in that company. On the facts Ven is quite clearly proposing to acquire shares in Robber Plc, the parent of Tot Ltd. The next step therefore is to ask whether there is financial assistance.

The principle underpinning the prohibition on financial assistance is to protect creditors from unlawful reductions of capital. Whilst financial assistance is defined very widely (but not exhaustively) in s152 of the Act it is worth bearing in mind the dictum of Hoffmann J in *Charterhouse Investment Trust Ltd* v *Tempest Diesels Ltd* (1986), that the prohibition is penal and ought not therefore to receive a strained construction in order to catch transactions not intended to be caught. This Hoffmann J stated required the court to look at the 'realities' of the transaction. Assistance by gift or guarantee is usually fairly easy to recognise. What however where, as in the instant case, there is a straightforward purchase?

Financial assistance is defined in s152 CA 1985 as including the following: assistance by way of loan or any other agreement whereby the obligations of the giver are fulfilled at a time when reciprocal obligations remain unfulfilled. Also 'any other assistance' which reduces the assets of the company. This part of the definition arguably catches any transaction whereby the assistance is not matched by the company acquiring assets of an equivalent value. Applying this to the facts of the instant case it can be seen that Tot Ltd is to pay £180,000 for a computer which is arguably worth £250,000. The assets of Tot Ltd are likely therefore to be swelled rather than reduced and so the transaction does not reduce the company's assets. There is therefore no financial assistance within the meaning of the Act.

In committing Tot Ltd to the purchase, are the directors abusing their fiduciary duty to act in the best interests of the company? It is difficult to discern any consistent thread running through the authorities on this area. The predominance of authorities concern directors' improper allotments eg where at least one of the purposes of the allotment is to destroy an existing majority or to create a new one: *Hogg* v *Cramphorn Ltd* (1967). The underlying principle is however the same. Can directors' actions be underpined by a dual purpose or must directors never act for any collateral purpose?

In *Re Smith & Fawcett Ltd* (1942), Lord Greene MR stated that directors should exercise their discretion in what they and not the court consider to be the best interests of the company, and not for any collateral purpose. The difficulty is of course that directors' actions are often motivated by any number of purposes. In *Mills* v *Mills* (1938), Latham CJ stated that where there is more than one purpose, the proper question to be asked is, 'What is the moving cause?' Provided generally that the moving cause is the benefit of the company then the course of action will not be upset by the court.

This view was subsequently adopted by the Privy Council in *Howard Smith Ltd* v *Ampol Petroleum Ltd* (1974). In particular Lord Wilberforce stated that the starting point would be to identify the power under consideration (eg, to allot shares) and then to examine the substantial purpose for which it was exercised. This approach seems at first glance very sensible. There may nevertheless be difficulties with it. It is presumably open to directors to attempt to protect themselves by passing a board resolution in favour of a particular course and to express as the dominant purpose what is in fact the subsidiary purpose. The courts will of course look at the factual reality of the situation as well as the declared intention of the directors. But the dominant purpose will be frequently difficult to ascertain. Once it is admitted that there is more than one purpose underpinning a particular act, how are the courts to determine dominancy? For example, as in the instant case, it may be that a new computer is very desirable (as is Ven's increased shareholding in Robber plc) rather than an absolute necessity.

It is useful to consider briefly the approach of the High Court of Australia in *Whitehouse* v *Carlton Pty Ltd* (1987). In this case the court preferred to ask whether the exercise of a power was causally connected with collateral purpose ie if the power would not have been exercised 'but for the' collateral purpose then the exercise of that power should not be upheld. This approach arguably avoids the difficulties occasioned by the dominant purpose test but at the same time is a more stringent one. Applying the above to the facts of the problem it would be sensible to advise the directors of Tot Ltd to direct their minds specifically to the dominant purpose of the purchase, and to proceed with it only if they conclude that they are principally motivated by benefit to Tot Ltd.

12 Minorities

12.1 Introduction

The general meeting is where shareholders exercise such power as remains with them. This comprises those matters for which statute prescribes a resolution of the general meeting, together with any powers reserved to the membership by the articles, ratification of otherwise improper acts by the directors, and a residual power to act where the board cannot or will not (see chapter 11: *Directors*).

As noted in chapter 10: *Meetings*, the general meeting operates on democratic lines. The concern, however, is that a group of 'wrongdoers' may gain control of the majority of votes and operate the company for their own benefit. This is more likely to happen in a small private company. Generally, the court has been reluctant to interfere with the exercise by the majority of their voting rights, unless there is clear bad faith, but there have been exceptions.

12.2 Key points

a) *The rule in* Foss *v* Harbottle

Fundamental to an understanding of minority protection is a grasp of the rule first formulated in *Foss* v *Harbottle* (1843) 2 Hare 461. The rule states that when a wrong is done to a company, the proper plaintiff is the company. Thus, the board will usually initiate an action. If the action is against the directors, the majority of shareholders must initiate it on behalf of the company. The minority cannot.

b) *Personal and derivative actions*

There are the following exceptions to the rule:

i) Ultra vires or illegal acts (see chapter 2: *The Memorandum of Association and Legal Capacity*).

ii) Resolutions passed by an incorrect majority (*Edwards* v *Halliwell* [1950] 2 All ER 1064).

iii) Personal rights of individual members (*Pender* v *Lushington* (1877) 6 Ch D 70).

iv) Fraud on the minority.

In these cases, the minority may be able to bring an action. Where his personal rights are involved, the plaintiff brings a 'personal action', but where the right of action belongs to the company and he is the one to bring it because wrongdoers control the company, it is termed a 'minority shareholders' action' or 'derivative action'. A derivative action is, however, brought at the court's discretion and will be disallowed if the plaintiff is a wrongdoer however, brought at the court's discretion and will be disallowed if the plaintiff is a wrongdoer himself, or if the company has gone into liquidation. The plaintiff need not have been a member of the company when the wrong was committed. Although the right of action belongs to the company, an order for costs may now be made in the plaintiff shareholder's favour (*Wallersteiner* v *Moir* [1974] 3 All ER 217).

c) *Fraud on the minority*

As noted above, the court will interfere where there is obvious bad faith, but it is difficult to find clear distinctions in the older decisions (contrast *Brown* v *British Abrasive Wheel Co* [1919] 1 Ch 290 with *Sidebotham* v *Kershaw, Leese & Co* [1920] 1 Ch 154). The general view of fraud is that it must involve actual dishonesty (*Derry* v *Peek* (1889) 14 App Cas 337). Misappropriation of company assets will certainly found a minority action on this ground (*Cook* v *Deeks* [1916] 1 AC 554) as being clearly dishonest, but there is doubt as to whether negligence, even if self-serving, is sufficient basis for an action (see *Pavlides* v *Jensen* [1956] Ch 565 which suggests it is not, and *Daniels* v *Daniels* [1978] Ch 406 in which a contrary view was taken). In *Clemens* v *Clemens* [1976] 2 All ER 268 the definition of fraud in this context was broadened to include the situation where a majority shareholder used her voting rights to increase the capital and dilute the minority shareholder's equity below 26 per cent. This case may be viewed on its particular merits and contrasts uneasily with the earlier decision in *Greenhalgh* v *Arderne Cinemas Ltd* [1951] Ch 286 where the fundamental point was not dissimilar but minority action was disallowed.

The plaintiff must usually show that the 'wrongdoers' are in control of the general meeting. In *Prudential Assurance Co Ltd* v *Newman Industries Ltd* [1980] 2 WLR 339 'control' was interpreted liberally to include de facto as well as de jure control.

d) *Companies Act 1985 s459*

This section confers a more general protection on minority shareholders than is mentioned above. It gives the court discretion to relieve against any course of conduct in the running of the affairs of a company which is unfairly prejudicial to the interests of some or all of its members, including at least the petitioning shareholder. 'Unfairly prejudicial' has been widely interpreted, and may include serious mismanagement (*Re Elgindata Ltd* [1991] BCLC 959). Section 461 gives the court power to make such order for relief as it thinks fit. Actions under this section have proved popular.

The courts' interpretation of this section has hitherto been liberal in comparison with its earlier restrictive attitude to s210 CA 1948. However, the recent decision of the Court of Appeal in *Re Saul D Harrison & Sons* [1994] BCC 475 suggests a narrowing of its scope. Here the court held that for a company to be wound up on grounds of directors acting for their own benefit, unless the directors had acted contrary to the company's constitution, it must be shown that they had acted wholly unreasonably or in bad faith.

e) *Winding-up petitions*

A more drastic remedy which may be available to an aggrieved member is to petition for the winding-up of the company. Under s122 Insolvency Act 1986 the court has a general discretion to make such an order if it thinks it just and equitable to do so. The usual basis for petitions of this kind has been the breach of the equitable obligations arising in quasi-partnerships. The leading case is *Ebrahimi* v *Westbourne Galleries Ltd* [1973] AC 360, where a minority shareholder/director removed from office by the other two shareholder/directors was awarded a winding up order. In other cases it has been held that the company should be wound up because the substratum of it has failed: *Re German Date Coffee Co Ltd* (1882) 20 Ch D 169. This is obviously a drastic remedy. It will not lightly be granted, and indeed an aggrieved shareholder should consider carefully before he seeks it. If the company is profitable, then winding-up is unlikely to be the most appropriate solution to the problem. It may be that this remedy is used less now than it used to be, because of the greater availability of lesser remedies under CA 1985 s459.

12.3 Recent cases

Re Little Olympian Each-Ways Ltd (No 3) [1995] 1 BCLC 636 – whether conduct is unfairly prejudicial must be decided objectively.

Re Macro (Ipswich) Ltd and Another [1994] BCC 781 – mismanagement as unfairly prejudicial conduct.

Re Tottenham Hotspur plc [1994] 1 BCLC 655 – unfairly prejudicial conduct – dismissed chief executive remaining as director.

Supreme Travels Ltd v *Little Olympian Each-Ways Ltd* [1994] BCC 947 – s459 relief sought against non-member.

12.4 Analysis of questions

Minority protection is a topic of immense importance in company law, and it is not surprising that it occurs so frequently in examinations. On the London LLB External it has appeared every year since 1985, sometimes in more than one question on the same paper. It is also a topic which can very readily be combined with other areas of the syllabus, notably directors, rules as to shares and the articles of association. It is thus a topic which cannot safely be neglected by students – a student who is not familiar with the rules as to minority protection is in danger of being unable to attempt a problem question despite having prepared adequately all the other topics which it covers. There is a growing body of case law, especially on s459 CA 1985 (as amended by CA 1989), and it is important to be familiar with this.

12.5 Questions

QUESTION ONE

Oak Ltd is involved with the film industry as production and recruitment consultants. Pat holds 51 per cent of its issued share capital and Quinn holds the remaining 49 per cent. The articles of association of the company are in the form of the 1985 Table A. Ria is the managing director and both she and the other directors are famous names in the film industry worldwide. For many years Pat and Quinn, who dislike each other intensely, have allowed the board to run the company without themselves becoming involved for they have no personal expertise and under the highly skilled management of the directors the company has prospered, yielding a rich harvest of dividends. The directors too have done well, receiving large salaries under very long-term service contracts.

In February 1994 Pat discovered that Shanti Ltd had broken its contract with Oak Ltd but that the directors of Oak Ltd were taking no action even though the litigation was potentially highly lucrative for Oak Ltd. Pat suspects that this is because Ria has been having an affair with the

the managing director of Shanti Ltd but he has no evidence of this. In March 1994 Pat himself commenced an action in the name of Oak Ltd against Shanti Ltd.

In April 1994 Quinn received anonymously through the post unequivocal evidence that Tim, one of the directors of Oak Ltd, was running his own private consulting business 'on the side' and was taking clients who would otherwise have become clients of Oak Ltd. He raised this with the other directors and with Pat but no-one wanted to do anything about it since Tim was one of the biggest names they had. In May 1994 Quinn commenced an action in the name of Oak Ltd against Tim.

The board of directors of Oak Ltd has now applied to strike out both actions and both applications have been consolidated into one hearing.

Discuss.

University of London LLB Examination
(for External Students) Company Law June 1994 Q7

General Comment

This question covers a number of areas. It requires a discussion on the relationship between the board of directors and the general meeting. In particular, it raises the important issue of who controls corporate litigation. Linked to this is the rule in *Foss* v *Harbottle*. Directors' service contracts, together with the possibility of removing the directors, also need to be considered.

Skeleton Solution

Relationship between the board of directors and the general meeting – art 70 Table A – the control of corporate litigation – the rule in *Foss* v *Harbottle* and the fraud on the minority exception – removal of a director under s303 – directors' service contracts ss318 and 319 – s459 unfairly prejudicial conduct.

Suggested Solution

Commencement of litigation by Pat

A company acts through two bodies. One is the company in general meeting, that is the shareholders. The other is the board of directors, who are appointed by the shareholders and to whom the management of the company is entrusted. The relationship between the board and the general meeting is a contractual one and depends upon the articles: *Automatic Self-Cleansing Filter Syndicate Co Ltd* v *Cunninghame* (1906).

Oak Ltd has articles in the form of the current Table A, art 70 of which provides that:

'Subject to the provisions of the Act, the memorandum and the article and to any directions given by special resolution, the business of the company shall be managed by the directors who may exercise all the powers of the company.'

The day-to-day management of the company then rests with the board of directors. Shareholder interference will only be allowed if a sufficient majority of the shareholders (75 per cent) either change the articles or give 'directions' to the directors.

The decision to litigate in the name of the company rests with the board of directors. It is a management decision: *Shaw* v *Shaw* (1935). Exceptionally, litigation has been allowed to commence by an ordinary resolution of the members but such cases represent a minority view and were decided on the basis of the older version of art 70, contained in the 1948 Table A: *Marshall's Valve Gear Co Ltd* v *Manning, Wardle & Co Ltd* (1909). There is probably no point in pressing for this minority view any longer following its rejection by Harman J in *Breckland Group Holdings Ltd* v *London & Suffolk Properties Ltd* (1989). Here, an injunction was granted to prevent a 51 per cent shareholder from continuing litigation which he had commenced in the name of the company.

Following the case of *Danish Mercantile Co Ltd* v *Beaumont* (1951), the court appears to have developed a practice whereby whenever there is a dispute as to authority to litigate, the case is adjourned so that the matter can be referred back to the general meeting. This practice now seems outdated where, as in this case, art 70 makes it clear that interference by the general meeting can only be by a special resolution.

The court is likely, therefore, to discontinue the proceedings in the name of the company against Oak Ltd, because according to art 70 this is a matter for the board of directors. As Pat is only a 51 per cent shareholder, he does not have enough votes to influence the directors' refusal to commence litigation.

Linked with the issue about who controls corporate litigation is the rule in *Foss* v *Harbottle* (1843). This rule states that the proper plaintiff, where directors in are in breach of duty, is the company itself. The company, acting through the board of directors, must bring the action.

It could be argued that by deciding to refuse to litigate the directors are exercising their powers for an improper purpose in breach of their fiduciary duty. A mala fide abuse amounts to a fraud on the minority: *Cook* v *Deeks* (1916). As such, it is an exception to the rule in *Foss* v *Harbottle* and Pat will have locus standi to sue in the name of the company. The difficulty here is that it will be very difficult for Pat to establish fraud. He has no real proof as to why the directors are refusing to sue Shanti Ltd for breach of contract, only a suspicion, which is not enough. It is very doubtful that Pat will be able to continue the litigation in the company's name.

An alternative course of action is for Pat to threaten the board of directors with removal under the procedure laid down in s303 Companies Act (CA) 1985. This only requires an ordinary resolution which Pat would be able to secure. This may put pressure on the directors to act. If they do not, then they may be removed and new directors appointed.

One drawback to removing the directors, however, is that they are receiving large salaries under very long-term service contracts. Removal under s303 will probably result in Oak Ltd having to pay a large amount in damages for breach of contract.

Pat should also enquire about the length of the directors' service contracts. As a member, he can inspect these under s318 CA 1985. Where such contracts cannot be terminated by the company by notice, or they can only be terminated in specified circumstances, then they must not be for more than five years, unless agreed to by the general meeting: s319 CA 1985. A breach of this section allows the company to terminate the contract on giving reasonable notice. The contract is also void to the extent that it exceeds five years.

Commencement of litigation by Quinn

What has been said about the control of corporate litigation in relation to Pat applies equally to Quinn. It is normally for the board of directors to commence litigation in the name of the company.

Tim is in breach of his fiduciary duties to Oak Ltd, as he has diverted customers away from Oak Ltd to a business which he has set up 'on the side'.

Quinn may be able to establish locus standi if he can establish one of the exceptions to the rule in *Foss* v *Harbottle*. The most likely one is the fraud on the minority exception. Here, Quinn will have to show that there has been a fraud on the minority, and that the only reason why the company itself will not bring an action is because the wrongdoers are in numerical or de facto control of the company: *Prudential Assurance Co Ltd* v *Newman Industries (No 2)* (1982). In such circumstances he can bring a derivative action in the name of the company: *Cook* v *Deeks*. In a derivative action, Quinn will not get the benefit of any judgment, which will go to the company, for in reality it is the company that is being defrauded.

A 50 per cent shareholder has been held to be a minority shareholder for the purposes of the exceptions to the rule in *Foss* v *Harbottle*: *Barrett* v *Duckett and Others* (1993), and so Quinn, who holds 49 per cent of the shares, is a minority shareholder.

Even if Quinn can establish fraud and wrongdoer control, the court may seek the views of the majority of shareholders independent of Tim, the wrongdoer. In *Smith* v *Croft (No 2)* (1988), for example, a minority shareholder was denied locus standi, where a majority of the shareholders who were independent of the wrongdoers did not wish proceedings to continue. This was because the defendants were the main assets of the company and to sue them might result in their leaving the company, thereby reducing the value of the shares.

This is very similar to the case of Oak Ltd. Pat, the majority shareholder, and the other directors do not want to do anything about Tim's activities, as Tim is one of the biggest names in the film industry. Despite the criticism which *Smith* v *Croft* has attracted, it remains to be seen whether it will be followed.

The problems of bringing a derivative action should not be underestimated. Quinn will have to consider the time, inconvenience and the disruption in management it will cause. Cost is also an enormous obstacle to an action, as legal aid is not available. A costs order under *Wallersteiner* v *Moir (No 2)* (1975) may, however, be available whereby the company has to pay the plaintiff's costs. The court must, however, be satisfied that it would have been reasonable for an independent board of directors to bring the action. In *Smith* v *Croft* (1986) Walton J held that this condition was not satisfied where the company's largest independent shareholder was opposed to the action and where the company was dependent on the services of the defendants, which outweighed suing them.

It is by no means certain that the court will refuse to strike out the action commenced by Quinn. An alternative course of action might be for Quinn to consider a petition under s459 CA 1985 on the grounds that the affairs of the company are being conducted in a manner which is unfairly prejudicial to the interests of the shareholders.

This is a much more flexible remedy, for which legal aid is available. Unfairly prejudicial conduct has been held to cover diverting business away from the company in circumstances similar to those of Oak Ltd: *Re Cumana Ltd* (1986) and *Re London School of Electronics Ltd* (1985).

Where unfairly prejudicial conduct is proved, the court may make a number of orders set out in s461. These include an order that the petitioner's shares be purchased by other members or the company itself. The court may also authorise civil proceedings to be brought in the name of the company and on behalf of the company. This latter order conveniently side-steps the rule in *Foss* v *Harbottle* (1843).

The alternative remedy in s459 would appear to be a much more attractive proposition for Quinn.

QUESTION TWO

Jumbo Limited ('the company') was formed to run the business formerly carried on in partnership by Arthur, Basil, and Charles, each of whom was appointed as a director of the company. Each owns 100 of the 300 issued shares. The articles of association of the company contain, among other provisions, the following regulations:

'28A Where any shareholder wishes to transfer his shares, he shall offer them for sale to the other shareholders who shall purchase them at an agreed or an arbitrated price.

80A A resolution for the dismissal of any director of the company will not be passed unless Arthur votes in favour of such resolution.'

After a number of years, a difference of opinion grew up between Arthur, on the one hand, and Basil and Charles on the other. The latter wished to expand the company's business, but Arthur was opposed to their plans.

The assets of the company were recently valued at £3m and Arthur has called on Basil and Charles to purchase his shares for £1m. They have refused and have proposed a resolution for the dismissal of Arthur from the board of directors of the company.

Discuss.

University of London LLB Examination
(for External Students) Company Law June 1991 Q4

General Comment

The question deals with a number of areas, the rules on transfer of shares and pre-emption rights, as well as minority protection under Companies Act 1985, s459 and s122 of the Insolvency Act 1986. The issue of removing Arthur where under the articles he has enhanced voting rights, there is a need to consider *Bushell* v *Faith* (1970), and if this clause can be changed under s9 CA 1985.

Skeleton Solution

Company is a quasi-partnership, therefore members must deal fairly with each other. Arthur may petition under CA 1985 s459 for his shares to be bought at a proper value or he may also petition for a winding up order under s122 Insolvency Act 1986, but this is a drastic measure – courts reluctant to wind up a running and viable business. Basil and Charles may wish to change the clause giving Arthur weighted voting rights but such a change must be bona fide for the benefit of the company.

Suggested Solution

Arthur, Basil and Charles have formed a company from what was previously a partnership. Prima facie the company has the characteristics of a quasi-partnership and in *Ebrahimi* v *Westbourne Galleries Ltd* (1973) Lord Wilberforce explained 'that such partnerships were formed on the basis of a personal relationship between the participants, and that there is an understanding that each of the participants will be concerned in the management of the business.' Where the relationship of trust has broken down, as seems to be the case here, it may be appropriate to make a winding up order under 'just and equitable' grounds by virtue of s122 Insolvency Act 1986. Success for Arthur is not guaranteed for the courts are reluctant to order the drastic remedy of winding up a solvent and viable company.

A less drastic and perhaps more attractive 'alternative' would be for Arthur to seek an order under s459 Companies Act 1985 for the majority to buy out his shareholding. In order to be eligible for this, Arthur would have to show that the affairs of the company were being conducted in a manner unfairly prejudicial to himself as he is part of the membership. Case law on this area seems to indicate that in cases of this kind the court may well be prepared to make a s459 order.

Further, s303 Companies Act allows a company to remove a director from its board by means of an ordinary resolution of the company in a general meeting; however the articles here contain a weighted voting clause in Arthur's favour. Such clauses were approved by the House of Lords in *Bushell* v *Faith* (1970). Although such clauses appear to contravene the principle that a director is always removable by ordinary resolution, the House of Lords in *Bushell* v *Faith* said that the clause merely affected the way in which the votes were counted on such a resolution, and therefore the likelihood of its being passed did not infringe the rule that such a resolution would be effective if passed. This seems a rather subtle distinction, but nevertheless the decision is still regarded as good law.

An alternative solution which Basil and Charles have considered is to seek to remove the *Bushell* v *Faith* clause and s9 Companies Act 1985 allows a company to alter its articles by special resolution. Basil and Charles could command the necessary majority. Arthur, as shareholder will presumably challenge the alteration as not being made bona fide in the best interests for the company. As in *Greenhalgh* v *Arderne Cinemas Ltd* (1946), the question to ask is whether the change benefits the aggrieved member. These authorities go to show that at least in a small company, the majority have to show due regard to the interests of the minority. Although on the face of it this seems a convincing solution, the difficulty here is that the company was set up on the basis that the directors would be protected from removal and the position is a finely balanced one Basil and Charles are by no means certain to succeed in their action.

The last possibility is an issue of further shares so as to reduce Arthur's holding to a level where the *Bushell* v *Faith* clause would no longer protect him. However, ss89–96 Companies Act 1985 including pre-emption rights to existing shareholders have to be considered. Arthur will be able to exercise these rights to defeat any scheme to dilute his shareholding. Basil and Charles may try allotting non-cash consideration, or may choose to ignore the pre-emption rights. However s92 Companies Act 1985 will give Arthur the right to compensation for any loss, damage or expenses resulting from such a breach and a further challenge can be made that such an allocation was for an improper purpose: *Hogg* v *Cramphorn* (1967). In such cases the court is likely to refer the matter to a general meeting to decide whether the shares have been properly allotted.

Basil and Charles, therefore, should consider buying Arthur's shares and can refer the purchase price to arbitration in order to fix a fair price, as it seems probable that Arthur will succeed in blocking their attempts to have him removed.

QUESTION THREE

'Despite many attempts by the legislature, no effective statutory remedy to safeguard the interests of minority shareholders has [been] or will be developed.' Discuss.

University of London LLB Examination
(for External Students) Company Law June 1985 Q1

General Comment

Some care is needed in dealing with this question. First, it asks about statutory remedies; thus, the *Foss* v *Harbottle* (1843) line of cases, which relate to a form of protection offered at common law, are not relevant (for an essay on this area see below). Secondly, the question refers to successive attempts by the legislature, and students therefore need to deal with the various provisions which have been enacted over the years, in addition to the present law.

Skeleton Solution

Main provisions are CA 1985 s459 and IA 1986 s122.

Section 459 gives court wide discretion, especially to order buy-out of shares – s459 more liberal than old s210 – now provides most effective and commonly-used remedy.

Section 122 is more drastic – various established situations for using it – especially quasi-partnership.

Question depends on how much protection is thought fair for minority shareholder – note general principle of majority rule.

Suggested Solution

Traditionally, relief has been afforded to the minority shareholder through two main routes. The first is the petition under Companies Act (CA) 1985 s459 (formerly CA 1980, replacing CA 1948 s210); the second is the winding-up petition under Insolvency Act (IA) 1986 s122 (formerly CA 1948 s222, then CA 1985 s517).

Section 459 by its terms allows the court to make a wide variety of orders in favour of the minority shareholder, including in particular the buying out of the shares of the dissentient minority. The practical effectiveness of this remedy depends, however, on the attitude of the courts. This has to be understood in the light of the history of s459. It was enacted in 1980 to replace the former s210, which had proved very unsatisfactory because of the need for a course of conduct rather than isolated acts of oppression ('oppression' was defined by Lord Simonds in *Scottish Co-operative Wholesale Society (SCWS)* v *Meyer* (1959) as 'harsh, burdensome and/or wrongful conduct', which placed a heavy burden of proof on petitioners) and because it was necessary to show that the facts would have justified a winding-up petition on the just and equitable ground. In view of this it is not surprising that there were only two successful petitions under s210: *SCWS* v *Meyer* and *Re HR Harmer Ltd*. The wording of s459 is more liberal, and the courts have interpreted it in a less restrictive way; thus, there is no requirement that the conduct be such as would justify a winding-up order: *Re London School of Electronics Ltd* (1986). A single act or omission can justify a petition, and s459 refers to 'unfair prejudice' rather than 'oppression', which appears to be a less onerous test (*Re a Company* (1983)) though it is difficult to say how much less onerous. Many of the s459 cases have concerned the valuation of shares for buy-out purposes (eg *Re OC Transport Services Ltd* (1984)). Relief under s459 is discretionary, and the court will expect the petitioner to come to court with clean hands: *Re Bird Precision Bellows Ltd* (1986), *Nurcombe v Nurcombe* (1984).

However, one restriction imposed by the old s210 is unchanged. It appears that the petitioner must still be affected in his position as member; thus, the removal of a director from office will not of itself entitle that director to bring a s210 petition, even if he is a member. This rule has been criticised, but it is submitted that it is perfectly justified; s210 is aimed at shareholder rights, and it would be invidious if a sacked director who is a shareholder were in a better position than one who is not a member.

Under IA s122 the court may order a winding-up of the company on the ground that it is 'just and equitable' to do so. Again, this gives the court a very wide discretion, but it is to be noted that there is only one remedy available under this provision, and that it is a drastic one. There are a few established categories of case where this relief is available: loss of confidence between the participants – *Loch* v *Blackwood Ltd* (1924); deadlock – *Re Bondi Better Bananas Ltd* (1952); failure of the substratum – *Re German Date Coffee Co Ltd* (1882). However, the leading case in this area, *Ebrahimi* v *Westbourne Galleries Ltd* (1973), shows that the discretion goes much wider than this. Where there is a special underlying obligation between the members that so long as the business continues each will be entitled to management participation, then it will be proper to subject the exercise of legal rights (such as removal of a director under CA 1985 s303) to equitable considerations, and a breach of the equitable obligations thereby arising may be sufficient grounds for a winding-up under s122. The kind of company where this principle will be invoked is likely to share certain of the characteristics of Westbourne Galleries Ltd eg that there is a personal relationship between the parties, that there is an understanding with regard to management and that there is a restriction on the transfer of shares. In these circumstances s122 is a potent weapon in the hands of a minority shareholder, though it is fair to say that the courts are reluctant to order the winding-up of a viable company and may prefer to make a buy-out order under s459.

In extreme cases it may be possible to bring a misfeasance action against a director or even to obtain a DTI investigation under CA 1985 s431 et seq, but these remedies are in practice confined to large public companies.

The question asks whether these remedies are effective to protect the minority shareholder. It must be understood that there can never be an automatic remedy for a disgruntled shareholder (it cannot simply be assumed that he is in the right). Company law operates on the principle of majority rule, and the only workable solution is to allow that majority rule to prevail in the great majority of cases. The present scheme, whereby the court is given a wide discretion and is then left to arbitrate on the merits of particular cases, is probably the best which can be devised, though it is arguable that s459 is still a little too restrictive.

QUESTION FOUR

'A major achievement of company law reform over the past decade has been the replacement of the old section 210 [of the Companies Act 1948] with, first section 75 [of the Companies Act 1980], and now section 459 [of the Companies Act 1985]. This has transformed a provision from which the judges systematically removed all the teeth into one which now bites deep into the administration of small private companies. We can now truly say that we have proper protection for minority shareholders – an indispensable ingredient to fairness in the principles of company law.'

Discuss.

University of London LLB Examination
(for External Students) Company Law June 1992 Q1

General Comment

The topic of minority shareholder protection in company law is always a popular question. It can be easily dressed up as a problem question, either self-contained or as part of a larger problem question, and also lends itself to analysis in an essay. This essay question is relatively easy to pass since it is only really asking for consideration of s459 in any detail and is thus confined in scope. In order to do well though the topic should have been fully considered and read around.

Skeleton Solution

Old provision of s210 Companies Act CA 1948 – need for reform – s75 CA 1980 and s459 CA 1985 – major differences – description of s459 in operation with case-law illustrations – assessment of its efficacy.

Suggested Solution

Prior to the enactment of s210 Companies Act 1948 (on the recommendation of the Cohen Committee) the only remedy available to a minority shareholder who felt his interests were being threatened by the actions of the majority shareholders in the way they were running the company was the somewhat drastic remedy of petitioning for a winding up on the grounds that it was 'just and equitable'. This solution is still, of course, available and found in s122(1)(g) Insolvency Act 1986, but is far from satisfactory since it means an otherwise viable business is dissolved perhaps in conditions in which it will not be possible to realise the best price for the company's assets and the minority shareholder may not fully realise the true extent of his interest, apart from it being a very 'all or nothing' type of solution. Section 210 was designed to empower the court to provide discretionary relief to a minority shareholder in a situation where the affairs of a company were being conducted in such a manner as to be oppressive to a minority shareholder. The facts had to be such, however, that they could also justify a winding up petition being granted, had one been sought, on the just and equitable ground. In spite of an auspicious start with the two successful petitions under s210 in *Scottish Co-operative Wholesale Society* v *Meyer* (1959) and *Re HR Harmer Ltd* (1959) the section quickly lost its effect through narrow judicial interpretation of 'oppression' and various procedural hurdles placed in its way. In order to constitute oppressive conduct the actions of the majority had to be extremely harsh, at the very least improper. There also had to be a continuing pattern of oppressive conduct so that one or two isolated incidents, no matter how unfair and harsh an effect they might have on the minority shareholder, would not be enough for a s210 petition to succeed.

Further reform was necessary and was called for by the Jenkins Committee on Company Law in 1962, but it was not until the Companies Act 1980 and s75 (now consolidated in s459 CA 1985) that s210 was overhauled. The most important change is the replacement of the requirement that the conduct of the company's affairs be oppressive with the less onerous and easier to establish requirement that 'the company's affairs are being or have been conducted in a manner which is unfairly prejudicial to the interests of some part of the members (including the [petitioner])': s459(1). Unfairly prejudicial is a more neutral and less pejorative term than oppressive, and indeed has been interpreted as such by the courts. Although the courts have been careful to leave the meaning of the term open, the most commonly quoted guidelines derive from Slade J, in *Re Bovey Hotel Ventores* (1981, unreported):

'Without prejudice to the generality of the wording of the section, which may cover many other situations, a member of a company will be able to bring himself within the section if he can show that the value of his shareholding has been seriously diminished or at least seriously jeopardised by reason of a course of conduct on the part of those persons who have had de facto control of the company, which has been unfair to the member concerned.'

The test of unfairness is an objective one and has been used to encompass situations which are inequitable not just illegal. Other examples of unfairly prejudicial conduct include the diverting of part of a company's business away from the company and to another company owned by the majority shareholder: *Re London School of Electronics Ltd* (1986).

Other improvements that s459 has wrought are; it is no longer necessary to establish such a severe business relationship breakdown that a winding up petition would also lie; there is no need to establish a course of conduct as being unfairly prejudicial since subs(1) clearly envisages a single act or omission as being capable of constituting unfair prejudice; the remedy can survive the death of a member and devolve on to his PRs (subs(2)); the Companies Act 1989 further increased the utility of s459 in that relief will now be available if it is in the interests of the members generally affected. So, just because all members suffer equally this does not prevent the section from applying.

Finally, s461 gives the court the broadest possible discretion to grant relief as the court may 'make such order as it thinks fit for giving relief in respect of the matters complained of' (s461(1)) and goes on to give a non–exhaustive list of examples of some of the extremely useful orders it may make including an order providing for the purchase of the shares of any member by the company or by other members (one of the most commonly sought in practice) and an order authorising civil proceedings to be brought in the name of the company (an improvement on s210).

Although the workings of s459 are not without their own set of difficulties, in particular finding a fair valuation mechanism on share purchase orders (see *Virdi* v *Abbey Leisure Ltd* (1990)), it has proved a vast improvement on its predecessor and is a popular and effective alternative to a s122(1)(g) Insolvency Act 1986 application or struggling with the difficulties of coming within the 'fraud on a minority' exception to the rule in *Foss* v *Harbottle*.

QUESTION FIVE

Alan, Barbara and Donald are the only three shareholders in Commodore Limited, each of whom owns one third of the issued share capital and each of whom is a director of the company. The business of the company is the manufacture and distribution of bottles and other containers. The articles of association are in the form of Table A. Alan and Barbara are anxious to introduce some new blood into the company, but Donald objects. Despite Donald's objection, Alan and Barbara force through a resolution at a directors' meeting enabling them to issue shares to their adult children. Donald is convinced that this will lead to his increasing isolation in the company. He has also just learned that a contract to supply bottles to a large jam factory for a period of three years has been diverted to another company of which Alan and Barbara are major shareholders.

Advise Donald.

University of London LLB Examination
(for External Students) Company Law June 1990 Q8

General Comment

This is a straightforward and relatively simple question. Little detail is provided which indicates that a relatively far-reaching discussion and advice to Donald is required. Do not be afraid to put alternatives forward depending on the answers to questions you need to ask to advise Donald properly. Knowing what questions to ask is often as important a skill as knowing advise Donald properly. Knowing what questions to ask is often as important a skill as knowing the answers.

Skeleton Solution

Pre-emption rights – exceptions – oppression of minority.

Directors' duties – *Foss* v *Harbottle* – exceptions.

Suggested Solution

Donald should be advised that his concerns fall under two broad heads: firstly the 'watering down' of his shareholding, presently one-third of the issued share capital, and secondly the diverting of the bottle supply contract. Allied to the second of these is the question of who is the proper plaintiff in an action where a wrong has been done to the company. Section 89 of the Companies Act 1985 grants all shareholders, subject to certain exceptions, the right to purchase additional shares where there is a new issue of equity securities issued for cash. These are the so-called 'pre-emption' provisions.

These pre-emption rights of Donald's may be excluded by the memorandum of articles of a private company: s91 CA 1985. However there is no evidence to suggest such an exclusion has been operated in this case. Should Donald's rights be breached then the company and guilty officers, in this case Alan and Barbara, are jointly and severally liable to compensate Donald: s92 CA 1985. Donald must be notified in writing of such pre-emption rights.

Further, any 'watering-down' of Donald's rights that constitutes oppression of Donald by the majority shareholders will be struck down by the court: *Clemens* v *Clemens* (1976). In this case, because Alan and Barbara are proposing to issue shares to their adult children (whether this means the adult children of *each* of Alan and Barbara, or the adult children of Alan and Barbara as parents together) the court would certainly have sufficient grounds to find that Donald was being so oppressed.

Majority shareholders do not have unrestricted rights to pass resolutions which are unfair to minority shareholders: *Estmanco (Kilner House) Ltd* v *Greater London Council* (1982). This weapon to fight oppression could be very useful to Donald, in case Alan and Barbara take advantage of the exceptions to the pre-emption requirements by, for example, having the shares paid for partly or wholly other than in cash, or by utilising the complex provisions of s95 CA 1985. This latter section permits a public or private company that has authorised its directors to issue shares to authorise to disapply the pre-emption provisions of s89 CA 1985.

The second issue is whether Alan and Barbara have breached their fiduciary duty as directors in diverting the long and probably lucrative contract to supply jam jar bottles to a different company which they control. Alan and Barbara have almost certainly breached this duty: *Regal (Hastings) Ltd* v *Gulliver* (1942). However, there is little Donald himself can do at this stage because, prima facie, the proper plaintiff to take proceedings in this, a wrong done to Commodore Limited, is Commodore Limited itself: *Foss* v *Harbottle* (1843).

However, there are exceptions to the so-called 'rule in *Foss* v *Harbottle*' that mitigate its draconian effect. These exceptions are best laid out in *Edwards* v *Halliwell* (1950) and fall into four categories.

Firstly, in cases where the act complained of is wholly ultra vires the company, then the rule has no application because there is no question of the transaction being confirmed by the majority. Secondly, where what has been done amounts to a fraud on the minority, and the wrongdoers are in control, then the rule is relaxed and that minority may bring an action.

Thirdly a minority shareholder can sue if a special resolution was only passed, say, by a simple majority, and finally there is an exception where the company has invaded the rights of an individual who can then sue as an individual member.

The diversion of the lucrative bottling contract smacks of fraud and so Donald will probably not be prevented by the rule in *Foss* v *Harbottle* from taking action against Alan and Barbara.

QUESTION SIX

Asa owns 99 of the 100 shares of Cafe Blue Ltd ('the company') which owns the restaurant business that Asa established 20 years ago. Last year Asa agreed to the takeover of the company by the sale of 75 shares to Eat-u-like plc. As part of the takeover deal it was agreed that Asa would be the sole director and managing director of the company for five years at an annual salary of £100,000. The articles of association of the company were also amended so as to include the following regulation:

'72A Asa shall be the managing director of the company for 5 years at an annual salary of £100,000 adjusted for inflation in accordance with the retail price index. No resolution of the company shall be taken as passed unless the votes of Asa are cast in favour.'

Asa was duly elected and assumed office as managing director. Management tensions between Asa and Eat-u-like plc soon erupted. Asa wanted the company to maintain the existing market whereas Eat-u-like plc wanted the company to increase business substantially by entering the lucrative lunch market. Asa suspects that Eat-u-like plc are trying to kill-off the company because they have refused additional capital to further develop the company until Asa considers their proposals. Eat-u-like plc are on record as saying that Asa is refusing to co-operate in the company's audit procedures and refusing to consider the views of Eat-u-like plc.

Eat-u-like plc has now requisitioned an EGM and cast its votes at that meeting to pass two resolutions: the first, to delete article 72A by special resolution and the second, to remove Asa as a director of the company by ordinary resolution.

Advise Asa.

University of London LLB Examination
(for External Students) Company Law June 1995 Q4

General Comment

This problem involves the question of validity of article 72A and of the two resolutions at the EGM in the light of a struggle for control of the company. It is necessary to look at the foundation of the capital structure and to see whether there are opportunities to seek the aid of the court to impose inequitable principles in assisting Asa.

Skeleton Solution

Validity of article 72A – common law limitations on powers to alter articles – validity of the two resolutions – effect upon Asa's contractual position – Ebrahimi principle – s122(1)(g) – s459 – conclusion.

Suggested Solution

The essence of the question is the validity of the alteration of the articles by article 72A and the validity of the two resolutions.

a) *The validity of article 72A*

The effect of this article is to prevent the passing of any resolution unless Asa votes for it, effectively giving Asa absolute control of the company as he is also sole and managing director. There is nothing to stop anyone buying shares without obtaining influence over the company (as with non-voting shares) but it is a very curious takeover arrangement where no control at all is obtained. Asa has attempted here to create a controlling class of shares for himself and he will need to consider, initially, whether he used the appropriate mode of alteration by special resolution: s9(1) Companies Act (CA) 1985 and *Bushell* v *Faith* (1970). He must then consider whether the alteration has created any conflict with any provision in the memorandum because, if so, to the extent of the conflict, the alteration will be void, *Ashbury* v *Watson* (1885). This sounds a distinct possibility here, considering the range of matters which might be covered in the memorandum. If Asa surmounts these obstacles he must then consider the common law limitations upon the power to alter articles that the courts have developed to prevent perceived abuses of company control. Probably the most important is that seen in *Allen* v *Gold Reefs of West Africa Ltd* (1900), that the power must be exercised bona fide for the benefit of the company as a whole. Much depends upon what 'the company as a whole' means. Obviously, when Asa was the only or possibly the major shareholder he would have met the description set out in *Greenhalgh* v *Arderne Cinemas Ltd* (1951), of 'the corporators as a general body' but the article could not be said to benefit the whole company if Eat-u-like plc is included. The view of the courts since Greenhalgh seems to be that the company's future prospects and, indeed, future members have to be considered, and the test is very much an objective one.

There is little doubt that an alteration which greatly increases or decreases the power of the majority shareholders can, in an appropriate case, be for the benefit of the company as a whole, as in *Rights and Issues Investment Trust Ltd* v *Stylo Shoes Ltd* (1965), but one which so completely excludes participation in control in the way that article 72A does would be likely to fail this test and the court, consequently, would strike it down.

b) *The validity of the two resolutions*

Clearly, if article 72A has validity, neither of the two resolutions would be valid. Assuming the article to be invalid, Asa will be greatly damaged in two respects here. He loses his ability to prevent any type of resolution of the general meeting and he loses his directorship. His voting control, if based upon an invalid article, was without foundation and he has, in truth, lost nothing. He still has his 24 shares and the attached voting rights. To this extent, the special resolution is unexceptionable and to the extent that deletion will remove the article providing the power to appoint Asa, similarly, little will be lost as he is already appointed and, presumably, has a contract on the basis of the article. The lack of capacity to employ him, if article 72A is invalid, will not affect the validity of the contract: s35(1) CA 1985. The problem is that there is the ordinary resolution to remove Asa and, provided that special notice had been given of this resolution (s303(2) CA 1985), this seems to have been properly done within s303. Asa will, of course, have an action for breach of contract if there is breach but it does seem that he is in an awkward position.

All may not be lost for Asa because there was, undoubtedly, some mutual contemplation

All may not be lost for Asa because there was, undoubtedly, some mutual contemplation that he would have substantial involvement in the day-to-day management of the company and he might be said to have a legitimate expectation of this continuing throughout at least the five years. Cases such as *Ebrahimi* v *Westbourne Galleries Ltd* (1973) and provisions such as s459 CA 1985 and s122(1)(g) Insolvency Act (IA) 1986 clearly illustrate that the law will, in appropriate cases, apply equitable principles to the exercise of legal rights where unconscionable or unfairly prejudicial behaviour would otherwise succeed. Even if there is some degree of inequitable conduct by the petitioner or plaintiff, this will not always bar relief as in *Re London School of Electronics* (1986) but there must be clear evidence: that both parties contemplated participation in control by the excluded party (*Re Tottenham Hotspur plc* (1994)); and that the agreement originated in some relationship of trust and confidence; and that some restriction exists upon a proper realisation of the party's interest in the event of a split (*Ebrahimi*).

It does seem that the real battle here is about the direction that the company's future development should take and the court may view this as more a test of who controls than one of minority oppression. Whatever view the court takes, the reality is of a quasi-partnership that has gone badly wrong, with little prospect of a reconciliation of views. There are various possibilities. On the basis that the company had proceeded from the equivalent of a partnership, it may be possible to achieve a winding up on the 'just and equitable' ground in s122(1)((g) IA 1986. In *Re Yenidje Tobacco Co Ltd* (1916) the deteriorating relationship between the two principal director/shareholders in a very profitable company made continuation impossible so the court ordered winding up. It might prove more difficult to persuade the court that the assertion of a controlling interest so as to pursue legitimate business policies is a matter within s122(1)(g) IA 1986 or that it is a matter within s459 CA 1985. Several cases under s459 involve removal and exclusion from control and office as in *Re Bird Precision Bellows* (1986) and *Re London School of Electronics*, but there has to be something more than an honest difference of opinion on policy to constitute unfair prejudice. An irreconcilable breakdown between a minor shareholder/director and the majority director which led to exclusion from office did not constitute unfair prejudice in *Re a Company (No 004377 of 1986)* (1987). The courts are not eager to consider competing views on company policies in these petitions or, indeed, in applications to set aside resolutions aimed at altering articles to further the interests of the majority shareholders: *Re Blue Arrow plc* (1987). Possibly, the best that Asa could hope for here is for the court to exercise its discretion under s461(2)(d) CA 1985, to order the purchase of his interest without discount for his minority position, as in *Re Bird Precision Bellows*. It is hard to see what else the court could do that would not create more problems than it solves.

13 Company Investigations

13.1 Introduction

13.2 Key points

13.3 Recent cases and reports

13.4 Analysis of questions

13.5 Questions

13.1 Introduction

To some extent this topic can be seen as overlapping with that of minority protection, since seeking an investigation into the company's affairs is one of the ways in which a disaffected minority can protect itself. Investigations are, however, a relatively minor part of that topic, since minorities now have more effective means of protection available to them. Further, investigations arise in circumstances other than that of a disaffected minority, and are worthy of independent treatment.

13.2 Key points

The Companies Act 1985 (as amended by the Companies Act 1989) gives the Secretary of State a number of powers (note that these are not duties) to investigate the affairs of companies and ownership of their shares. The principal provisions to note are:

a) Section 431 CA 1985 gives power to appoint an inspector on the application of members of the company or the company itself. In the case of a company with a share capital, the minimum number of members is 200 holding not less than one-tenth of the issued shares. The application must be supported by sufficient evidence and the applicants may have to give security for costs.

b) Section 432(2) CA 1985 gives power to appoint an inspector if there are circumstances suggesting one or more of the following grounds:

   i) conduct with intent to defraud creditors or unfairly prejudicial to some part of the membership;

   ii) an act or proposed act or omission of the company which would be so prejudicial, or the company has been formed for a fraudulent or unlawful purpose;

   iii) persons concerned with the formation or management of the company have been guilty in connection with it of fraud, misfeasance or other misconduct towards the company or its members;

   iv) the members have not been given all the information with respect to the company's affairs that they might reasonably expect.

c) Section 447(1)–(3) CA 1985 give the Secretary of State power at any time if he thinks there is good reason to require the company to produce documents at a specific time or place, or to produce them to his duly appointed officer (who will usually attend at the company's offices without prior notice). This is the most used power, for obvious reasons, and there are criminal sanctions for non-compliance. A person charged with such an offence may have a defence if the documents are not in his possession or it is not reasonably practicable to produce them.

d) Section 448 CA 1985 provides that a warrant may be obtained from a Justice of the Peace (JP) for the police to search the company's premises for documents. Usually a s447 demand must already have been made, but the CA 1989 amended the provision by adding subs(2), so that a warrant may nevertheless be issued if the JP is satisfied that:

i) there are reasonable grounds for thinking an indictable offence has been committed and there are documents on the premises relating to it;

ii) the applicant has the power to require production; and

iii) there are reasonable grounds for believing that if production were required, the demand would not be complied with and the documents would be removed, hidden, tampered with or destroyed.

e) Sections 442–446 CA 1985 contain powers relating to the appointment of inspectors to investigate the ownership of shares in a company. Section 446 CA 1985 sanctions investigations into suspected improper dealings by a director or a person connected with a director of the company.

13.3   Recent cases and reports

Fayed v *United Kingdom (Case No 28/1993/423/502)* (1994) The Times 11 November (European Court of Human Rights) – inspectors' reports did not violate Article 6(1) of the European Convention on Human Rights.

Companies in 1994–95 – a report by the DTI revealing a record number of company investigations mainly for fraudulent trading and theft. 529 directors were disqualified in this period.

13.4 Analysis of questions

This is in some ways a rather obscure topic, and one which relatively few students are likely to prepare. Nevertheless it has occurred twice on the London LLB External paper since 1983, and is worthy of some attention.

The topic has always arisen in essay form, and it is likely that it will continue to do so; in view of the other forms of protection available it would be a very contrived problem question in which the bulk of the answer was concerned with company investigations.

13.5 Questions

The two questions which have been set on this topic are printed below. It can be seen that both run along very much the same lines, asking about two matters, the adequacy of the powers in a legal sense and the strength of the political will to use those powers. The suggested essay which appears below the questions would do equally well for either question and, it is thought, for any other essay question on this topic which is likely to appear. It may be observed in passing that students who are not well versed in the relevant legislation would be well advised to steer clear of this topic if at all possible – this is not an area in which intelligent students can bluff their way through.

QUESTIONS

'Although the investigative powers of the Department of Trade have been substantially extended by recent legislation, that Department still lacks both the powers and the will to act as a watchdog for minority shareholders.' Discuss.

University of London LLB Examination
(for External Students) Company Law June 1984 Q3

'Statute has now provided sufficient machinery for any type of corporate investigation which may be necessary. What is lacking is the will to use that machinery.' Discuss.

University of London LLB Examination
(for External Students) Company Law June 1987 Q1(a)

Skeleton Solution

Powers contained in CA 1985 Part XIV.

Appointments of inspectors to investigate and report – Secretary of State may act on their report.

Investigations into company ownership and dealings in shares – petitions to wind up company.

Powers are extensive – major problem seems to be reluctance to use them in practice.

Suggested Solution

One of the duties of the Secretary of State is to ensure that companies conduct their affairs in an appropriate manner and that the interests of creditors are properly protected. Part XIV of the Companies Act 1985 gives the Secretary of State considerable investigative and regulatory powers to assist him in carrying out this duty. Amendments to Part XIV by Companies Act 1989 have strengthened the Secretary of State's powers.

Under s431 of the Act the Secretary of State can appoint one or more inspectors to investigate the affairs of a company. This may be done on the application of certain interested parties or on the application of the company itself. The Secretary of State must be satisfied that there are good reasons for making the application, though the statute does not define what these reasons may include.

Under s432 the Secretary of State may appoint inspectors without the need for any application if he suspects that the company's affairs are being conducted in a manner prejudicial to the interests of creditors or if he suspects fraud. He is not subject to the rules of natural justice in deciding whether to appoint inspectors under this provision: *Norwest Holst Ltd* v *Department of Trade* (1978). Section 432 also allows the court to require the Secretary of State to appoint inspectors.

Once appointed, inspectors are given certain powers by the Act. They may require the production of documents and may take statements under oath from officers and others concerned with the running of the company. They may make interim reports to the Secretary of State and must make a final report. It is a contempt of court to obstruct the inspectors in their enquiries. There is no privilege against self incrimination when required by inspectors to answer relevant questions. See, for example, *Bishopsgate Investment Management Ltd* v *Maxwell* (1992). Once the report is made the Secretary of State may take civil proceedings on behalf of the company if he judges it expedient to do so – s438.

In addition to the above the Secretary of State has the power to order investigations into company ownership (s442) and into dealings in the shares of a company (s449). These powers are supplemented by powers to enter and search premises (s448) and require production of documents (s447). It is a criminal offence to destroy relevant documents in such cases (s450).

In practice the inspector has to work on his own initiative, and the success of the investigation will depend heavily on the energy and perseverance which he brings to his task – see, for example, *Re Pergamon Press* (1971) and *Maxwell* v *Department of Trade* (1974).

Finally, the Secretary of State may petition for the winding-up of the company under Insolvency Act s122 on the just and equitable ground and can apply for a disqualification order against a director or shadow director of a company under s8 and Sch 1, Company Directors Disqualification Act 1986.

The above clearly indicates that a wide range of powers is available, and recent years have seen an increased willingness to exercise those powers, especially in cases such as the Guinness scandal, which attract considerable public interest. The major difficulty seems to be that there is a reluctance to take legal proceedings against those involved in running the company, even when the inspector's report points clearly to serious wrongdoing. It is at this latter point that the regulatory system seems to break down; no change in the law can remedy this, since it is a political issue rather than a legal one.

14 External Influences: the EC and Corporate Governance

14.1 Introduction

14.2 Key points

14.3 Recent cases and materials

14.4 Analysis of questions

14.5 Questions

14.1 Introduction

Not all influences on Company Law come from statute and case law. In recent years, thinking about the structure and management of companies has been affected by outside influences, notably the European Community's harmonisation programme and the increasing pressure for good corporate governance. Both of these topical issues have appeared in recent London papers, and it is convenient to deal with them together here.

14.2 Key points

a) *Company Law Directives*

A number of Directives have been issued by the EC in connection with its programme of harmonising the company laws in the member states of the European Community in order to achieve the aims of the Treaty of Rome. A Directive is not incorporated directly into the law of the Member State but requires the Member State to change its law to conform with the provisions of the Directive. Since Britain's accession to the EC there have been some 12 Company Law Directives, although some are still in the draft stage, and not all of those issued have yet been complied with. When considering the provisions of an EC Directive, it is worth remembering that most of the Member States do not have a common law jurisdiction, and many favour a different way of dealing with certain corporate problems than has been favoured in England and Wales.

Of the Directives, the most important have been:

i) *The First* – which became the notorious s9 European Communities Act 1972 (see chapter 2: *The Memorandum of Association and Legal Capacity*), and was finally translated into ss35 and 35A Companies Act 1985.

ii) *The Second and Fourth* – which led to the more detailed regulation of public companies and directors originally contained in the Companies Acts 1980 and 1981.

iii) *The Twelfth* – on single member private companies, which was implemented by Statutory Instrument.

iv) *The Directive on Insider Dealing* – implemented by Part V Criminal Justice Act 1993 (see chapter 15: *Insider Dealing*).

Still proceeding are the Thirteenth Directive on Takeovers, the Draft Fifth Directive (two-tier boards) and the Draft Ninth Directive (groups). Of these, the Fifth is perhaps the most fertile ground for questions. The vexed question in relation to the Fifth, which is highly controversial at least so far as Britain is concerned, is 'co-determination'. In Germany, where the concept of supervisory boards (which oversee the operation of the managerial board) originated, worker-directors (or employee-directors) play an important role on those boards. In the late 1970s, the idea of worker-directors gained some popularity in Britain with the publication of the Bullock Report (Report of the Committee of Inquiry into Industrial Democracy (Cmnd 6706)) which recommended employee representation in the decision-making process, although not necessarily at board level. There is, however, a great deal of opposition to the idea from British industrialists. Their views are supported by the current Government and have prevailed to the present day, thus the recommendations in the Report have never been implemented.

Although, as the Fifth Directive is presently drafted, it is thought that the English idea of a unitary board with majority non-executive director representation will be sufficient compliance, the Directive undoubtedly requires a significant employee representation in the decision-making process (even if only in a consultative role) and it is to this that the present Government policy is opposed, hence the delay in adopting the Directive.

b) *Corporate governance*

'Corporate governance' is not a legal term of art but a convenient label which has been attached to problems concerning the way in which a company is managed and, in particular, abuse by public company directors of their position.

i) The Cadbury Report

The takeover fever of the 1980s led to 'scandals' involving directors and senior employees of certain public companies being investigated or put on trial in connection with alleged criminal offences. These included Guinness plc, County NatWest (a subsidiary of National Westminster Bank), Queens Moat Houses plc, Brent Walker plc, Polly Peck plc, and the Robert Maxwell group of companies. Not just directors, but well-known City professionals came under public scrutiny and the City, led by the Stock Exchange, was required to bring in self-regulatory measures in an attempt to prevent a recurrence.

The Committee of Inquiry into the Financial Aspects of Corporate Governance was set up under the chairmanship of Sir Adrian Cadbury, and published its Report (known as the Cadbury Report) and Code of Best Practice in 1993. The Report made a large number of recommendations concerning accounting practices and the management of public companies. Most important for company law purposes are the provisions of the Code which recommend significant non-executive director representation on boards for supervisory purposes. It also recommends the establishment of audit and remuneration committees and the separation of the roles of chairman and chief executive.

Compliance with the Code is not mandatory, but companies have to state in their annual report whether or not they comply with it. Most now do. The main problems with this approach, however, are that it is hard, given the relatively small pool of suitable persons and the interlocking nature of board membership in large public companies, to find suitably independent non-executive directors (indeed there may be no incentive to try), and there are signs that some of these directors resent having to occupy a monitoring role within the company.

ii) The Greenbury Report

Despite the Cadbury recommendations concerning remuneration committees, there was a recent public outcry over the remuneration packages awarded to directors in public utility companies. The Greenbury Committee was set up to look into this and published its recommendations early in 1995. One of these, that share option schemes should be taxed, was implemented immediately and then withdrawn by the Government when it was seen to affect employees other than directors. Changes have also been made to the Stock Exchange Listing Rules to secure prior shareholder approval of long-term incentive schemes and the publication of a company policy statement on share options and incentive schemes.

iii) Self-regulation

This topic may be approached from the point of view of asking whether self-regulatory systems can ever be effective. It may then be combined with the regulation of takeovers and mergers, which is supervised by the Takeover Panel of the Stock Exchange. In favour of self-regulation, it is said that Government and the courts should not interfere too much in the conduct of business, such interference causes delay and is bad for business confidence. Against, it may be argued that self-regulation provides no effective sanctions and that, in the present business climate, something stronger than the disapproval of their peers is required by those prepared to act unethically in order to make a profit.

14.3 Recent cases and materials

Anyone interested in this topic is recommended to read the Cadbury and Greenbury Reports and also the newspaper accounts of company collapses and trials in the latter half of the 1980s. Relevant cases are *Guinness plc* v *Saunders* [1990] 2 AC 663, *R* v *Seelig; R* v *Spens* [1991] 1 WLR 624 and *R* v *Maxwell* (1996) unreported.

14.4 Analysis of questions

The topic has begun to appear only recently, but there is a good deal of scope for the future and developments should be noted. Questions on harmonisation may be set in the form of the question below. The subject of corporate governance is a very wide one, and very topical, and there are many guises in which a question might appear, although the Cadbury Report is the most likely focus (see Question 3 on the 1994 London paper and Question 3 on the 1995 London paper, below).

14.5 Questions

QUESTION ONE

'The effect of our entry into the EEC has had, and will continue to have, an almost entirely malign effect on the overall development of English company law.'

Discuss.

University of London LLB Examination
(for External Students) Company Law June 1993 Q2

General Comment

A fairly simple question provided that the candidate has a sufficient working knowledge of the underlying subject matter. A good opportunity for candidates to illustrate that they have their finger on the pulse.

Skeleton Solution

Impact of Community law upon UK company law – aims of secondary legislation – difficulties.

Examples of secondary legislation translated into Companies Acts – are the difficulties with the implementation conceptual or practical? – has the UK achieved the aims of the secondary legislation?

The future – proposals for increased worker participation – a supervisory board for the plc.

Suggested Solution

That Community law has already had a tremendous impact on English company law cannot be doubted. To maintain that its effect upon English company law is and will continue to be entirely malign is demonstrably inaccurate. Such inadequacies as have appeared to date may be properly attributed to our own parliamentary draftsmen who experience difficulties in expressing secondary legislation in terms appropriate to the domestic canvas. Hence many Community reforms were introduced in CA 1985, but have only recently been properly implemented 'second time around' by virtue of CA 1989. That the problems are not conceptual is best illustrated by considering some of the principal (and almost entirely beneficial) changes that have been made to our domestic law.

Perhaps the most significant changes to domestic law can be seen in the form of the new ss35, 35A, 35B as implemented by s108 CA 1989. In its original unamended form s35 CA 1985 represented the codification of Article 9 of the First Directive on Company Law of 1968. Its greatest flaw was that s35 attempted to deal in an instant with the doctrine of ultra vires but without distinguishing between ultra vires and directors' want of authority. This and the wording of the section itself led to difficulties of interpretation, for example, when does a person 'deal' with a company? What was meant by 'good faith'? Did the transaction have to be expressly approved by all of the directors? Lawson J's judgment in *International Sales & Agencies Ltd* v *Marcus* (1982) is famous for providing answers to some at least of these questions. But it is more significant for present purposes to note that the directive itself made no mention of 'dealing' or 'good faith'. These constructions were the product of our own draftsmen. Thus the fault lay not with the aim of the Commission but with our implementation of the directive.

These problems were largely ironed out by s108 CA 1989 which noticeably avoids any reference to 'dealing' and provides guidance as to the meaning of 'good faith'.

The beneficial effects of Community intervention may also be seen in the area of consolidated accounts and in particular the obligations imposed by virtue of the Seventh Directive (Part VII and Sched 4A CA 1985). By virtue of these amendments there is a new (and more stringent) definition of parent and subsidiary and there is also an obligation on companies to include unincorporated subsidiary 'undertakings' (eg, partnerships) owned by the group in the accounts. The value of this practice is that companies are now less likely to be able to borrow massive amounts via subsidiaries but to keep the subsidiary and therefore also the subsidiary's borrowing off the group balance sheet. The effect is entirely beneficial since the investing public is less likely to be misled into investing in a group that appears to be more solvent than it in fact is.

The above directives represent a fraction of the law that has passed into our statute books in the area of company law. If there is to be a complaint about the impact of Community law then it must be largely centred around the piecemeal approach of the Commission to reform. Thus as directives are issued the national states make legislation without knowing (with any certainty) whether a further directive will require alteration of the legislation based upon the preceding directive.

Before concluding we must ask whether there are likely to be any future malign consequences of our membership of the EEC. Again, because of the piecemeal approach (referred to above) little more can be done than to consider briefly some of the proposed changes that may or may not become law.

Two notable changes may be found in the draft Fifth Directive. Firstly it provides for more effective monitoring of management in the case of plcs by making a division between directors responsible for management and those responsible for their supervision. Especially significant is the proposal that directors are to be jointly and severally liable except to the extent that the individual director can prove that no fault is personally attributable to him. If implemented such a proposal can only serve to better managerial standards and hopefully go some way towards preventing the reoccurrence of commercial catastrophes like the Maxwell and/or Polly Peck sagas.

Secondly, the Fifth Directive contains proposals to increase worker participation, possibly by guaranteed representation at board level. The precise degree of participation afforded to workers is a matter for debate, but it cannot be doubted but that an informed and well represented workforce is likely to be more productive. This last proposal may however be significantly at odds with the government policy of some member states and depending on political viewpoint may be a malign prospect. In the final analysis however, our entry into the EEC must be seen on balance to have had and be likely to have overwhelmingly beneficial consequences.

QUESTION TWO

'It is quite pointless to think that we can discuss any questions of "policy" [in law reform] in the abstract ... when the reality of the matter is that it is Europe that has loomed largest in the minds of everyone who has been concerned with companies legislation in recent years ... For we have to accept that, so long as we are in Europe, there will be pressure for changes in Company Law, and this pressure will not go away.' (Sealy)

Discuss.

Is there a need for clearer policy in Company Law reform?

University of London LLB Examination
(for External Students) Company Law June 1994 Q1

General Comment

A fairly difficult question requiring a critical appreciation of the impact of European Community law upon our domestic company law.

Skeleton Solution

Need for domestic reform – hitherto impact of European Community law on domestic company law.

Domestic legislation – potential conflict with Community law – need for clearer policy.

Likely ambit of domestic and Community legislation – continuing need for formulation of policy.

Suggested Solution

Taken at face value, Sealy appears to be suggesting that accession to the European Community has paralysed domestic reform of company law and, moreover, that it has rendered both the consideration of reform and the adoption of policy a sterile exercise. At any rate from a domestic view point. There is indeed a need for clearer policy in company law reform. While it cannot be doubted that simple domestic reforms may have a very limited shelf life, in so far as they may be rendered superfluous by Community law, it will always be necessary to formulate policy at domestic level. Only then can the United Kingdom address the challenge of taking a more active role in the preparatory stages of Community legislation.

Since 1972, the major changes to domestic companies' legislation have been underpinned by numerous directives, eg the first, second, third, fourth, sixth, seventh and eighth directives. The impact of the directives has been almost entirely beneficial; for example, the substantial abolition of ultra vires, the general liability of promoters upon pre-incorporation contracts and the new rules governing the preparation of group accounts. However, with company law, as with other areas of law, the legal translation of directives into domestic legislation has not proved altogether smooth, eg see s35 Companies Act 1985 (unamended).

The possibility of domestic legislation being superseded by Community directives is a real one. It has the consequence that the legislature is likely only to pass consequential or amending legislation, without tackling some of the fundamental and perennial problems which face the courts regularly, eg should parent companies be liable for the debts of wholly owned subsidiaries? Professor Gower in *Principles of Modern Company Law* (5th ed, p70) puts it thus:

'... the reaction has been to add to the existing framework without ever re-examining its foundations to ensure that they are sufficiently sound to bear the weight of the expanding superstructure.'

It should also be borne in mind that Community law will be enacted only in so far as it is necessary to 'harmonise' the domestic laws of member states. The Companies Division of the Department of Trade and Industry produces an annual report entitled 'Harmonisation of Company Law and Related Law in the European Community: Progress of Draft Directives and Proposals'. A cursory glance at the report reveals the array of proposals which may or may not eventually become Community law. Against this background of potential Community law it is almost impossible for domestic legislation to be formulated (or at least implemented) in any lasting or meaningful way.

Domestic reforms are therefore likely to be of a very technical nature without any attempt being made to address fundamental problems, except to the extent that harmonisation requires that they be addressed. There is, however, a tendency to forget that Community law is decided upon collectively by member states. Logically, the way forward should be for much-needed domestic policies and proposed reforms to be pursued into the European arena.

QUESTION THREE

'In spite of the growth in the number of superficial legal restrictions imposed on them in recent years, directors are in fact as free as ever to misuse their powers. The self-regulatory approach advocated in the Cadbury Report merely serves to underline the government's abdication of responsibility for providing a suitable legal framework.'

Discuss.

University of London LLB Examination
(for External Students) Company Law June 1995 Q3

General Comment

The proposition can be dealt with by examining the foundations of directors' power and the rationale for the freedoms that lead to abuse. This raises consideration of whether the abuses can be ended without reducing the discretion given to directors to act in the best interests of the company. The question requires an overview of directors' powers and duties, and the consequences of a directors' powers regime based upon other foundations.

Skeleton Solution

Legal rationale of English director law – directors' powers, origin, purpose, scope for setting limits – wide or narrow scope of powers – significance of director/shareholders – concept of director as fiduciary – duty owed to company – alternative basis of powers likely to remove discretions and fiduciary basis – existing safeguards – conclusion.

Suggested Solution

The proposition suggests the possibility of a legislative framework of controls which would prevent, as distinct from punishing, the misuse of directors' powers. Such controls would necessarily have to operate without substantial restrictions upon the management of the company's affairs. It is submitted that the proposition fails to take into account the legal rationale of directors' powers, and the great importance of individual and collective freedoms and discretions that are given to directors in managing the affairs of the company so as to achieve the fullest potential of the corporate form in providing benefits to company, director, member, employee, creditor and society generally. It is necessary to consider the origin and nature of directors' powers in order to assess whether any alternative regime would be as effective, overall, as the present one:

a) *Directors' powers*

A company as a legal, non-natural person, cannot act for itself but must necessarily act through the agency of the Board or the General Meeting. The powers of the Board are determined largely by the memorandum and the articles which, subject to the Companies Act, divide powers and functions of the company between either the Board or the members in General Meeting. Table A art 70, allows for the Board management of the company's business and the exercise of all the company's powers subject only to the 1985 Act, the memorandum, the articles and the special resolution of the General Meeting. From this, it follows that the extent of the Board's powers is initially determined by the purposes of the founders of the company and, subsequently, by its controllers. The appointment, remuneration, retirement, circumstances of dismissal and even the regulation of directors' proceedings such as Board meetings can be prescribed by the articles: see Table A CA 1985 arts 64–98. The obvious consequence of this is that the width of directors' powers can range between the case of one who exercises little power at all to another who is almost omnipotent and is, in reality, subject only to the power of the courts in applying the companies legislation. The problems of potential width of powers are amplified by the possibility that the directors may also be shareholders and may well be responsible qua member for the scope of their own powers as directors. This is where the real potential for abuse lies and it is hard to see what legislation can do to remedy the problem of controllers giving to directors such powers as they think appropriate. The only possible way to deal with the near-infinite permutations of company control and management is by a clear and well-established doctrine of directors' duties which the courts can apply to all company directors, irrespective of the width of powers that they exercise, coupled with a wide range of sanctions for breach of the duty. The flexibility of the directors' duty concept lies in the principle that the duty is one of good faith and that it is owed to the company itself, generally to the exclusion of, or in priority to, duties owed to others. Thus, even the owner of most of the shares in a company, if he is a director, will owe duties to the company which he ignores at his peril.

b) *Directors' duties*

Directors' duties are of a fiduciary nature and really come down to the necessity for each director to act honestly, carefully and with such skill as he possesses in the best interests of the company as a whole. This has to be seen in the context of the business world, where speculation and some risk-taking is often necessary, so that the duties are somewhat different to those of a trustee or an agent as regards discretion to act. A clear illustration of the flexible but effective use of duty as a check upon abuses is seen in the cases concerning claims that the directors owe duties to persons other than the company. These cases all show that the powers must be exercised for the benefit of the company itself, that is the members collectively rather than for: the directors themselves *(Regal (Hastings) Ltd* v *Gulliver* (1967)); or company officers or employees *(Parke* v *Daily News Ltd* (1962)); or the company's subsidiary or holding company *(Charterbridge Corporation Ltd* v *Lloyd's Bank Ltd* (1970)); or a section of the membership *(Multinational Gas & Petrochemical Co Ltd* v *Multinational Gas & Petrochemical Services Ltd* (1983)).

It does not follow from this general rule that no duties at all are owed to others by the directors. There are circumstances where the directors will be found to owe fiduciary duties to members as illustrated by *Allen* v *Hyatt* (1914) and *Dawson International* v *Coats Paton plc* (1989) and, of course, there can be liability towards members on a *Hedley Byrne* basis *(Hedley Byrne & Co* v *Heller and Partners* (1964)) for negligent misstatement: see *Caparo Industries plc* v *Dickman* (1990). The general rule remains that the duties are to protect the good of the company as a whole. Even the statutory duty owed by directors in performing their functions (to have regard to the interests of employees) is owed to the company alone: s309 CA 1985.

It can be seen that the English law view of the director as a fiduciary justifies the width of powers that may be given to him at the instance of the incorporators, provided breaches are remediable. Any attempt to replace this system with a statutory code, breach of which would be punishable according to the statutory penalties, would almost certainly lead to many directors being unwilling to continue upon such a basis, as their freedom to act would be considerably compromised. The existing investigative and punitive safeguards under CA 1985, Insolvency Act 1986 and Company Directors (Disqualification) Act 1986, the growing use of minority oppression petitions under s459 CA 1985 combined with the wide and comprehensive case law on directors' duties should be found capable of containing abuses to a publicly acceptable level for the foreseeable future. This depends upon sufficient political will and funding to enforce regulatory and disqualification proceedings. The safeguards upon any insolvency involving abusive directors will continue to be used with vigour by the wide and increasingly experienced body of insolvency practitioners, and it is submitted that the existing legal framework is perfectly adequate and should be used to maximum effect rather than trying to replace it with something which may damage the corporate form considerably.

15 Insider Dealing

15.1 Introduction

15.2 Key points

15.3 Recent cases and statutes

15.4 Analysis of questions

15.5 Questions

15.1 Introduction

This chapter deals with the situation where a person who is in possession of unpublished price-sensitive information about a company uses that information to deal in the securities of that company so as to make a profit for himself. In some circumstances this is a criminal offence under the Part V Criminal Justice Act 1993 which came into force on 1 March 1994, repealing and replacing the Company Securities (Insider Dealing) Act 1985.

15.2 Key points

a) *Background*

It has been a matter of some dispute whether the law should prohibit insider dealing. It is often referred to as a 'victimless crime' and some have argued that exploitation of inside information provides a useful incentive for directors and other entrepreneurs. On the other hand, it is argued that small investors in particular are at a disadvantage and that regulation is necessary to preserve confidence in the integrity of the market, and these arguments have been accepted. Against this, however, the legislation provides no remedy for those small investors who are disadvantaged, and it may be said they are perenially at a disadvantage when compared with institutional investors who have closer access to company sources and are 'courted' by companies and invited to special briefings. The law does nothing to redress this imbalance nor, at the other end of the scale, does it seem to have succeeded in combatting large-scale organised insider dealing. The first real attempt to control insider dealing, the Company Securities (Insider Dealing) Act 1985 attracted harsh criticism, including charges that the defences were too wide, the definitions too loose and that a civil remedy was not provided, as well as more practical criticisms concerning enforcement and evidence. Part V of the Criminal Justice Act 1993 was enacted not so much in response to such criticism but to implement Community Directive No 89/592/EEC which requires Member States to regulate insider dealing, and proclaims itself as a 'restatement' of the law. It may be seen, therefore, as having amended the form rather than the substance of the 1985 Act and its main effect has been to tighten the definitions laid down by its predecessor.

b) *The offence*

Section 52 provides that an individual who has information as an insider is guilty of insider dealing if he deals in price-affected securities in relation to that information, encourages another to deal or discloses the information otherwise than in the proper performance of his employment, office or profession. The dealing must be on a regulated market or through a professional intermediary.

c) *The defences*

Section 53 provides the following defences:

i)   the accused did not at the time expect the dealing to result in a profit attributable to the fact that the information was price sensitive;

ii) at the time he believed on reasonable grounds that the information had been disclosed widely enough to ensure that no one taking part in the dealing would be prejudiced by not having it;

iii) he would have done what he did even if he had not had the information.

The defences to a charge of disclosing inside information are:

i)   he did not at the time expect any person to deal in the securities because of the disclosure;

ii) he did expect this but not that it would result in a profit attributable to the fact that the information was price sensitive;

d) *Definitions*

Sections 56–60 define the terms used in the substantive parts of the legislation. The most important are:

i)   Inside information (s56(1))

   This relates to a particular security or issuer of securities and is not general, is specific or precise, has not been made public and if it were would be likely to have a significant effect on the price of any securities.

ii) Insider (s57(1))

   A person has information as an insider if, and only if, it is (and he knows it is) inside information, he has it and knows he has it from an inside source.

iii) Inside source (s57(2))

   An inside source is someone who: has information through being a director, employee or shareholder of an issuer of securities; or has access to the information by virtue of his employment office or profession; or has been given the information by a director, employee or shareholder of an issuer of securities.

e) *Penalties (s61(1))*

On summary conviction, a fine up to the statutory maximum or six months' imprisonment and, on indictment, an unlimited fine and/or seven years' imprisonment.

15.3 Recent cases and statutes

Most of the convictions obtained under the CS(ID)A 1985 concerned one-off transactions by single persons in relation to small companies. The important reported cases concerned the interpretation of provisions of the Act which are now repealed. There is virtually no case law on the provisions of the new legislation.

15.4 Analysis of questions

Insider dealing has from time to time been topical, especially in the light of the City 'scandals' which emerged in the late 1980s and early 1990s such as Guinness, Blue Arrow and Maxwell (although in fact insider dealing itself has not been an issue in any of the cases brought so far). As there is virtually no case law on the new legislation, the candidate attempting a question must rely on a thorough knowledge of Part V Criminal Justice Act 1993 and the problems connected with regulating insider dealing.

15.5 Questions

QUESTION ONE

Toucan plc is a large public company. Three of its directors are Cedric, John and Bill. Each holds 5,000 £1 shares. Cedric discovers from Pete (a director of Distilation plc) that Distilation plc is likely soon to make a generous offer for the shares of Toucan plc in order to effect a takeover. Cedric passes on this information to John and Bill and all three borrow money from Toucan plc to buy themselves more shares in that company.

John is worried about the effect that the impending takeover will have on the value of his wife's holding in a rival company. He suggests to his wife that she should pay for their annual holiday not from their savings account as she usually did, but by selling her shares in the rival company.

The loan from the company to John, Bill and Cedric comes to light and at a general meeting a motion to take legal proceedings against them is defeated only by the votes of John, Bill, Cedric and one other director, who himself authorised the loan.

Adrian has a small shareholding in Toucan plc, is disgusted by the behaviour of the directors and asks you if there is any legal action he can take. You are asked to advise on the possible civil and criminal liability of Cedric, John, Bill and Pete.

University of London LLB Examination
(for External Students) Company Law June 1987 Q8

General Comment

This question deals mainly with Part V Criminal Justice Act 1993, though the provisions of Companies Act 1985 relating to loans to directors are also of significance.

Skeleton Solution

Insider dealing – CJA 1993: the offence – definitions: insider; inside information; inside source – defences – sanctions and remedies – s459 CA 1985 – fiduciary duty.

Loans to directors – criminal sanctions – void – accountability.

Financial assistance.

Suggested Solution

The first issue in this question is whether Pete, Cedric, John or Bill is guilty of insider dealing contrary to Part V Criminal Justice Act (CJA) 1993 (the following section numbers refer to that Act).

The offence is defined in s52 CJA 1993: an individual who has information as an insider is guilty of insider dealing if he deals in price-affected securities in relation to that information, encourages another to deal, or discloses the information otherwise than in the proper performance of his employment, office or profession. Pete and Cedric both disclosed the information concerning the intended takeover bid, and Cedric, John and Bill all dealt in securities of Toucan plc. (Dealing is required to be on a regulated market or through a professional intermediary as defined. The problem does not state whether this was the case but it is assumed to be so.) Cedric might possibly argue that he disclosed the information in the proper performance of his office, as it may have been his duty as a director of Toucan to disclose it to the other directors.

Only someone who has information 'as an insider' is caught. This phrase is defined in s57(1) CJA 1993 to mean if and only if he knows the information is inside information and he has it and knows he has it from an inside source. An 'inside source' is someone who has information through being a director, employee or shareholder of an issuer of securities, or has been given it by such a person, or has access to it by virtue of his employment, office or profession (s57(2) CJA 1993). Clearly Pete is an inside source. Cedric, in his turn, knows Pete to be so. Cedric may not have disclosed to John and Bill where he obtained the information, but it is likely that he did so. The source may be direct or indirect (s57(2)(b) CJA 1993), and therefore the fact that the information has come to them via Cedric does not prevent them being 'insiders'.

Finally, it is necessary to decide whether the information itself is 'inside information'. Section 56(1) CJA 1993 provides that it must relate to a particular security or issuer of securities, must be specific or precise, must not have been made public and, if it were to be made public would be likely to have a significant effect on the price of any securities (price includes value). The information concerning the takeover bid would appear to satisfy all of these criteria.

Each of Pete, Cedric, John and Bill would appear then to have committed an offence. In addition John, although he may not have disclosed the information to her, encourages his wife to deal (dealing includes disposals) in the shares of a rival company which he believes may be affected. As these shares are probably price-affected securities in relation to the information, this is likely to be a further offence. It then remains to consider whether any of them would have a defence. The defences are contained in s53. Subsections (1) and (2) contain identical defences in relation to dealing and encouraging others to deal respectively. These are:

a) the accused did not at the time expect the dealing to result in a profit attributable to the fact that the information was price-sensitive;

b) at the time he believed on reasonable grounds that the information had been disclosed widely enough to ensure that no one taking part in the dealing would be prejudiced by not having it;

c) he would have done what he did even if he had not had the information.

There is nothing in the facts of the question to suggest that any of these defences would be available to Cedric, John or Bill. The defences to a charge of disclosure are (a) that the accused did not at the time expect any person to deal in the securities because of the disclosure; and (b) that he did expect this but not that it would result in a profit attributable to the fact that the information was price-sensitive. As Cedric is himself concerned in the dealing and the financial arrangements surrounding it, it is unlikely he would be able to avail himself of either of these defences. Pete, on the other hand might be able to take advantage of (a).

The sanctions are entirely criminal and any of the participants could be sentenced to an unlimited fine and/or seven years' imprisonment, but the courts have been notoriously reluctant to impose heavy penalties. Adrian must be advised that the CJA 1993 does not provide compensation for 'disgusted' shareholders and that he has no remedy against any of the directors on this ground, although he might consider whether it would be possible to bring an action against them under s459 Companies Act (CA) 1985 on the basis of conduct unfairly prejudicial to the members of Toucan plc. The main bar to such an action would be the argument that none of the shareholders has actually suffered a loss. Nor would it help to argue that the directors were in breach of their fiduciary duties since these duties are owed to the company, not the shareholders (*Percival* v *Wright* (1902)).

The issue of the loans is somewhat different. Section 330 CA 1985 prohibits a company from lending money to its directors, except in small amounts not exceeding £2,500 in aggregate. It seems probable that in the present case the limits are exceeded. Contravention of s330 is a criminal offence by the company, and directors who permit such a contravention will also be guilty of an offence. It is submitted that the company cannot validly ratify a criminal act, so that the attempted ratification is ineffective. However, in contrast to the CJA 1993, CA 1985 provides civil remedies in connection with loans to directors in s341: the loan itself is void and the borrowers must repay the loan and account for any gains made from the money. The company therefore has a remedy and Adrian can bring a derivative action if the directors control the majority.

There would also seem to be an offence under s152 CA in that financial assistance has been given for the purpose of assisting a purchase of the company's own shares, and the company and each of its officers who is in default are liable to a fine.

QUESTION TWO

'There are many examples of conduct in the administration of companies which are controlled both by being criminalised by statute as well as being remediable by civil suit at the instance of the victim. Yet in the case of insider trading, there is only a criminal penalty. If insider trading is to be effectively brought to an end, it is essential that a civil remedy should be provided.'

Discuss.

University of London LLB Examination
(for External Students) Company Law June 1992 Q2

General Comment

This question is not, as it may seem to some, simply asking for a straightforward exposition of the law on insider dealing. Such an answer, while it might pass if comprehensive and accurate, would not earn a good mark. Instead it is asking you to think more deeply and critically about the market phenomenon of insider dealing and how the law should best (if at all) control it and prevent it.

Skeleton Solution

Examples of conduct statutorily criminalised and also remediable civilly – outline of criminal penalty for insider trading – assessment of efficacy – arguments for and against proscription of insider trading – utility of a civil remedy for 'victim' – reforms in consequence of EC Directive.

Suggested Solution

Company law is awash with instances of multiple layers of legal protection in that the Companies Act 1985 renders criminal many specific acts and omissions of directors (imposing fines and in some cases the possibility of imprisonment) which will also be of relevance in a civil action by the company itself against the directors. An example is the prohibited loans to directors' provisions in s330 Companies Act 1985, contravention of which by a director can result in criminal liability under s342 and civil liability under s341 in that a director must account for any gain to the company and indemnify the company against any loss or damage. A general action for breach of fiduciary duty will also be available for a company against its directors in many cases where they have committed other specific statutory offences – for example s206 Insolvency Act 1986 (fraud in anticipation of winding up).

The criminal prohibition on insider dealing, however, although it is wide in the category of persons to whom it can apply (including not just directors but also a number of others concerned in the administration of companies including recipients of inside information or 'tippees'), is not specifically backed up with any civil remedy to compensate the victim of an insider trader. The prohibition is contained in the Criminal Justice Act 1993, Part V, and applies to dealing in securities on a recognised stock exchange on the basis of unpublished price-sensitive information. The offence also extends to encouraging someone else to deal on the basis of such information and communicating such information to another person expecting that person to deal in the securities resulting in a profit due to the price sensitivity of the information. Thus rings and networks of insiders are technically within the legislation. It is not just persons connected with the company (most obviously directors, officers and advisers privy to sensitive information) who are within the scope of the offence. The consequences of contravention of the Act are purely criminal though s61 imposes up to seven years imprisonment and/or a fine. In fact s61 expressly provides there are to be no effects on the validity of transactions in contravention of the Act and nowhere does the Act provide for any specific civil remedy for the victim(s) of an insider trader.

The enforcement and efficacy of the Act have been strongly criticised. It is sometimes argued that the courts have been hesitant to use their power of imprisonment and fines have been too light, and that a civil remedy which somehow required the insider to disgorge his profits (as pertains in the USA) would have an additional deterrent effect. However the whole idea of a specific civil remedy calls for closer analysis, for who exactly is the victim of an insider trader? Is it his market counterparty? If so then couldn't it be argued that they suffered no actual loss since they were willing to make the trade when they bought from or sold to the insider at that price? Is the victim the company whose securities are the subject of insider trading? If so then what is the actual damage suffered by that company for listed securities are bought and sold daily for a thousand different reasons? Some commentators have even argued that insider trading is efficient since it improves the rate of dissemination of new information to the market and hence benefits efficiency. At the moment the only sustainable legal argument that a civil remedy exists can be made in the limited circumstances where the insider owes a fiduciary duty to Company A (eg he is a director of Company A) and in the course of the discharge and performance of his duty he comes into possession of unpublished price sensitive information about the securities of Company B. If he deals on his own behalf on the basis of that information then it can be argued that he is liable to account for any gain he makes to Company A in action for breach of fiduciary duty brought by Company A against him: *Regal (Hastings) Ltd* v *Gulliver* (1942) and *Phipps* v *Boardman* (1964). In addition a counterparty to an insider trade could always try to argue fraudulent misrepresentation.

16 Corporate Crime

16.1 Introduction

16.2 Key points

16.3 Analysis of questions

16.4 Question

16.1 Introduction

The expression 'corporate crime' relates to the question of the company's possible liability for criminal and/or tortious acts carried out on its behalf by its agents.

16.2 Key points

a) *Criminal liability*

The principal difficulty of fixing a company with criminal liability is the problem of imputing mens rea. This problem is circumvented in the case of offences relating specifically to corporations by making them crimes of strict liability, which do not require mens rea. However, this leaves other offences where it is indisputable that the acts which constitute the actus reus have been committed in the name or in the course of the business of the company.

English law, therefore, identifies the company with its 'organs' (organic theory), the leading case in the area being *Tesco Supermarkets Ltd* v *Nattrass* [1972] AC 153. Here, the actual perpetrator of the offence was the manager of one of the many supermarkets belonging to the company, and the House of Lords held that the company could not be held responsible. For there to be corporate liability, the commission of the offence had to be by an organ of the company – individuals who are part of the 'directing mind and will' of the company – which effectively means the board. However, in the earlier case of *R* v *ICR Haulage* [1944] KB 551 it was held that the company could be liable for a managing director's acts, even when he was acting outside the normal scope of his duties.

Because of the mandatory sentence of life imprisonment, it is assumed that a company cannot be charged with murder. However, in recent years, interest has focused on attempts to make corporations liable for manslaughter, highlighted in the recent unreported prosecutions brought against PLO (1990) and OLL Ltd (1994) as a result of disasters in which members of the public lost their lives. In these cases, at least, the courts remained faithful to the principles enunciated in *Tesco* v *Nattrass*.

However, some commentators claim to have detected a recognition by the courts in other recent cases of the limitations of the *Tesco* concept of liability, where the offence in question was statutory and liability turned on an interpretation of the statute. In *Re Supply of Ready Mixed Concrete (No 2)* [1995] 1 AC 456, *Tesco Stores Ltd* v *Brent London Borough Council* [1993] 1 WLR 1037 and *Meridian Global Funds Management Asia Ltd* v *Securities Commission* (1995) The Times 29 June the House of Lords, the Divisional Court and the Privy Council respectively inclined towards a more direct application of the principles of vicarious liability (see below). In *Seaboard Offshore Ltd* v *Secretary of State for Transport* [1994] 2 All ER 99, where the House of Lords had to consider the application of a new statutory offence created in response to the *Herald of Free Enterprise* disaster, the Lords refused (on a construction of the statute) to impose vicarious liability for all the ship's employees but suggested it may be possible to establish liability by showing that the company failed to establish a safe system. On this basis, it has been suggested that the law may be moving towards a 'systems and procedures' approach.

b) *Tortious liability*

The law of tort has long imposed liability on employers for the tortious acts of their employees committed in the scope of their duties (vicarious liability), and companies are no different from any other employer in this regard. It is necessary to establish that the tortfeasor was an employee of the company, and that he acted within the scope of his employment. The company has a right of indemnity against the employee who committed the tort. *Lennard's Carrying Co* v *Asiatic Petroleum* [1915] AC 705 is perhaps the leading tort case where it was held that a company could be liable for the default of its managing director. There are many other cases where companies have been held vicariously liable for torts committed by employees but, as this topic falls within the ambit of the law of tort, it is highly unlikely that a candidate would be expected to analyse them in a company law paper.

It will rarely be the case nowadays that an executive director of the company who commits a tort is not an employee, but if this should be the case, the company may be held liable on agency principles if the tort was committed within the scope of the director's authority.

16.3 Analysis of questions

This is a somewhat obscure topic; many company law courses ignore it entirely, but it appeared on the London LLB External in 1985, and is included for that reason. The 1985 question was an essay question, and it would seem unlikely that this topic will appear as a problem question. It is thought likely that the topic will appear by itself rather than being combined with other area of the syllabus. The question set on the 1985 paper covers the two major parts of the topic – tortious liability and criminal liability.

16.4 Question

To what extent can (a) tortious and (b) criminal liability be imposed on companies?

University of London LLB Examination
(for External Students) Company Law June 1985 Q3

General Comment

This question requires examination of both the major problem areas – tort and crime.

Skeleton Solution

Tort: Vicarious liability for acts of employees within scope of their employment. Also for acts of directors/managers acting in that capacity. Ultra vires acts can also be the basis of liability.

Crime: General principle is that acts of 'directing mind' of company are company's own acts. This is question of fact. Company may escape if act is through 'default of another'.

Suggested Solution

It is clear that a company, like an individual, is vicariously liable for torts committed by its employees when they are acting within the scope of their employment, even if the tort includes wilful malice: *Citizens' Life Assurance Co v Brown* (1904). The same principle applies to criminal liability if the statute creating the liability imposes liability on employer as well as employee and the employer is a company.

In some cases the court has interpreted a statute as imposing liability on the company when the offence was committed by an officer of the company acting within the scope of his employment: *DPP v Kent and Sussex Contractors Ltd* (1944). More recently, though, there has been some reluctance to impose such liability unless the persons who generally manage the company have actively participated in the crime. In *Tesco Supermarkets Ltd v Nattrass* (1971) the company was charged under s11(2) Trades Descriptions Act 1968 with advertising goods at a lower price than that at which they were sold. The situation arose because the manager of the particular Tesco store had failed in his duty to ensure that the goods advertised were in fact available. The company had a sophisticated supervisory system designed to prevent this sort of thing from happening, but it had broken down on this occasion. Tesco pleaded that the offence was due to the default of another (the manager) and that they had taken all reasonable care. This defence is specifically allowed under the 1968 Act. The defence succeeded; Lord Reid pointed out that a company must act through living persons; in some circumstances that person is the embodiment of the company rather than its agent, and no question of vicarious liability can arise. However, it was the board of directors here which was the embodiment of the company, and its authority had not been delegated to the store manager, who was therefore to be treated as a separate person.

This case requires to be treated with some caution, for the 'default of another' defence was contained within the 1968 Act, but is not generally available to companies charged with criminal wrongdoing. The case does illustrate, however, that not every act by every junior employee will be considered to be the act of the company for the purposes of the criminal law.

Two major areas of difficulty have arisen here, and these have not so far been explored in any detail by the courts. First, for what acts of the board of directors is the company to be held responsible? So far as tort is concerned the company is responsible for the tortious acts/omissions of those who manage the company when they are acting in that capacity. In *Lennard's Carrying Co v Asiatic Petroleum* (1915) the company was held liable for the default of a single managing director who ought to have known that a particular ship was unseaworthy. It was said that the managing director was the directing mind and will of the company (or, as it is sometimes expressed, the company was his alter ego).

The search for the directing mind and will of the company is not restricted to looking at the formal provisions of the memorandum and articles; rather, this is a question of fact to be determined in all the circumstances. This is so equally in criminal cases, and if the company is to be convicted it must be proved that the (natural) person in question controlled the management of the company: *R v Andrews Weatherfoil Ltd* (1972). A difficulty arises here where a sole director is charged with conspiring with the company: conspiracy necessarily requires two independent minds, and these cannot be found if it is established that the company has no mind or intelligence independent of the will of the sole director: *R v McDonnell* (1965).

In *R v ICR Haulage* (1944) it was held that the company could be criminally liable for the wrongful act of its managing director even though the act was outside the normal ambit of his duties. *Lennard's Carrying Co* v *Asiatic Petroleum* suggests that the position would be the same in tort.

Most recent criminal cases (eg *Re Supply of Ready Mixed Concrete (No 2)* (1995)) have turned on the question of whether, on an interpretation of the statute in question, vicarious liability could be attributed to the company. In one recent case, however, the House of Lords has suggested that a company could be held liable for failing to establish a safe system (*Seaboard Offshore Ltd* v *Secretary of State for Transport* (1994)). Again the case concerned interpretation of a particular statute and it remains to be seen whether the courts are prepared to develop that approach.

It may be noted finally that one effect of the 'alter ego' doctrine is to circumvent the problem of imposing liability for offences which require a specific intent; even if the company cannot form the intent, its alter ego presumably can, and this is enough to found liability.

17 University of London LLB (External) 1996 Questions and Suggested Solutions

UNIVERSITY OF LONDON
LLB EXAMINATIONS 1996
for External Students
PARTS II EXAMINATION (Scheme A)
THIRD AND FOURTH YEAR EXAMINATIONS (Scheme B)
GRADUATE ENTRY LEVEL II (Route A)
GRADUATE ENTRY THIRD YEAR EXAMINATIONS (Route B)

COMPANY LAW

Tuesday, 4 June: 2.30 pm to 5.30 pm

Answer FOUR of the following EIGHT questions, including at least ONE from Part A and at least TWO from Part B.

PART A

1 'The elimination of the ultra vires doctrine and the *Turquand* doctrine by the Companies Act 1989 has done much to improve company law.'

Discuss.

2 'English company law has become more and more out of touch with business and its needs ... and has lost sight of the commercial values and priorities which it ought to recognise and serve ... The challenge for us now is to find some way forward which ensures that the law does respond to business needs and moves in sympathy with commercial trends.'

Discuss. What should be the 'way forward' for company law?

3 'In permitting the creation of fixed charges over shifting assets the law has taken an unfair step, for such charges combine all the advantages of a floating charge but with none of the usual disadvantage.'

Discuss.

PART B

4 Wheels Ltd was formed five years ago to provide lorry transport facilities to the computer industry. It has an issued share capital of £500 divided into 300 'A' shares of £1 each and 400 'B' shares of 50 pence each. Alf, Bob, and Colin are the directors of the company. Alf and Bob each hold half the 'A' shares and Colin holds all the 'B' shares. The articles of association of the company provide that:

i) The 'A' shares carry two votes each and the 'B' shares carry one vote each.

ii) Colin is to be a director of the company at a salary of £20,000 per year.

Until 1993 the three directors worked well together and the company prospered. However, at a board meeting in August of that year, Alf and Bob disagreed with Colin over a

153

fundamental matter of business policy and the meeting ended abruptly when Colin hit Alf. Colin was later fined £50 for assault by local magistrates. Since then Alf and Bob have continued to run the company but the business policy pursued after the meeting in August 1993 has clearly proved unsuccessful and, although the company is still solvent, it has made no profits since then. Colin continued to received his salary after the August meeting but has attended no board meetings since then, even though Alf and Bob have periodically invited him to do so.

Three months ago Alf and Bob stopped payment of Colin's salary. Colin is now saying that he will attend the next board meeting as he intends to 'make one last effort to lick the company into shape.' Alf and Bob do not want him back and want to run the company without him.

Advise Alf and Bob, and Colin.

5   Ace plc, which is engaged in manufacturing washing machines, has an issued share capital of one million £1 shares and is listed on the Stock Exchange. At 10.00 am on 11 March 1996 the directors of the company received a report that most of the machines recently supplied by the company would need to be replaced free of charge because of the presence of a dangerous electrical fault caused by faulty manufacture.

At 12.00 noon that day, Bob, one of the directors, telephoned his brother Colin and said, simply, 'Get out of washing machines'. At 12.30 pm Colin sold all his 10,000 shares in Ace plc, on the Stock Exchange, at a price of £8 each.

At 2.15pm Daisy, one of the waitresses in the directors' dining room overheard the directors discussing the morning's bad news. At 2.30 pm she sold all her 200 shares in Ace plc, on the Stock Exchange, at £7 each.

At 3.00 pm Eric, one of the directors, sold half his holding of 2,000 shares in Ace plc, on the Stock Exchange, at £6 each, intending to use the money to pay for his daughter's wedding which was due to take place on the following Saturday.

On 12 March 1996 the Financial Times newspaper published an article revealing the problems with Ace plc's washing machines and the share price quickly fell to £5 per share.

Discuss.

6   Blue plc is a major conglomerate which has several wholly owned subsidiaries. One of these subsidiary companies is Sky Ltd. Sky Ltd specialises in the lending of money. Blue plc wished to further expand its operation and were in negotiations with Red plc to merge some of their operations. As part of this reconstruction, Red plc were proposing to acquire a substantial number of shares in Blue plc but due to an unexpected delay in obtaining finance from their bank, Red plc proposed delaying the purchase of the shares until July 1996. Blue plc were unhappy about the delay because the share price of Blue plc was falling and this was having an adverse affect on the financing of several other takeovers which were based on Blue plc's share price. The board of directors ('the board') of Blue plc proposed that they should give Red plc some help to purchase the share immediately. The board procured a loan from Sky Ltd arguing that the loan 'was in good faith in the interests of Sky Ltd.' The directors of Sky Ltd were concerned about their future employment and felt unable to refuse making the substantial loan, despite the fact that the loan breached their normal rules of business on lending.

Advise the directors of Sky Ltd.

7   The issued share capital of Moon Ltd, which was incorporated in 1992, consists of 100,000 £1 ordinary shares and 15,000 £1 'A' preference shares and 15,000 £1 'B' deferred shares. Holdings of the shares are spread out unevenly between 20 different people, including the three directors.

The memorandum of association of Moon Ltd provides, inter alia, that:

1) The 'A' preference shares shall carry such rights as may be specified in the articles of association.

2) The 'B' deferred shares shall carry no rights to vote, save in class meetings, but shall carry unalterable rights to an annual 16 per cent deferred dividend payable only after the ordinary shares have received an initial annual dividend of 10 per cent and further, to participate rateably in any dividends paid to the ordinary shareholders after their initial 10 per cent.

The articles of association provide, inter alia, that:

i) The 'A' preference shares shall carry rights to an annual 13 per cent preference dividend but shall carry no rights to vote, save in class meetings.

ii) Repayment of shares in a reduction of capital shall be deemed to be a variation of the rights attached to those shares.

iii) All provisions in the company's memorandum and articles may be altered by special resolution without the need for any further procedures of any kind.

The directors of the company are proposing to make the following changes:

a) To reduce the share capital of the company by paying off the 'A' preference shares at par in a reduction of capital.

b) To reduce the annual dividend of the 'B' deferred shares to 8 per cent.

Advise the directors, who wish to know whether their proposals can be carried out, and if so, how.

8   Jill and Ben are directors of Safety Belts Ltd, a successful company which specialises in installing safety belts in buses. Wishing to raise additional finance for expansion, they decided to convert it to a plc, and offer the shares to the public in the UK and throughout Europe.

They sought advice from Bankers, a leading merchant bank. Bankers agreed to underwrite the issue of shares and advised Jill and Ben that they should make an application for admission to the Alternative Investment Market rather than listing on the Stock Exchange. Bankers suggested that other market professionals might be willing to subscribe for all the shares that were to be issued and that Jill and Ben should also consider limiting the persons to whom the offer was addressed.

Jill and Ben cannot decide which course of action they should follow. They need to raise finance, but wish to avoid being subject to onerous regulations and wish to avoid potential liability and risks. They are particularly concerned about the preparation of documents as they are unaware of their duties and responsibilities for documents being issued to the public.

Advise Jill and Ben.

QUESTION ONE

'The elimination of the ultra vires doctrine and the *Turquand* doctrine by the Companies Act 1989 has done much to improve company law.'

Discuss.

University of London LLB Examination
(for External Students) Company Law June 1996 Q1

General Comment

Analysis of this proposition requires some discussion of the foundation and effects of both the ultra vires doctrine and the rule in *Royal British Bank* v *Turquand*. The statutory provisions now covering these areas should be described and an outline of the perceived improvements in company law given, with particular emphasis on the distinctions between the powers of the company, the powers of the directors (as a Board and individually) and the position of third parties dealing with the company. The provision to 'internalise' problems should be discussed.

Skeleton Solution

Background and effect of ultra vires doctrine – the rule in *Turquand* – statutory changes affecting the ultra vires doctrine – statutory changes affecting the rule in *Turquand* – changes to the position of the company – the position of Board of Directors – the position of individual directors – third parties dealing with the company – 'internalisation' of problems – conclusion on the proposition.

Suggested Solution

The ultra vires doctrine in English law had achieved a considerable degree of refinement well before company law began to be codified by the Companies Acts in the nineteenth century. The doctrine had its origins in the idea that statutory corporations could only properly do those acts which were authorised by the legislation under which the corporation was constituted and functional. After some initial doubts as to whether this doctrine applied to companies under the new Companies Acts, the House of Lords in *Ashbury Railway Carriage and Iron Co Ltd* v *Riche* (1875) confirmed the point that the statutory requirements for objects to be set out in the memorandum of incorporation and for the implication of a covenant between the company and its members to observe the company constitutions, could only make sense if the doctrine did apply to companies under the Companies Acts.

The effects, in summary, of this rule were that a member could usually obtain injunctive relief to prevent the ultra vires acts (a right which is still preserved and which is discussed below) and, of greater importance, contracts made by the company which were not within the express or implied powers of the company were void at common law as against both parties and could not be saved by ratification, even if all members agreed to ratify. This rather draconian approach was subjected to some softening where a company's objects clause was drawn in such a way as to display some ambiguity and the third party had no good reason to think that an ultra vires object was being attempted by the company. In this situation, the court would often allow the third party to enforce the contract (but, obviously, not the company) as in *Rolled Steel Products (Holdings) Ltd* v *British Steel Corporation* (1986).

The rule in *Royal British Bank* v *Turquand* (1856) is a fairly broad principle, sometimes known as the 'indoor-management' rule, which protects a third party dealing with the company in transactions where the third party deals in good faith with officers of the company but there is some defect of procedure within the company which undermines the validity of the transaction. The effect of the external appearance of correct procedures is that a true outsider or third party will not be affected by constructive notice of the internal defects within the management of the company. It is otherwise where the third party is not a true outsider, as illustrated in *Morris* v *Kanssen* (1946) where the House of Lords refused to apply the rule. This is often accompanied by arguments concerning the ostensible authority as agents of company employees but the rule stands quite independent from agency principles and is founded upon the particular needs and formal foundation of Companies Act registered companies.

The statutory inroads upon the ultra vires doctrine began with s9(1) European Communities Act 1972, the process being continued by the Companies Act 1985 (CA 1985) with the present ss35, 35A and 35B being inserted into CA 1985 by the Companies Act 1989 (CA 1989). The general effect of these changes has been to bring English company law very much into line with European law on the point and to end, as against third parties dealing in good faith, the ultra vires doctrine. The position of third parties is greatly improved by this change and s35A(1) gives great protection to persons who deal with the Board of Directors or persons empowered by the Board to deal with third parties. The effect of all this is not to undermine the requirement for companies to act within their objects clauses but simply to prevent the invalidation of contracts where the company fails to do so.

The rule in *Turquand*'s case has been very much affected and superseded by the new s35A in situations where the dealing is with the Board or persons authorised by the Board. In such cases the powers of the Board are deemed to be free of any limitation under the company's constitution. This does not, however, extend to the position where a single director or a part only of the Board is dealing with the third party or authorising others to do so. Here, the *Turquand* rule will continue to apply as it will to other situations where the Board is not involved at all in the dealing or the authorisation thereof.

The position of the company after these changes is that it has lost some protection in that it will be tied to contracts which formerly might have been avoided but this protection is also lost to the other contracting party who could previously rely upon the doctrine to escape an unfavourable bargain: *Bell Houses Ltd* v *City Wall Properties Ltd* (1966). The company will undoubtedly, have much less trouble in drafting objects clauses which are designed to protect it against its own directors than as in the former situation, where the clause had to protect against the third parties also. The new s35(3) makes the position of the company against its directors, where they exceed their limitations under the memorandum, crystal clear. They will be liable to the company unless their liability is relieved by a separate special resolution, independently of any ratification of their act.

The position of the Board of Directors is spelt out with considerable clarity by the new provisions and the general effect is likely to be of an increase in awareness, by the Board, of the limitations upon its freedom to act. The new s35(2) expressly confirms the power of members of the company to bring proceedings to restrain ultra vires acts that have not already taken place or which are not in fulfilment of a prior legal obligation of the company.

An individual director who acts without the authority of the Board is, undoubtedly, placing himself in a much more vulnerable position than was formerly the case. Given that an act, by him alone, would not fall within the deeming provision of s35A(1), so as to bind the company, he would be likely to have to fall back upon the vagaries of the common law such as in *Turquand* and ostensible agency and might find himself facing the alternative possibilities of an action for breach of director's duty for causing loss to his company or an action by the third party for breach of warranty of authority as an agent. He would do well to act only with the blessing of the Board and obtain the protections afforded by s35.

Third parties dealing with the company are clearly in a better position than formerly. Much of the former constructive notice that was deemed to affect third parties has been swept away by ss35B and 711A as inserted by CA 1989, and the only question really remaining is whether the third party is affected by any matter where he has failed to make reasonable inquiry: s711A(2).

It is very clear that the general effect of the new sections is to 'internalise' the question of ultra vires acts as being a matter to be dealt with within the company itself. As regards third parties, the effect is to largely confirm the *Turquand* rule by statute but at the same time to remove the problem of any lack of vires as affecting the validity of transactions.

In summary, it may be said that whilst the ultra vires and *Turquand* doctrines have not been completely eliminated, their treatment, by CA 1989, has substantially clarified and improved the position for all parties and for English company law.

QUESTION TWO

'English company law has become more and more out of touch with business and its needs ... and has lost sight of the commercial values and priorities which it ought to recognise and serve ... The challenge for us now is to find some way forward which ensures that the law does respond to business needs and moves in sympathy with commercial trends.'

Discuss. What should be the 'way forward' for company law?

University of London LLB Examination
(for External Students) Company Law June 1996 Q2

General Comment

This question offers a wide range of possible themes to the well-read student. The premise is clearly that English company law is too inflexible to meet 'business needs' and 'commercial trends'. An answer can be framed according to the candidates view of social legal and economic functions of company law, as it stands, and of the merits or disadvantages of deregulation. The suggested solution below is based upon the view that the corporate form has always been seen, and will continue to be seen, by the unscrupulous as a convenient vehicle for fraud, tax evasion and dishonesty of all types in the absence of close regulations of companies, directors and members. Answers favouring the views expressed in the quotation would be equally acceptable if supported by good argument.

Skeleton Solution

Origins of modern Companies Acts, legislation seen as the answer to abuse of the corporate form – use and abuse of corporate form as a legal entity – strict view of English law of directors as fiduciaries – consequences for commerce and business of further deregulation – attempts to ease the regulatory burden – conclusion, values and priorities can vary according to the standpoint of the observer.

Suggested Solution

Modern English company law is the result of a very long process in which the courts and Parliament have attempted to harness the beneficial, socially useful and responsible employment of the corporate form by entrepreneurial persons to the public good. The only reasons why the law should get involved in this area at all are to resolve disputes where there is uncertainty and to prevent abuses by unscrupulous and dishonest persons. Anyone reading through the evidence given to Mr Gladstone's Select Committee on Joint Stock Companies (1843), out of which the modern Companies Acts were born, could not fail to understand that the companies of that relatively unregulated period were a byword for fraud and dishonesty. No doubt there were companies which exercised probity but these appear to have been few and far between. The possibility of any further useful development of the corporate form (other than as an engine of fraud) was, in the absence of strict regulation, nil. The urge to make a quick profit by the many was too strong for the honest few. This, of itself, shows that 'commercial values and priorities' can be looked at from very different perspectives.

One of the early problems for the law (and one upon which the quotation is premised) is that regulation stifles the spirit and frustrates the intentions of the entrepreneur. This question of regulation without stultification came squarely to the fore in the well known case of *Salomon* v *Salomon* (1897), where the question for the House of Lords boiled down to one of whether a man of business could, within the law, adopt the corporate form for his own already established business, see that business fail disastrously within a short time and still walk clear from the wreckage, relatively untouched, the loss having fallen on the corporate creditors. The answer was that he could, the creditors having dealt with the incorporated entity. The point being that the regulating and frustrating aspects of the law were more than outweighed by the privilege of the limitation of the corporation or members' liability. No doubt, if the 'way onward' for English company law involved some loss of protection from personal liability there would be even louder complaints that the law has 'lost sight of commercial values'. One cannot have one's cake and eat it as well.

The courts have long recognised the dangers of legislative stifling of the competitive and acquisitive urges that contribute so much to the success of all types of companies upon which the economic health of the nation depends. The maximum degree of flexibility is given to the courts by the simple stratagem of allowing discretionary principles of equity to have an important role in company matters. Such diverse matters as the treatment of directors as fiduciaries to their company as in *Industrial Development Consultants* v *Cooley* (1972); the application of equitable principles to the control and ownership of closely-held companies as in *Ebrahimi* v *Westbourne Galleries Ltd* (1973); the unfair prejudice remedy provided by s459 CA 1985; the 'proper purposes' doctrine for the exercise of director powers as in *Parke* v *Daily News Ltd* (1962) or as in *Howard Smith Ltd* v *Ampol Petroleum Ltd* (1974) and innumerable other situations illustrate that the courts are very aware that only the flexibility of equitable principles will cover the enormous variety of shapes, sizes and types into which registered companies fall. Short of having a very large number of different legislative and common law frameworks for the widely varying company types, involving enormous problems of demarcation, the present combination of common law, legislation and equity seems to be the best compromise between unlimited freedom to run a company by whoever controls it and complete regulation by the state.

The short term consequences for commercial and business interests of further deregulation may appear to be highly attractive. The opportunity to make a quick 'killing' and to get clear leaving

leaving a disastrous situation to someone else to clear up has very different consequences in the long term. In a very short time, indeed, highly deregulated companies would find that the supply of persons willing to deal with them and extend credit to them would rapidly shrink. Distrust and uncertainty would bring the trade of such organisations to a halt and capital availability, whether by share or under debenture, would dry up.

This is not to say that there have not been attempts to ease the burden of regulation. The Companies Act 1989 introduced the so-called elective regime for private companies which allows the company, on receipt of elections by all members entitled to vote at a general meeting, to agree to a written resolution and to act without a meeting being held at all: s381A(1) CA 1985 as inserted by s113(1) CA 1989. This resolution may be used to by-pass fundamental requirements of CA 1985 such as extending the statutory period for dealing with unissued shares or dispensing with annual accounts, direction and auditors reports etc being presented to the AGM, dispensing with the AGM and adjusting the requisite voting rights necessary for majority control. This regime may prove to be of very considerable importance in the development of the private company as distinct from public companies and could influence group development plans but it has considerable potential for abuse. Time alone will show whether this potential is realised.

In conclusion, it is submitted that the dangers and problems identified by Mr Gladstone's Select Committee in 1843 have not disappeared altogether. Even with close regulation, company fraud and director wrongdoing has been at very high levels in recent time. The dangers in further deregulating are obvious and the 'commercial values and priorities' which company law 'ought to recognise and serve' should be seen in their true perspective. It all depends upon who holds the value or the priority.

QUESTION THREE

'In permitting the creation of fixed charges over shifting assets the law has taken an unfair step, for such charges combine all the advantages of a floating charge but with none of the usual disadvantage.'

Discuss.

University of London LLB Examination
(for External Students) Company Law June 1996 Q3

General Comment

This question calls for some discussion of the nature of fixed and floating charges and the general question of priorities as between such charges and also against other creditors. An overview of the case law is required and the standpoints of the different parties to such a question must be considered in order to assess the validity of the proposition.

Skeleton Solution

The nature of fixed charges – case law development of the concept of fixed charges – the nature of floating charges – perceived advantages of the different types of charge – priorities – effects of the case law developments – conclusion.

Suggested Solution

The question of just what distinguishes a fixed charge over company assets from a floating charge is one that has come before the courts on many occasions. In plain cases there is no problem but the borderline between the two types of charge can be very difficult to ascertain when the subject matter of the charge is debts owed to the company. The traditional view of the nature of a fixed charge is that the property that is charged is identifiable at the time that the charge is created and that it remains identifiable throughout the duration of the charge. It does not signify at all if the company has yet to acquire the property or even if it is yet to come into existence at the date of charge, provided that once it is acquired or created, it is readily identifiable in the company's hands. In *Illingworth* v *Houldsworth* (1904) the Yorkshire Woolcombers case, this view expressed by Vaughan Williams LJ in the Court of Appeal was approved by the House of Lords and has not been seriously disputed since.

The fact that the property must be identifiable does not mean that its precise form or scale should remain frozen as at the date of charge. A building that is charged may be improved or extended, a block of shares may gain or lose rights by dilution or otherwise. A quarry or mine may become worked out and exhausted. Because of this acknowledged and accepted feature of fixed or specific charges, the courts have not found too much difficulty in accepting that in certain circumstances, a charge created over the book debts of a company, is capable of being seen as a specific charge. The book debts are readily identifiable and distinguishable from other company assets both at the date of charge and subsequently. The chargee is obviously willing to accept the risk that the value of these debts will fluctuate as they are discharged by the debtors of the company. It is this fluctuating quality that has created a certain amount of case law and which is at the root of the question's proposition.

The peculiar problem attaching to book debts is that, in the usual situation, as the debt is discharged the money received is dealt with by the company in its normal course of business without restriction or inhibition as to its use. This obviously creates a problem, as will be seen when the nature of floating charges is discussed below, as this freedom to use the asset is something of a distinctive mark of a floating charge. The problem evaporates completely when it is realised that the debt ceases to exist both as a debt and as a subject of the charge the minute that it is paid off. If the charge is on book debts simpliciter, it cannot bite upon the receipts of a discharged debt. This is the explanation of the decision in *Siebe Gorman & Co Ltd* v *Barclays Bank Ltd* (1979) where there was a charge order over the book debts accompanied by an undertaking by the chargor company to pay the receipts into a bank account controlled only by the chargee. The book debts were always identifiable and the receipts never fell into the hands of the company to deal with in the normal course of their business. This case must now be viewed in the light of the more recent Court of Appeal decision in *Re New Bullas Trading Ltd* (1994) which is discussed below.

The nature of the floating charge is quite different to the fixed charge in that it can never be a legal charge but takes effect in equity by reason that it is intended to 'hover above' assets which are essentially changeable and ambulatory in form and with which, during the duration of the floating charge, the company is completely free to deal in the normal course of its business. The charge is brought to its consummation by some circumstance or act which causes the charge to 'crystallise' or fix upon the assets as they exist at the date of the crystallising event and the charge assumes the characteristics and effect of a fixed charge at that time. The events precipitating crystallisation are any of the matters so specified in the instrument which creates the charge, appointment by the court or the chargee of a received, commencement of winding up or ceasing to function as a going concern. The leading case on this type of charge is *Illingworth* v *Houldsworth* mentioned above.

There are considerable perceived advantages to both types of charge and the question of which is adopted often is as much a feature of the bargaining powers of the parties as of the nature of the charged asset. The floating charge has the flexibility such that it can attach to the whole of a company's undertaking and assets regardless of the form or nature of the particular asset. The real crux of the problem is the question of the priorities as between the different types of charge. Although the whole question of priorities is complex, there is a basic principle that a properly-created fixed charge will take priority over a floating charge hovering over the same assets: *Wheatley* v *Silkstone & Haigh Moor Coal Co* (1885). This is subject to the caveat that the fixed charge was not created later than a crystallising event having transferred the floating charge into a prior fixed charge and also that the fixed charge was not created in breach of a prohibition upon the creation of later superior or equal ranking charges contained in the floating charge instrument. If such a prohibition exists, a later chargee with notice of the prohibition will lose precedence even if he holds a fixed charge: *English and Scottish Mercantile Investment Co* v *Brunton* (1892).

Re New Bullas Trading Ltd is the case that has, arguably, provided the basis for the question's proposition. The problem that was raised in that case was that book debts, subject to a company charge, were paid into a particular designated account as in *Siebe Gorman* v *Barclays*, but the account was, itself, within the scope of a floating charge. The question for the court was whether the receipts from the debts, pending payment into the specified account, were subject to the fixed charge or not. The Court of Appeal held that the question must be decided in accordance with the intentions of the parties to the fixed charge. The intention, in this case, was a fixed charge over the debts and over the receipts representing the debts after discharge up until the transfer into the designated account. Consequently, the company was not free to deal with those moneys up until that time, except as required by the fixed charge.

The reality of this is of course, that there is no question of 'creation of a fixed charge over shifting assets'. The chargor company knew, or ought to have known, that all book debts would be completely unavailable for its use or dealing until, at the earliest, the payment into the designated account. A book debt cannot 'shift'. It is a fixed liability between the company and its debtor and is as certain and identifiable as a building or a piece of equipment. The fact that book debts tend to be discharged and fresh ones arise does nothing to alter the fixed nature of individual debts. Note that the charge is upon the plural 'debts', not upon the singular and collective norm 'debt'. In conclusion, it is submitted that the question's proposition is misconceived and based upon a mistaken notion of the concept of 'shifting assets'.

QUESTION FOUR

Wheels Ltd was formed five years ago to provide lorry transport facilities to the computer industry. It has an issued share capital of £500 divided into 300 'A' shares of £1 each and 400 'B' shares of 50 pence each. Alf, Bob, and Colin are the directors of the company. Alf and Bob each hold half the 'A' shares and Colin holds all the 'B' shares. The articles of association of the company provide that:

i)   The 'A' shares carry two votes each and the 'B' shares carry one vote each.

ii)   Colin is to be a director of the company at a salary of £20,000 per year.

Until 1993 the three directors worked well together and the company prospered. However, at a board meeting in August of that year, Alf and Bob disagreed with Colin over a fundamental matter of business policy and the meeting ended abruptly when Colin hit Alf. Colin was later fined £50 for assault by local magistrates. Since then Alf and Bob have continued to run the company but the business policy pursued after the meeting in August 1993 has clearly proved unsuccessful and, although the company is still solvent, it has made no profits since then. Colin continued to received his salary after the August meeting but has attended no board meetings since then, even though Alf and Bob have periodically invited him to do so.

Three months ago Alf and Bob stopped payment of Colin's salary. Colin is now saying that he will attend the next board meeting as he intends to 'make one last effort to lick the company into shape.' Alf and Bob do not want him back and want to run the company without him.

Advise Alf and Bob, and Colin.

University of London LLB Examination
(for External Students) Company Law June 1996 Q4

General Comment

The question calls for examination of the principles governing the 'closely-held' company and the exclusion of members from participation in such companies. Some discussion of the enforceability of rights provided by the articles of association is needed and a general appreciation of the law on minority protection is necessary. A range of remedies is available and, within time constraints, should be dealt with.

Skeleton Solution

The nature of the company: closely held companies – quasi-partnership – unfair prejudice, the principle of majority control and s459 CA 1985 – provision (ii) of the articles, s14 CA 1985 – remedies open to Alf and Bob – remedies open to Colin.

Suggested Solution

Wheels Ltd is a private company of the 'closely-held' or 'quasi partnership' variety and this point must be considered in advising the parties here. The essence of this type of company is that it is usually formed by and controlled by a small number of persons acting as the directors of the company. The aim usually is for a far greater involvement by the participators than mere investment. The leading case on this type of company and situation is *Ebrahimi v Westbourne Galleries Ltd* (1973) where Lord Wilberforce made the point that the fact of a company being small and private is not, by itself, enough to justify applying equitable principles to the normal questions of company majority control and management. There is also a need to illustrate that other features are present such as evidence that the company was formed or continues to rest upon the basis of personal and mutual trust, indications of agreements that members have and should continue to have participation in management and, usually, some restrictions upon the member withdrawing his membership and capital by transferring it.

If these factors, or some of them, are present the approach of the courts to disagreements between the members goes quite a long way towards recognising a relationship analogous to a fiduciary one between the parties. If the problem cannot be resolved in any other way the court may order a winding up of the company on the 'just and equitable' ground in s122(1)(g) IA 1986 as happened in *Ebrahimi* itself (under the equivalent statutory provision at that time). This is similar to the old quasi-partnership agreement used to justify winding-up in the old but well known case of *Re Yenidje Tobacco Co Ltd* (1916).

The modern remedy which has been most frequently applied to situations such as this is provided by s459 CA 1985 (as amended by CA 1989), which is designed to offer a range of solutions to situations where it is alleged that the affairs of the company are being conducted in a manner which is unfairly prejudicial to the interests of all or part of the membership which includes the petitioner. The nature of the remedy offered here is essentially equitable because, in many situations considered under the section, the petitioner is being subjected to majority control which is the general principle underlying English company law. The idea under lying this section is that, so far as possible, the company should not be wound up but the successful petitioner should achieve redress from his prejudiced situation. The jurisdiction to grant relief under this section is amazingly wide but the one area that seems to be clearly outside of the remedy is the situation where the court is expected to consider questions of the business or management policies of the company: *Re Macro (Ipswich) Ltd* (1994). This is, of course, entirely consistent with the court's approach in supporting the majority rule and delegated director powers principles. This is subject to the caveat, in all cases, that directors should make decisions bona fide in the interests of the company as a whole, ie the corporators as a body. This can be seen in cases on alterations to the company constitution as in *Greenhalgh* v *Aderne Cinemas Ltd* (1951) or in situations affecting the reduction or dilution of controlling interests as in *Howard Smith Ltd* v *Ampol Petroleum Ltd* (1974) and innumerable other cases.

A point that should be considered is whether the provision in the articles concerning Colin's directorship can be enforced in any way by reliance upon the statutorily implied contract, provided by s14 CA 1985, between the company and its members inter se, on the basis of the memorandum and articles. The short answer is that it does not. This section can only assist the member in his capacity qua member and not in respect of rights given in any other capacity such as director or secretary etc: *Hickman* v *Kent or Romney Marsh Sheepbreeders' Association* (1915).

The remedy that Alf and Bob really are seeking is that of excluding Colin from control and management of the company. Colin is a director and a holder of 40 per cent of the voting rights. Procedurally, s303 CA 1985 allows the company by ordinary resolution to remove a director notwithstanding anything in the articles. Alf and Bob can achieve the ordinary resolution, the question is whether Colin could rely upon the *Ebrahimi* principle, or s459 to prevent this. This is, in truth a position of irretrievable breakdown between Colin and the other pair and Colin refuses to attend Board meetings to resolve the matter. The cases seem to show that it is not unfairly prejudicial for the majority shareholding directors in a quasi-partnership to openly arrange a general meeting and vote for dismissal: *Re a Company* (1987); and to invoke provisions in the articles allowing the majority to buy out the minority at a fair price. We do not know whether it is easy or difficult for Colin to get clear of the company with his capital reasonably intact. Much would depend upon this and the one thing that Alf and Bob could not do is to force him to sell his shares at an unfair price, the principles being well explained in *Re Bird Precision Bellows Ltd* (1984).

Colin would not be able to use s459 to interfere with the policies pursued by Alf and Bob as the Court will not look into such matters. The question of a winding up under *Ebrahimi* and s122(1)(g) IA 1986 looks very unlikely as there appears to have been no disagreements at all other than over business policy and no deception or fraud has been practiced by Alf or Bob. As Colin is still a director until such time as the other pair resolve to dismiss him under s303, he is entitled to his contractual remuneration and to attend Board meetings if he so wishes. He would not necessarily be in breach of his duties if he did not attend as his duty is owed to the company itself and it is only a duty to act honestly, with reasonable care having regard to knowledge and experience, for the benefit of the company: *Re Brazilian Rubber Plantations and Estates Ltd* (1911). The company will be in breach if he is not paid or notified of meetings.

If Bob and Alf decide to remove Colin as a director, they will need to alter the articles of association. Section 303 will override the effect of the existing article and although a special resolution is required under s9 CA 1985 to alter the articles, the court will have the power on a s459 petition (which would almost certainly occur) to authorise alterations to the company's memorandum or articles: s461(4) CA 1985.

QUESTION FIVE

Ace plc, which is engaged in manufacturing washing machines, has an issued share capital of one million £1 shares and is listed on the Stock Exchange. At 10.00 am on 11 March 1996 the directors of the company received a report that most of the machines recently supplied by the company would need to be replaced free of charge because of the presence of a dangerous electrical fault caused by faulty manufacture.

At 12.00 noon that day, Bob, one of the directors, telephoned his brother Colin and said, simply, 'Get out of washing machines'. At 12.30 pm Colin sold all his 10,000 shares in Ace plc, on the Stock Exchange, at a price of £8 each.

At 2.15pm Daisy, one of the waitresses in the directors' dining room overheard the directors discussing the morning's bad news. At 2.30 pm she sold all her 200 shares in Ace plc, on the Stock Exchange, at £7 each.

At 3.00 pm Eric, one of the directors, sold half his holding of 2,000 shares in Ace plc, on the Stock Exchange, at £6 each, intending to use the money to pay for his daughter's wedding which was due to take place on the following Saturday.

On 12 March 1996 the Financial Times newspaper published an article revealing the problems with Ace plc's washing machines and the share price quickly fell to £5 per share.

Discuss.

University of London LLB Examination
(for External Students) Company Law June 1996 Q5

General Comment

The question requires an overview of the law on insider dealing in shares and in particular, the defences available to various types of person who come into possession of the type of unpublished price sensitive information which is the basis of the liability. The precise nature of the information received and the capacity in which it is received, as well as the state of the recipient's knowledge as to the status of the information must be considered.

Skeleton Solution

Insider dealing: the nature and scope of the prohibition – status of the report indicating faults – Bob's situation: defences available to one who 'encourages' insider dealing – Colin's situation: is he an 'insider'? – Daisy's position: is she an 'insider'? – Eric's position: the time of his sale; has the information become public knowledge by this time?

Suggested Solution

The situation here clearly points towards the possibilities of 'insider dealing' having taken place. This occurs when an individual who is in possession of unpublished price sensitive information which relates to particular securities, or the issuer of those securities, either deals in those securities on a regulated market such as the Stock Exchange or encourages another person to do so or simply discloses the information to another. This has proved a difficult question for the law to deal with as the prevailing view of the English courts has been that it will not interfere to set aside agreements to deal in shares between insiders and non-insiders (*Percival* v *Wright* (1902)), although where there is some fiduciary aspects to the dealing, as in *Allen* v *Hyatt* (1914), the court is able to impose a duty to account based upon the law of trusts.

The solution eventually arrived at, after some particularly disgraceful examples of such dealing in modern times, was to attempt to protect the integrity of market dealing by creating criminal liabilities for certain types of insider dealing. The legislation has proved very difficult to get right and is currently contained within Part V Criminal Justice Act (CJA) 1993, replacing the Company Securities (Insider Dealing) Act 1985. This is supported by the Insider Dealing (Securities and Regulated Markets) Order 1994. All statutory references are to CJA 1993.

The first point to consider is whether the report that the directors received at 10.00 am was, itself, the sort of information sufficiently unpublished to ground liability upon. If there were any question that the report contained information which could be derived from information already in the public domain, eg previous press or TV publicity about the faults, the report would be viewed as already having been 'made public' so far as the price sensitive information is concerned: s58(2)(d) CJA 1993. It is assumed for the purposes of this question that the information is not public.

Bob has clearly decided to attempt to prevent his brother making a loss – his words indicate knowledge that Colin has some holdings in 'washing machines'. Bob is likely to be caught by s52(2)(a) for encouraging another person to deal in the price-affected securities, having reasonable cause to believe that Colin would deal on a regulated market in the shares. Bob will have great difficulty in providing a defence to this charge and the only one that seems available might be contained in s53(1)(a), that he believed on reasonable grounds that the information had been disclosed widely enough to prevent prejudice to others dealing with Colin. This seems an unlikely prospect in view of the short period of time, two hours, between receipt and disclosure of the information.

Colin is what is sometimes referred to as a 'tippee'. The question of whether he is likely to be treated as an insider is dealt with in s57. Colin will be taken to have his information as an insider if and only if he knows that it is inside information and he also knows that it came from an insider (s57(1)) having received it directly or indirectly from a director, employee or shareholder in the company issuing the price-sensitive shares (s57(2)(b)). This is purely a question of fact and there seem to be strong possibilities for him to argue that, because of the non-specific nature of the advice, he did not realise that he had inside information relating specifically to Ace plc shares. Of course, if Colin only held Ace shares in washing machines and both brothers were aware of this, this would carry a very strong implication of knowledge of the inside nature of the information. The question of the specific nature of advice is dealt with by s56(1)(b).

Daisy's position is that, like Colin, she has received information from a director, albeit indirectly by overhearing it. It would be very difficult to hold the directors liable for encouragement on disclosure in this circumstance. Daisy would need to show that she did not have the information as an insider within the meaning of s57. It does sound, from the speed with which she sold her shares (all of them within 15 minutes) that she fully understood that the information was likely to be price-sensitive. This seems to carry the implication that she knew that it was inside, rather than public information. Apart from this possibility, she does not seem to be able to meet any of the defences within s53.

Eric's position is that he has delayed in dealing in the shares for five hours, during three of which the price has been falling. Although Eric will clearly be an insider, the information has fast been moving into the public domain. Any information which has been 'made public' is not insider information: s56(1)(c). Section 58(2) defines some circumstances in which information is made public and, s58(2)(d) fits Eric's circumstances, which establishes that information derived from information that the public already know about, is taken to be made public. This will still be the case even though the information can be acquired only by observation and deduction therefrom: s58(3)(c). The movements of the Ace plc shares were public knowledge and it seems that Eric may just have timed his sale to coincide with the time at which some problems with the company had become sufficiently notorious to remove the 'inside' quality from the information. He may well have expected that the dealing had almost reached the stage at which the price had settled so that no profit could have been taken by reason only of the inside information, giving him a defence within s53(1)(a).

The detailed publication in the *Financial Times*, although causing a fall of £1 was, almost certainly, dealing with a matter which had already been made public within the meaning of s58.

The common law principle supporting the validity of transactions made on the basis of inside information is preserved by s63(2) which prevents the dealings being avoided. The penalties on conviction, if summary trial, are for alternative of maximum £2,000 fine or six months' prison or, on indictment, unlimited fines or up to seven years in prison, or both.

QUESTION SIX

Blue plc is a major conglomerate which has several wholly owned subsidiaries. One of these subsidiary companies is Sky Ltd. Sky Ltd specialises in the lending of money. Blue plc wished to further expand its operation and were in negotiations with Red plc to merge some of their operations. As part of this reconstruction, Red plc were proposing to acquire a substantial number of shares in Blue plc but due to an unexpected delay in obtaining finance from their bank, Red plc proposed delaying the purchase of the shares until July 1996. Blue plc were unhappy about the delay because the share price of Blue plc was falling and this was having an adverse affect on the financing of several other takeovers which were based on Blue plc's share price. The board of directors ('the board') of Blue plc proposed that they should give Red plc some help to purchase the share immediately. The Board procured a loan from Sky Ltd arguing that the loan 'was in good faith in the interests of Sky Ltd.' The directors of Sky Ltd were concerned about their future employment and felt unable to refuse making the substantial loan, despite the fact that the loan breached their normal rules of business on lending.

Advise the directors of Sky Ltd.

University of London LLB Examination
(for External Students) Company Law June 1996 Q6

General Comment

The question has two aspects which must both be addressed. The first aspect is the question of the extent to which a company can assist in the purchase of its own share capital and how this fits in with the notion of holding companies and wholly owned subsidiaries. The second aspect concerns the limits for the purposes for which directors can exercise their powers and the relationship with their fiduciary duties towards the company.

Skeleton Solution

The maintenance of capital principle, rationale, scope and mechanisms – the emotional circumstances where assistance is allowed – the position of Sky Ltd – the position of Sky Ltd directors in agreeing to the loan – consequences and sanction

Suggested Solution

The problem that is posed for Blue plc and Sky Ltd here is that the proposed actions may be seen as offending against the long-established company law principle that the share capital base of a company must be jealously guarded and maintained for the protection of creditors and all persons dealing with the company, and any reduction of that capital must be carried out in accordance with the Companies Acts. The current provisions can be found in Part V ss151–158 Companies Act 1985 and the relevant provisions are ss151–158, which deal with companies providing financial assistance for the purchase of their own shares or the shares of a company's holding company to another person. The general rule is that such transactions are unlawful: s151(1). This is, however, subject to numerous exceptions that are set out in s153 and a special regime is given in s155 for private companies who provide assistance. Section 155 recognises the more relaxed approach that can be taken for private companies and those with private holding companies in situations where it is clear that net assets are not reduced by the financial assistance or the assistance is provided out of distributable profits.

The question is, therefore, whether Sky Ltd can be seen to fall within any of the excepted circumstances. Section 155 cannot help here because, although Sky Ltd seems to fall within the section, it has no application at all where the assistance is provided for purchasing shares in a public holding company or where, in a chain of holding companies, there is one which is public: s155(1) and (3). Another possibility is seen in s153(1) which exempts the situation where the providing company's principal purpose in assisting is not the giving of the assistance but is 'an incidental part of some larger purpose of the company' and the assistance is given in good faith in the interests of the company: s153(1)(a) and (b). The problem for Sky Ltd's directors is that they will have some difficulty in showing such a larger purpose (it is Blue plc which has a 'larger purpose') and their concern is not bona fide in the interests of the company but is really about their own future employment prospects as they cannot hold shares in what is a wholly owned subsidiary company.

The question becomes one of whether the Sky Ltd directors can properly take the view that as Blue plc really own Sky Ltd, does Blue plc's 'larger purpose' constitute a larger purpose of Sky Ltd? In other words, can a company have a 'purpose' which is not that of its shareholders? It is submitted that it cannot, and that the larger purpose of Blue plc in expansion of the group as a whole is also the larger purpose of Sky Ltd. The problem with this provision is that the cases decided on the point, *Brady* v *Brady* (1989) and *Plant* v *Steiner* (1988) show a strict construction given to 'purpose' and difficult distinctions are drawn between the reasons why assistance may be given and the purpose of giving the assistance. In this situation the reasons are those of expansion and reconstruction of the group. On a strict construction of 'purpose', the purpose is purely to assist in purchasing shares, a prohibited matter. *Plant* v

Steiner shows the pitfalls particularly well and there could be real difficulty in persuading the court of a larger purpose of Sky Ltd.

Another possible exception can be seen in s153(4)(a) where the 'lending of money is part of the ordinary business of the company, the lending of money by the company in the ordinary course of its business' is not prohibited. The problem here is whether the breaching of Sky Ltd's normal rules of business is enough to take the loan outside 'the ordinary course of its business'. This is probably more a question of fact than of law. If the breach was of a fairly minor procedural rule, the exception might be available but if the breach is more serious the subsection will not protect Sky Ltd. As Sky Ltd is obviously an English company there is no assistance to be gained from the recent first instance decision in *Arab Bank plc v Mercantile Holdings Ltd and Another* (1993) which held that the prohibition does not apply to foreign subsidiaries of English holding companies .

The position for the directors of Sky Ltd is clearly very difficult. If they decide that they might rely upon the 'larger purpose' argument in s151(1)(a), the point may be raised as to whether they were acting 'in good faith in the interests of the company'. It does seem that in many respects, the 'company', if viewed as being really Blue plc, has an interest in making the loan. The directors, in going along with this, are incidentally observing their own best personal interests but provided that there is no conflict of these interests, the directors will not breach their fiduciary duties towards Sky Ltd. The vice for any director is to put himself in the position where his interests and the company's may conflict, as in *Industrial Development Consultants v Cooley* (1972).

If the directors put their faith in s153(4)(a), the lending of money in the ordinary course of business, they will have to be able to explain to the court why the breach of rules does not take the matter outside the ordinary course of business. If it did so, they might be in the unenviable position of being in breach of the prohibition in s151 and also in breach of their fiduciary duty towards Sky Ltd itself for which they could be required to account. This would involve an investigation as to the extent of the directors' powers, as given by the memorandum and articles of association, to disregard lending rules.

The directors of Sky Ltd should be made aware that any company acting in contravention of s151 is liable to a fine and every officer of it is liable to imprisonment or fine or both: s151(3). The consequence of all this is that Sky Ltd's directors should begin to question themselves as to how closely they investigated the claim by the Blue plc board of directors to be speaking in the name of the members of Sky Ltd. If they failed to address this point, the matter may come back to given them difficulties in the future. One course of action that might help the directors is to show their bona fides in respect of s153(1) and to protect them from charges of breach of fiduciary duty towards Sky Ltd by calling an EGM of Sky Ltd and seeking ratification of their acts by ordinary resolution as in *Bamford v Bamford* (1970) or, if the breach of rules was an ultra vires act, by special resolution along with a separate special resolution relieving the directors from liability under s35(3) Companies Act 1985 as substituted by s108 Companies Act 1989.

QUESTION SEVEN

The issued share capital of Moon Ltd, which was incorporated in 1992, consists of 100,000 £1 ordinary shares and 15,000 £1 'A' preference shares and 15,000 £1 'B' deferred shares. Holdings of the shares are spread out unevenly between 20 different people, including the three directors.

Company Law

The memorandum of association of Moon Ltd provides, inter alia, that:

1) The 'A' preference shares shall carry such rights as may be specified in the articles of association.

2) The 'B' deferred shares shall carry no rights to vote, save in class meetings, but shall carry unalterable rights to an annual 16 per cent deferred dividend payable only after the ordinary shares have received an initial annual dividend of 10 per cent and further, to participate rateably in any dividends paid to the ordinary shareholders after their initial 10 per cent.

The articles of association provide, inter alia, that:

i) The 'A' preference shares shall carry rights to an annual 13 per cent preference dividend but shall carry no rights to vote, save in class meetings.

ii) Repayment of shares in a reduction of capital shall be deemed to be a variation of the rights attached to those shares.

iii) All provisions in the company's memorandum and articles may be altered by special resolution without the need for any further procedures of any kind.

The directors of the company are proposing to make the following changes:

a) To reduce the share capital of the company by paying off the 'A' preference shares at par in a reduction of capital.

b) To reduce the annual dividend of the 'B' deferred shares to 8 per cent.

Advise the directors, who wish to know whether their proposals can be carried out, and if so, how.

University of London LLB Examination
(for External Students) Company Law June 1996 Q7

General Comment

This question will require the student to consider the relationship between the protection and alteration of class rights, the company's constitution as set out in the memorandum and articles of association, and the provisions of Companies Act 1985. This will necessitate identification of the source of the rights attaching to the different classes of share and consideration of the correct procedures required to vary such a right.

Skeleton Solution

Identification of the different classes of share and analysis of the basis of the rights attaching to each class – consideration of the methods required to vary each class right – inconsistencies between the company's constitution and Companies Act 1985 – inconsistencies between the memorandum and the articles – alteration of the memorandum itself.

Suggested Solution

The directors of Moon Ltd, themselves shareholders (although we do not know of which class of share), wish to get rid of the 'A' preference share class altogether and to alter the contractual rights attaching to the 'B' deferred shares. It is important to examine where the rights attaching to the shares originate because the procedure for varying such rights depends

170

upon their origins. The 'A' shares are given their rights by the clear direction of the memorandum that they are to have such rights as are specified in the articles. This must mean that the source of the 'A' class rights will be taken to be the articles rather than the memorandum. The 'B' class shares, on the other hand, are very clearly given their rights by the memorandum itself.

The directors will undoubtedly meet resistance from the 'A' preference holders, particularly as article (ii) deems this to be a variation of the share rights. Although there is a good deal of case law to the effect that the cancellation of a class of preference shares in this way is not prima facie treated as a variation of class rights (*Prudential Assurance Co Ltd* v *Chatterley-Whitfield Collieries Ltd* (1949)), this principle has to give way to express provision in the articles that it will amount to a deemed variation, as in *Re Northern Engineering Industries plc* (1994). This is supported by the effect of s125(8) that references to variation include references to abrogation.

The directors may consider that their difficulties here can be eased by the use of article (iii) to alter article (ii) by special resolution. We do not know whether they can control the voting to this extent but, assuming that they can, this would seem to allow for changes to prevent this being a deemed variation of rights. It is normally permissible, where the memorandum provides a method of altering class rights or where it states that alterations can be made by methods set out in the articles for changes to be made in the prescribed way: *Re Welsbach Incandescent Gas Light Co Ltd* (1904). In Moon Ltd's case, however, there is apparently no reference in the memorandum to methods for altering class rights and, in any case, the *Welsbach* principle has no application to situations of alterations involving reduction of share capital.

In this situation there is a mandatory requirement in s125(3)(c) Companies Act (CA) 1985 that where the memorandum or articles contain provision for varying class rights and the variation is connected with, inter alia, reduction of share capital, the rights are not to be varied without the written consent of holders of three-quarters of the nominal value of the 'A' class or the sanction by the extraordinary resolution of a separate general meeting of the 'A' class. This will clearly override the apparent effect of article (iii) and the directors must obtain such agreement or they will be open to an application to the court by the 'A' shareholders to prevent the reduction. There will still be a need for the special resolution of the company in general meeting: s125(3)(c)(ii).

The 'B' deferred class is in a different position because its rights are found in the memorandum and are expressed to be 'unalterable'. These rights are effectively entrenched because a company may not alter the conditions contained in its memorandum except in the situations expressly provided for by s2(7) CA 1985. This renders the inconsistent article (iii) ineffective as there is a broad general rule that in the event of an inconsistency between the memorandum and the articles, the articles will be read as subject to the memorandum (*Re Gilmour (Duncan) & Co Ltd* (1952)), and this point is expressly provided for, in the context of alteration of class rights, by s17(2)(b) CA 1985.

The correct procedure for this situation is set out in s125(5) CA 1985 which provides that where rights are attached to a class and the memorandum or articles do not contain provisions to vary the rights, those rights may be varied with the agreement of all the members of the company. The ineffective article (iii) will not cause the situation to fall outside s125(5). This is, of course, subject to the possibility that the memorandum contains, elsewhere, a provision that all class rights are subject to variation in accordance with the articles, which would have the effect of incorporating article (iii) into the memorandum by reference and would create a real inconsistency within the memorandum between the entrenching provision of 'unalterable rights' and the article (iii). This would probably need the intervention of the court to construe the matter.

The directors might feel that they could short-circuit the whole process by simply altering the wording of clauses (1) and (2) in the memorandum itself. There may be in the memorandum an identical clause to article (iii). If this were the case, this would alter the situation drastically but, without such a clause, any amendment to the wording will need the same consents as are required for the variation of class rights themselves. In this situation, the consent of all the members of the company would be required. This will, of course, include all shareholders of whatever class, whether voting or non-voting.

QUESTION EIGHT

Jill and Ben are directors of Safety Belts Ltd, a successful company which specialises in installing safety belts in buses. Wishing to raise additional finance for expansion, they decided to convert it to a plc, and offer the shares to the public in the UK and throughout Europe.

They sought advice from Bankers, a leading merchant bank. Bankers agreed to underwrite the issue of shares and advised Jill and Ben that they should make an application for admission to the Alternative Investment Market rather than listing on the Stock Exchange. Bankers suggested that other market professionals might be willing to subscribe for all the shares that were to be issued and that Jill and Ben should also consider limiting the persons to whom the offer was addressed.

Jill and Ben cannot decide which course of action they should follow. They need to raise finance, but wish to avoid being subject to onerous regulations and wish to avoid potential liability and risks. They are particularly concerned about the preparation of documents as they are unaware of their duties and responsibilities for documents being issued to the public.

Advise Jill and Ben.

University of London LLB Examination
(for External Students) Company Law June 1996 Q8

General Comment

Jill and Ben's situation calls for an overview of the duties and obligations involved in the flotation and marketing of companies, and the various options open to controllers of companies who wish to broaden the share capital base of their company. This will involve some analysis of the balance of advantages and risks in each course of action.

Skeleton Solution

Stock Exchange official listing, listing particulars and liabilities – the Alternative Investment Market, perceived advantages as against full listing – the European context – consequences of not making an offer to the public – common law remedies.

Suggested Solution

Jill and Ben will need to be very careful in deciding about their future plans if they are desirous of avoiding potentially heavy obligations and liabilities, both in their personal capacities as well as in respect of their company, whatever form it takes. Their overwhelming need is to bring in fresh capital and they wish to do this by issue of shares rather than by loan. The matter is governed by the Financial Services Act (FSA) 1986 and the subordinate legislation thereunder. The first situation to consider is whether Bankers' advice of avoiding a full listing on the Stock Exchange is supportable. It is a fairly drastic step to go from what may possibly be quite a small company to becoming a public company with a full listing on the Stock Exchange.

The general rule is set out in s142 FSA 1986 that no investment can be admitted except in accordance with Part IV FSA 1986 which includes meeting the requirements of listing rules made under the 'competent authority', which is the UK International Stock Exchange. These listing rules are found in the Yellow Book and require, inter alia, that for a company to obtain a full listing that it should have a record of trading of at least three years duration, a market value of its listed shares of at least £700,000 and a minimum of 25 per cent of any class of its shares in the hands of persons other than institutional shareholders. The other very important requirement from Jill and Ben's standpoint is the necessity for submission, approval and publication of listing particulars, which is the equivalent requirement to the former Companies Act concept of a prospectus, setting out the details and intentions of the proposed issue: s144(2A) FSA 1986. There is a very considerable duty of disclosure concerning the assets, liabilities, financial position, profits and losses of the issuer of such securities (s147(1)(a)), as well as the rights attaching to those securities (s147(1)(b)) and a requirement to keep this information updated by supplementary particulars up to the time of commencement of dealing (s147). There is a statutory right to compensation in respect of persons who suffer loss as a result of untrue or misleading information in the listing particulars (s150(1)) and the right is against persons responsible for the particulars, which will include both the issuer, Safety Belts plc, and the directors at the time that the particulars are submitted. Jill and Ben are well advised to be wary of such a large step even if they are of such a size as to make it.

As to the suggestion concerning the Alternative Investment Market (AIM), this is the successor to the Unlisted Securities Market (USM). The rules on the USM were formerly contained in Part V FSA 1986 but this part was repealed by the Public Offers of Securities Regulations 1995, Part II of which deals with public offers of securities, which are not listed or the subject of a listing application. The general rule applicable to such securities is that there is a requirement for publication and availability, free of charge, of a prospectus containing much the same information as in listing particulars with similar provisions as to compensation and the scope of liability, including the duty of disclosure. There is, however, an added sting in the tail of possible imprisonment for up to two years for persons, other than members of recognised self-regulating investment organisations, who contravene certain regulations within the 1995 Regulations or who assist other persons to contravene the specified provisions. This means, of course, that Jill and Ben will need to be no less careful in respect of an application to the AIM than with a full listing, but there are not the requirements for the preconditions relating to trading record, market valuation or non-institutional shareholdings.

Jill and Ben might be well advised in considering Bankers' suggestion as to limiting the offers of shares to certain persons and the use of market professionals. The reason for this is that reg 7 of the 1995 Regulations sets out certain exempt situations which are deemed not to be offers to the public in the United Kingdom. Several of these are of significance here: reg 7(2)(a) covers offers to persons who acquire, hold or dispose of investments for the purpose of their investments; reg 7(2)(b) applies to offers to a maximum of 50 persons; reg 7(2)(d) applies to offers to restricted circles of persons reasonably believed by the offeror to be knowledgeable as to the risks involved; and reg 7(2)(c) covers bona fide underwriting deals.

It seems that Bankers are offering good advice here because a normal practice in such a situation is the use of 'placing', to place blocks of the issue with a small number of professional investors, which would bring the matter within more than one of the exempt circumstances in reg 7. A particular point that might be worth exploring is reg 7(2)(5), that the securities offered are Euro-securities, which are not the subject of advertising likely to come to the attention of persons who are not professionally experienced in investment. A Euro-security is defined in Sch 11A, para 3 FSA 1986 as an investment underwritten and distributed by a syndicate at least two of the members of which have their registered offices in different countries, or territories, such securities to be offered on a significant scale other than in the country of the issuer and can only be acquired through a credit or financial institution.

The consequences of Jill and Ben pursuing a course which fits within a reg 7 exemption is that all of the statutory liabilities imposed by the Regulations cease to apply. They will be treated as making private offers of securities which will be traded on the AIM as unlisted securities of a public company. This does not mean that they are without liability or risk in the matter. They will not have to face the prospectus and disclosure requirements imposed by the FSA 1986 and the 1995 Regulations, but they will, without doubt, have to provide a good deal of information to persuade the offerors of the shares to take up the offer. There are, however, a number of other common law and statutory remedies available against Jill and Ben and they must take care to consider these. The possibility of rescission of contracts and indemnity payments must be thought about as in *Lynde* v *Anglo-Italian Hemp Spinning Co* (1896), as well as damages for the tort of deceit along *Derry* v *Peek* (1889) lines. Non-fraudulent misrepresentations may be pursued under the Misrepresentation Act 1967 as well as simple negligent misstatements which do not amount to representations under *Hedley Byrne* reliance principles (*Hedley Byrne & Co* v *Heller and Partners* (1964)). In all or any of these circumstances, there exists the possibility of personal liability for Jill and Ben so they should be advised that they will be unable to avoid some element of liability and risk, whichever course they follow.

Methods of Research in Law

by Dr Charles Chatterjee

When conducting research in law, a thorough knowledge of the subject area is not enough. The research must also follow a method and apply techniques for analysing facts and data.

Methods of Research in Law is a guide to the techniques of carrying out research and developing ideas. The work deals with:

Ethics in Research
Certain Important Terms and Concepts
Tools of Research
Research Planning and Research Design
Sources of Information
Techniques of Interpretation of Documents
Layout of Thesis, Footnoting and Bibliography

It is an essential handbook for those students whose degrees demand an element of legal research, or those who are carrying out research for a postgraduate degree. Within the broad area of social sciences, there are a number of common elements of research which will also make this book of interest to those studying economics, business studies and international relations.

Professor Chatterjee has many years of experience in supervising postgraduate students in law, and as well as having completed a number of pieces of original research.

ISBN 1 85836 070 6
Published January 1997
Price £9.95
336 pages

To order your copy, please contact:

Claudine Pryce
Old Bailey Press
200 Greyhound Road
London
W14 9RY

Telephone No: 00 44 (0) 171 385 3377
Fax No: 00 44 (0) 171 381 3377
E-Mail Address: hlt@holborncollege.ac.uk

Law Update 1997

Law Update 1998 edition – due March 1998

An annual review of the most recent developments in specific legal subject areas, useful for law students at degree and professional levels, others with law elements in their courses and also practitioners seeking a quick update.

Published around March every year, the Law Update summarises the major legal developments during the course of the previous year. In conjunction with Old Bailey Press textbooks it gives the student a significant advantage when revising for examinations.

Contents
Administrative Law • Civil and Criminal Procedure • Commercial Law • Company Law • Conflict of Laws • Constitutional Law • Contract Law • Conveyancing • Criminal Law • Criminology • English Legal System • Equity and Trusts • European Union Law • Evidence • Family Law • Jurisprudence • Land Law • Law of International Trade • Public International Law • Revenue Law • Succession • Tort

For further information on contents, please contact:

Mail Order
Old Bailey Press
200 Greyhound Road
London
W14 9RY
United Kingdom

Telephone No: 00 44 (0) 171 385 3377
Fax No: 00 44 (0) 171 381 3377

ISBN 0 7510 0782 X
Soft cover 234 x 156 mm
396 pages   £6.95
Published March 1997

Using the Net for Research in Business, Law and Related Subjects

by Kevin McGuinness, Steele Raymond, Professor of Business Law
and Tom Short, Principal Lecturer and Researcher,
both at Bournemouth University

Using the Net is an essential guide for all lawyers and business people using the Internet worldwide. Starting with a general introduction to gaining access to the Internet, the book goes on to provide analysis of sites of interest under a series of subject headings. These include:

Advertising Law

Banking

Bankruptcy and Insolvency

Civil Procedure

Contract, Consumer and
**   Commercial Law**

Corporate Law and Securities

Expert Witnesses

Finance

Insurance

International Law and Relations

Law Practice Management

Negotiation and ADR

Newspapers

Patents and IP

For ease of use, a disk is included with the book giving direct access to 2,000 primary sites linking to 100,000s of specific sources of information.

This book assimilates a vast body of invaluable information for lawyers, business people, accountants and financiers and particularly for those conducting research in any of these fields.

For further information on contents, please contact:

Claudine Pryce
Old Bailey Press
200 Greyhound Road
London
W14 9RY
United Kingdom

Telephone No: 00 44 (0) 171 385 3377
Fax No: 00 44 (0) 171 381 3377

Published February 1997
ISBN 1 85836 072 2
Price £19.95   298 pages approx
E-Mail Address: hlt@holborncollege.ac.uk

2nd edition
publishing
January 1998

Old Bailey Press

The Old Bailey Press integrated student library is planned and written to help you at every stage of your studies. Each of our range of Textbooks, Casebooks, Revision WorkBooks and Statutes are all designed to work together and are regularly revised and updated.

We are also able to offer you Suggested Solutions which provide you with past examination questions and solutions for most of the subject areas listed below.

You can buy Old Bailey Press books from your University Bookshop or your local Bookshop, or in case of difficulty, order direct using this form.

Here is the selection of modules covered by our series:

Administrative Law; Commercial Law; Company Law; Conflict of Laws (no Suggested Solutions Pack); Constitutional Law: The Machinery of Government; Obligations: Contract Law; Conveyancing (no Revision Workbook); Criminology (no Casebook or Revision WorkBook); Criminal Law; English Legal System; Equity and Trusts; Law of The European Union; Evidence; Family Law; Jurisprudence: The Philosophy of Law (Sourcebook in place of a Casebook); Land: The Law of Real Property; Law of International Trade; Legal Skills and System; Public International Law; Revenue Law (no Casebook); Succession: The Law of Wills and Estates; Obligations: The Law of Tort.

Mail order prices:

Textbook £10

Casebook £10

Revision WorkBook £7

Statutes £8

Suggested Solutions Pack (1991–1995) £7

Single Paper 1996 £3

Single Paper 1997 £3.

To complete your order, please fill in the form below:

Module	Books required	Quantity	Price	Cost
		Postage		
		TOTAL		

For UK, add 10% postage and packing (£10 maximum).
For Europe, add 15% postage and packing (£20 maximum).
For the rest of the world, add 40% for airmail.

ORDERING

By telephone to Mail Order at 0171 385 3377, with your credit card to hand

By fax to 0171 381 3377 (giving your credit card details).

By post to:

Old Bailey Press, 200 Greyhound Road, London W14 9RY.

When ordering by post, please enclose full payment by cheque or banker's draft, or complete the credit card details below.

We aim to despatch your books within 3 working days of receiving your order.

Name

Address

Postcode   Telephone

Total value of order, including postage: £

I enclose a cheque/banker's draft for the above sum, or

charge my   ☐ Access/Mastercard   ☐ Visa   ☐ American Express
Card number

☐☐☐☐ ☐☐☐☐ ☐☐☐☐ ☐☐☐☐

Expiry date   ☐☐☐☐

Signature: ....Date: ....